Salsa for people who probably shouldn't

To our mothers, Marlen and Anna

SALSA
FOR PEOPLE
WHO PROBABLY
SHOULDN'T

MATT RENDELL

MAINSTREAM
PUBLISHING

EDINBURGH AND LONDON

First published in Great Britain in 2011 by
MAINSTREAM PUBLISHING COMPANY
(EDINBURGH) LTD
7 Albany Street
Edinburgh EH1 3UG

ISBN 9781845963996

A catalogue record for this book is available
from the British Library

Printed in Great Britain by
Clays Ltd, St Ives plc

1 3 5 7 9 10 8 6 4 2

CONTENTS

1

ENTRE FAMILIA

(Ay Júlia) Ahora yo voy a bailar.
(Ay Júlia), Now I'm going to dance.
'Júlia', composed by Yin Carrizo,
performed by El Gran Combo de
Puerto Rico

(Eleven years ago.)
Night falls fast over a crowded street in a foreign city. As
the last of the light is sucked out of the sky, griddle trolleys
take over the street corners, sizzling with scorched fat and
beef entrails that unthread into the air the sweet-edged
stench of rotting flesh just beginning to caramelise. You
salivate involuntarily: if there were a chance of keeping it
down, you might be tempted. It is that time of day.
  '*Arreglo la de presión.*'
  For hours the shout has filled the air, and what you hear
is, 'I can cure depression,' although he's really offering to
repair your pressure cooker. He's gone now, along with the
street hawkers shouldering their great sprays of brooms
and the men who walk miles each day with a pot of corn
broth in each hand, calling '*Mazamorra!*' up at the apartment
buildings. A cyclist weaves through the evening gridlock
with plantains hanging from the handlebars. A taxi driver

rests the hand he uses to grip a mattress laid across the car roof. Energised bodies shifting cargoes with any means to hand.

They, and the well-dressed office workers who ignore them, are mainly focused on the journey home, but you're tall enough and white enough to be obviously foreign in a place where most people are shorter and darker and where the few foreigners they see are sometimes up to no good, so the glances thrown your way don't always leave time for anything reciprocal. But, even in the darkness, black and white play too excitedly in their eyes to let their looks pass unnoticed.

Invisible speakers set somewhere among the stalls emit a recorded rhythm, the lilt of leathery hands with weight and warmth, hands and arms on which the forces of the physical world act, slapping a beat from an ancient drum, although no one pays too much attention. Close up, a brass section and vocals loom into earshot, then fade, and all that's left is the contagious, cryptic drumming.

Which was when I noticed him shadowing me along the sidewalk. He had decided I wasn't dangerous, which didn't feel like much of a compliment, although I needed to think about that and he didn't give me time.

'You're not from here.'

Not knowing quite how to reply and not wanting to appear defensive, I said, 'No, I'm from England,' which was more than I intended.

'What do you think of Colombia?'

'Enchanting,' I said, without thinking, or thinking too much, which amounted to the same thing.

'Where are you going?'

'The metro.'

'Me too. There's a free concert at the stadium. Why don't you come?'

I knew how I would have reacted at home. But this wasn't home and I fought the urge to withdraw into myself. Even so, when I replied, 'Why not?', I surprised myself again.

His name was Diego and his reserve had been loosened by the liquor that still hung on his breath. He'd been arguing with his wife. It didn't seem polite to ask whether he had started drinking before the fight or whether he had hit the bottle for the same reason he was going to the concert, the same reason he had approached the harmless-looking foreigner: to step for a few hours outside the everyday precincts of his life. Either way, I thought, 'Why not? A few stops out, some music, a few stops back. Nothing life-changing.'

Except that neither of us, it transpired, knew Medellín. Diego had moved here recently from Bogotá. I had come in on the early flight, although the early flight was late and I had swept across town and made a meeting in the nick of time, only to find it had been cancelled. So, my sensibilities doubly offended, I checked into a hotel off La Playa, failing to notice the tell-tale stains of swatted cockroaches on the walls, and, with little else to do, set off for the metro to see the city from the overhead train.

By the time I reached the platform I was with Diego.

Medellín's overhead metro is spotless. Passengers talk to each other here and, if you eat or smoke, they will ask you in all politeness to desist. So, when Diego says we have to change trains two stations down the line, a young woman standing within earshot corrects him: 'No, *señor*, you change at the next stop for the stadium.'

It's courtesy, not flirtation, but in an instant Diego's attention has shifted from me to the girl, dressed discreetly in jeans and a light jersey, heading home, not out, but beautiful.

'*Gracias, negra,*' says Diego, all charm.

I'm suddenly uncomfortable. Colombian men use the term *negra* all the time as a term of endearment for women, even those whose skin tone is not at all dark. The light-hearted use of a word that could easily cause offence

9

probably creates an air of confidence. All the same, it's not a word I could ever use. Too many cross-cultural complexities: man, woman, English, Colombian, white, black.

As I ponder the tragic sweep of history, Diego moves fast, steering the girl round to the topic of an evening out. 'Are you going to the concert?'

She isn't. She's been at a work do and she's going home.

The exchange draws to an end but the train comes to a halt before the next station, so Diego has another shot. 'Come with us.'

'I don't know you.'

'I don't know *him*.'

All this time, I've been gazing rather deliberately through and past and over her to convey the impression that I haven't really noticed her, but when Diego says *'him'* he means me, so, not entirely failing to pull myself together, I mutter something like, 'I've got nothing else on,' and smile.

Diego tells her I'm German, which I think is a reference to skin colour, not nationality, although I correct him anyway, with more emphasis than the occasion really demands. It's as well I do. It's just what's needed to break the ice. We're all smiling now, and Diego says, 'Let's all go to the concert, then we can take the metro home.'

The girl agrees and, together, we head off to the stadium.

By the time the concert finished, the metro had closed for the night. Diego was fairly far gone, gripping the woman I now knew as Viviana by the hand and strafing her with drunken compliments. He was insisting on a taxi to a nightclub but I was tired and un-streetwise, and I didn't want to get into a fight over a woman, so I let them get some way ahead and hailed a passing taxi. I called out, 'I'm in the Villa de la Candelaria in the centre. Call me if you like. You're the only people I know here,' before driving off.

Two days later, incredibly, reception put the call through.

Incredibly, because Viviana had every reason to be angry with me. There'd been something protective in her decision to come with us to the stadium. She'd wanted to keep an eye on me. She had also hated the music: songs of social protest sung by and for radical students and white-skinned intellectuals. None of the Afro-Caribbean warmth her tastes required. But she'd put up with it for me and I'd repaid her by abandoning her, not realising she didn't have the cash to pay for a taxi. She'd made it home, just, no thanks to me, by climbing in next to Diego, giving the driver her address and leaving Diego, who was too drunk to object, to pick up the tab. The following day she had told her family about her evening. It was her mother who encouraged her to make sure I'd made it back in one piece.

She was one of those women who seem to contain their countries. There was a slowness to her, a refusal to rush I initially took for a variety of shyness. It was only much later I understood it as a deeply rooted style of being. She moved from her centre, the spot below the navel where gravity acts on the body mass, the place where changes of direction, weight shifts and spinal fluidity begin, beneath the deep breathing apparatus. It was the movement of someone with a clear sense of who she is. Perhaps that was why I was drawn to her.

Twice that week, I visited the flat she shared with two brothers and her mother, Marlen, with whom, I discovered, she also shared her upright carriage. Their looks and languid body language flowed down the maternal line. They had the same handwriting and couldn't be told apart on the telephone. Expert in the rhythms of dialogue, they would talk from the moment they arrived home after work until bedtime. Vivi's brothers would come in, eat, go out again or disappear upstairs, but when they came back to the kitchen the conversation would still be in full flow. Strangers to that wonderful womanly facility for speech,

11

they'd ask, 'Still talking? What do you talk about?'

They talked about their day, was the answer. Vivi had earned the best matriculation mark in her school, then her father had left home so she had paid her own way through university, getting up at five to fit in work and study. She'd gone out to work to bring money into the family home, managing a busy office, ten things at a time, four years distributing industrial dyes, three years with a US multinational. There'd been no time for unrealisable ambitions or adolescent rebellions. Her moral education was also severe, given that Marlen was a social worker who held parenting sessions for poor and displaced women, helping them with the skills needed to raise decent children in deprived areas that had been devastated by drug-related violence.

It seems to me now that those long evening exchanges were part of the simple assimilation of experience, where wisdom lies. Marlen was a woman of charisma, adept in the negotiations that take place as men, women and children teeter together over the abyss of incompatibility. She kept a ready supply of cautionary tales that could raise a smile, calm anxieties and smooth the way to modesty and reason. She told me the story of a large woman who used to beat her much smaller husband so often and so severely it scandalised the neighbourhood. When she grew ashamed and mended her ways, her husband was dejected. It was only when she beat him, he said, that he knew she loved him. Between people from such different worlds, so strangely hewn to the same sharp edges, at times such strangers to themselves, how could the barriers dissolve and love ensue? With Marlen, everything had this same sense of fun and mystery.

During my first visits, Vivi put on a tape of her favourite music, which was also her mother's. A background drumming, with bursts of colour from the trombones and trumpets, and an almost operatic voice singing songs that were also stories, accompanied the conversations between the three of us. And although it seems strange now, it didn't seem at all odd then to sit there with my future wife and her mother, being vetted, as you would probably have to call it, because I suppose it was a test of some sort, not of my Spanish or sense of rhythm, but as if my response to the music would tell them something they needed to know before our relationship went any further.

I remember we stopped to listen to a funny song about a lazybones who spends his days apparently preparing to go to work, without ever leaving the house, and I had to ask them to repeat lines I couldn't understand, and Vivi got up and danced with a tiny French poodle named Kiwi who stood on his rear paws and evidently knew a lot more about salsa than I did.

I'd been visiting Colombia regularly for five years. I'd produced a television documentary and the beginnings of a book which gave a semblance of purpose to what was never in reality more than a baffled searching, the real scope of which might well have been the avoidance of things I had no words to describe, things I probably had with me all along. I suppose there was also the vague intuition that your life can become visible to you if you take enough distance from it.

When I was there, the street choreography seeped into me through the pores. It seeped out again, sadly, when I left, and leaving had become part of the work I did – going out into the world, gathering what fragments I could and coming home to shape them into written form. I thought it was the responsible thing: to distance myself from brute experience then burnish it until it glistened with objectivity. But childhood memories were involved, too, of the vicarage I grew up in and my maternal grandfather, a reader of Hebrew and Greek, disappearing into his study to write among leather-bound books of strange alphabets on tissue-paper pages. A withdrawal from physical reality into the world of the mind.

Dance had been low on the agenda when I was growing up in the battlefield of British family life that was the 1970s. My grandparents knew the pleasure of two gently interlaced bodies moving together in time, but I never saw them dance, and pair-dancing had gone out of fashion before my parents ever got together. My mother, when she was a teenager in Liverpool, went to the Cavern and probably shook to The Quarrymen before they became The Beatles, but that was before I was born and by the time my memories begin we were a one-parent family and she had no one to dance with anyway.

It certainly wasn't something my generation had much time for. Dance steps sounded too much like being told what to do. We went in for spontaneous, improvised, delirious, ad hoc and, for some, more adventurous than me or just more reckless, drug-induced self-expression. We were too busy hanging loose, too caught up in our own identities to dance properly. So, as a ten-year-old, I flailed the occasional limb at the school disco, and as a teenager I pogoed and head-banged a bit, and that was about it, before I grew into one of those people whose sense of personal space extended several feet in every direction and in whom the slightest physical contact, in a rush-hour train with a fellow traveller, for instance, produced something close to panic. The sort of person who burbles 'Sorry' in the event of a near miss when no actual physical contact has taken place.

*

I sometimes wonder if it was an instinctive, unconscious desire for some sort of therapy that drew me to salsa. In about 1981 three of Cuba's most famous bands began to take annual residencies at Ronnie Scott's Jazz Club, packing the place out: Irakere, led by a piano virtuoso named Chucho Valdés; the Arturo Sandoval group, led by Irakere's former trumpeter; and the island's most popular band, Juan Formell's Los Van Van. I went to see them all every year, but I either stood in the crowd at the back or sat at a table near the stage. It never occurred to me to dance.

Five or six years later, with a group of friends, I became a regular at a night club near Old Street in the City of London. It was called the Bass Clef and they had started holding a Latin night on Fridays. There was a DJ and the occasional band called Picante or Palenque with musicians like Roberto Pla or Chucho Merchán. There were a few Latin Americans among us, although, since most of the City's Spanish-speaking Caribbeans were cleaning office floors through the night for less an hour than we were paying for our Tequila slammers, there were probably more of them playing than dancing.

I remember preparing to take my first step on the apparently solid dance floor when – *boom!* – the bass, anticipating the downbeat with a punch, jolted the earth beneath me and knocked me strangely off balance, and suddenly I was plunging through a rush of sound and movement into the tropical storm of Caribbean classical music. Then, *bam!*, just as suddenly, the bass was back with something solid under my feet. And so it went on, *boom!*, the ground speeding away, then *bam!*, rushing back to find me. It was like a funfair ride. There were many rhythms but it was the bass, speeding ahead of the pulse and then relaxing almost too far to let me catch up, that commanded me to shape my body to the music and embark on this exhilarating journey against the shifting sound-scenery.

The music I found so captivating derived from the folk genres of the Spanish-speaking Caribbean, which had been mixed together and given a driving, urban feel. Recorded by mostly New York-based bands in the 1960s and '70s, and marketed aggressively under the catch-all label of salsa, it was ten or fifteen years old and already had an aura of nostalgia.

How people danced to it depended on where they came from. In Latin America, revellers fused together movements from local folk dances, Mexican movies and films of the New York clubs into improvised interpretations of the music. Until the teaching industry mobilised itself, there was no such dance as salsa; you simply made it up as you went along. Except, of course, that, where I came from, dance didn't really figure in people's lives, so there wasn't much raw material to make it up with.

That pattern of deep punches that forestalled the downbeat, then paused until the following measure had a name: *tumbao*, 'fallen over', 'wrong way up'. In Central American slang, *tumbao* also meant 'duped' or 'robbed', as in 'You fell for it', as if the beat had been stolen and had turned up somewhere unexpected, putting you suddenly out of kilter. In the first verse of the song '*Pedro Navaja*' by Rubén Blades, the anti-hero is described as walking *con el tumbao* – with the swagger, the lilt – *que tienen los guapos al caminar* – that marks him out as a street thug. And, as every fighter knows, it's the blow you don't see coming that floors you: it punches the mind towards delirium, shocks the body into movement, steeps the senses in rhythmic blows, beats the spirit towards demonic possession, a cultic obeisance to a higher will.

My gait marked a simple rhythm, despite the sense of peripheral drift affecting otherwise simple movements. It was like walking in a fast-flowing river or with my eyes turned skywards as clouds rushed past overhead. The landscape moved, the horizon shifted, the thing I called 'I' was suddenly elsewhere and the 'me' I discovered existed only in relation to the sound and motion on the dance floor.

While most of our group made our personal, if rather similar, interpretations of the music, alone as part of the crowd, embracing nothing more sentient than a bottle of beer, the Chilean boyfriend of one of my fellow students guided her through a succession of semi-embraces, spicing their movements with the lightest notations of a tendency towards a kiss. I probably thought of it as salsa, although it was really *cumbia*, a Colombian dance that had caught on in Chile in the 1950s and reached Britain 20 years later, brought by émigrés fleeing Pinochet. A dance displaced twice in as many generations and washed up on an English shore by a wave of Latin American immigration in the 1970s. It had a dreamlike quality. I found it irresistible.

Soon afterwards, the musicians boycotted the Bass Clef over wages and conditions, and the place closed. It reopened under new management and there were no more Latin nights, but, while they lasted, for those of us with a student grant to squander on London ticket and bar prices, it was magnificent.

Across the water, the Generalísimo was still in power and continuing his contribution to the political violence that was rife across Central and South America. In London, solidarity campaigns had sprung up to lobby Parliament, pressure the media and raise public consciousness. I joined thousands on sponsored bike rides to help the cause, and attended smaller, more earnest bashes for El Salvador or Nicaragua in church halls and people's homes with concerned university lecturers and radical students, plus a few migrants and refugees who must, at times, have felt like laboratory specimens. I had no idea how Central Americans handled hellos and welcomes. The English organisers, true to local practice, handled them rather badly, with no introductions or outstretched hands or welcoming smiles, but nor were there enough people present to allow you to go unremarked. It wasn't at all clear whose etiquette rules applied or what the appropriate language was, although I spoke little or no Spanish at the time, so I didn't have much choice. I tried drifting casually into conversation with whoever was closest but little came of it. There was always the unspoken suspicion that the next man's concern or involvement might not be sufficiently informed or profound or authentic, although not knowing salsa was part of it. Not that there was that much actual dancing. But there were also at these gatherings occasional immigrant couples who, when the music started, entered that enchanting, itinerant embrace, momentarily in their own world, surrounded by an aura of suspended childhood. I made a mental note.

At the bigger fundraisers, there were live bands. Central American mothers with toddlers swayed to the music beside embarrassed English husbands trembling half-heartedly in attendance. Even those doggedly determined to shine in public mingled the visible strain of going the whole hog with a distinct awareness of doing something deeply foreign. The sheer intensity of our respect for the particularities of other people's ways of life imprinted on our faces the hazy smiles of amateur actors who quote but never quite become their parts.

I'm not sure how much of a danger all this posed to Augusto Pinochet. I felt threatened enough to enrol in evening classes at a dance academy near Euston Station. This was long before today's proliferation of lessons. The early enclave of salsa education to which I gravitated was called The Place. I was barely out of my teens and hopelessly tongue-tied with women, and part of the attraction, apart from the overarching politics, of course, was the prospect of weaving my limbs into those of a pulsating female body or two.

The only thing was, until the decisive moment, I hadn't given much thought to the prospect of getting extremely close to a member of the opposite sex and making sustained eye contact. I knew no language of flirtation that would allow any affection thereby kindled to survive our unremitting gaze. There was every danger my initial glance would decay into something exposed and shivering. The life of the eyes was too raw.

There were other deficiencies: an inability to move body parts without looking at them, or to stand in proximity to another human body without going into generalised muscular spasm. My shoulders were tense and my elbows clenched to my sides. I shambled around, unconscious of the co-ordination of my clothes or the condition of my hair, perhaps because etched into the scattered contents of my personality was a resistance to style and elegance, deposited there by members of my lineage who had torn down rood screens and stained-glass windows because surface elegance was a godless distraction from deeper realities, and who duly regarded dance as a lewd, groping, pestiferous vice. What was I thinking when I involved myself in an activity in which these things really, genuinely mattered?

My class, sure enough, had more women than men. It was 1989 and lambada was in the air: the song was in the charts and our teacher was a Brazilian woman who added the sort of full-on sensuality that was a long way from the make-believe quality I'd glimpsed in my classmate's *cumbia*. There were moves I found frankly embarrassing, especially given the presence of a slight, curveless thing in a tiny orange lambada-style skirt whose hem rose more than it fell, driving the few men in the class to distraction. But she turned out to have a steady boyfriend, and the midwifely calls of 'Hips forward', 'Bend your knees' and 'Don't forget to breathe' had the effect of stifling the call of the erotic. The classes were too slow for me anyway, too group orientated, nowhere near *foreign* enough, so, although I was still desperate to learn, after three or four sessions, I dropped out.

Then two things happened. The first took place in Colombia, years after those first lessons but still before I met Vivi. I visited a bar in Pereira, in the heart of the coffee-growing region, and watched workers trudge out of the night, some scraping mud from their boots, and move towards a dance floor already crammed with thickset, paired-off frames. There they merged into salsa's gentle role play of concealment, detection, false revelation and rediscovery. Each space was filled with more heaving human matter than seemed plausible although the impression was not of mass but of weightlessness. The bodily submission to rhythm and melody, each gesture matching an inner release, shook off the day's burdens.

I thought I recognised dancers who descended more deeply into the music than others. It wasn't that they were more elegant or rhythmic, or showed the lightness of touch of the professional dancer. They had something harder to define – the ability to respond in dance to each change of musical colour, each pun or threat or amorous declaration of the lyrics. There was a sense of a world behind the world: rituals of touch and distance, steps, words, notes, opening out on to something inexhaustible.

I would have liked to let my body mingle with theirs but I had been brought up not to be taken in by such enactments. I had or feigned no belief in role play, my own or other people's. In any case, as a foreigner in a provincial town, local perspectives on my presence pressed on me there, and the dance floor represented not a *Saturday Night Fever*-style platform for showing off but the promise of anonymity, a shedding of self. The dark enticing rhythms of the Afro-Caribbean might have given me somewhere to hide, a background to merge into – if only I'd known how to dance.

The second thing that happened to me was meeting Vivi. The more I learned about her, the more Colombia's passion for music and dance imposed itself. Movement and rhythm were tied to lineage, inheritance and the land.

The maternal line of her family came from the Chocó, Colombia's poorest, blackest region, overwhelmingly populated by the descendants of slaves brought in colonial times from Central Africa and the territories now called Nigeria and Ghana to work the gold mines. The Bantú,

Yoruba, Ibo and Akan inheritance of the Chocoans left them with a seemingly inexhaustible reservoir of rhythmic body movement.

Vivi's great-great-grandmother was a strong, black Chocoan woman called Colomba, whose daughter married a Spaniard named Cosme Damián, a police inspector in a Chocó village called Valencia, who was also a spectacular dancer. He was ambitious too, so, in the 1930s, when the plan to build a highway to connect the interior to the Pacific was announced, Cosme set off upwards and eastwards through the dense forest, sensing an opportunity.

A month into his journey, he stumbled on a place towering with palm trees. Most of the Chocó suffers 24-hour heat and humidity, but this was 3,575 feet above sea level. At night, a mist descended on the forest, meaning no mosquitoes, meaning in turn that it would be the perfect stop-off point for the road project and then a trading post for the migration that would surely follow. So, on 19 March 1938, the Feast of St Joseph, he founded a town there and called it San José del Palmar, or Palmar, for short. Snakes came slithering in from the trees, and, as Cosme didn't like to kill them, the other settlers called him the snake charmer.

The snake charmer's daughter, named Colomba after her grandmother, attracted the attention of a merchant named Sigifredo from Antioquia, the region whose capital was Medellín. He had nous and a salesman's way with words and he was a typical Antioqueño: hardworking, adventurous, self-reliant, commercially shrewd. He started buying maize and cocoa from producers around Palmar and loading them on to trains of mules for the journey over rough ground to the town of Cartago. He returned the same way with food, medicine, cloth, shoes, crockery: everything the settlement needed.

Although Sigifredo was from a Conservative family and Colomba was a Liberal, they never argued over politics, despite the tensions in the country which led to violence even before the assassination in April 1947 of Jorge Eliécer Gaitán, the Liberal presidential candidate.

Too dark-skinned to have been accepted by the ruling elite, Gaitán had polarised the nation, flaunting crooked, outsized teeth, sweating profusely, even foaming at the mouth as he delivered inflammatory speeches to huge crowds. Music and dance were integral to his presidential campaign: not the delicate *bambuco* of the ruling classes, but *porro*, a genre of dance music full of Caribbean flavour, one of the precursors of Colombian salsa. The white ruling class of both parties disapproved.

The political violence reached Palmar in 1949. Colomba escaped the machete by hiding under the houses and then making her way inland with her children. Marlen was three years old, and the memory of crawling through body parts, and of going to collect water and finding corpses bobbing in the tank, stayed with her for the rest of her life. Years later, excavating to improve the sewers, they found bones from the mutilations and killings. There were months when neither of Marlen's parents knew whether the other was alive.

Sigifredo and Colomba eventually had ten children together, Marlen being the second born, and, when peace returned, Colomba imposed her considerable charisma over those who met her, with the patience and collectedness of mind of an ancient African ideal. She organised the choir in the San José del Palmar chapel. She sang beautifully and played boleros on the church harmonium. Black maids filled the house with their singing voices, and Marlen listened to music in the stockroom of her father's general store, where peasant farmers sat among sacks of coffee, cocoa and maize, and the music of a station called Radio Sutatenza rang out from the town's only wireless and mingled with the pungent smells. She liked to slip out in the evening to dance, which was why Colomba had to cover for her when Sigifredo noticed their daughter's absence.

When Marlen was sent away to study in the departmental capital, Quibdó, even Sigi couldn't isolate her from music and movement. Marlen learned *cumbia, porro, merecumbé* – a mixture of *merengue* and *cumbia* – and *son chocoano*, intense dances signifying contact with the earth and its gods. They gave shape to her life and led her to love and the birth of her three children.

Marlen shared her mother's qualities. They were both unflinching in their moral strenuousness, but also sympathetic to the imperfections of living and full of motherly kindness towards life. Their deep Catholicism, their guardianship of religion in their family homes, made me think of ancient household shrines under feminine protection.

This was Vivi's inheritance, although she learned to dance not in Palmar, nor even in Medellín, high in the mountains, but in her father's home city, Cartagena de Indias, the yellow-walled citadel town where the conquistadors once stored their loot before shipping it back to Spain, in the heat of the Caribbean coast.

Among the Costeños, dance was a long-ripened generational rite, a taken-for-granted part of development through which, at a certain age, children continue their developing relationship with their own bodies and those of others. Walking but not yet speaking, perhaps not even two, Vivi had danced with her cousins after meals, half-guided, half-bullied by her father's mother, Julia Carmona, a happy woman, always laughing, always dancing, with a husband who never danced in his life yet fathered nine children, all male, all expert on the dance floor. Vivi's father Luis – Lucho – was the eldest. He and his brothers left the coast to study in the high-altitude inland cities of Bogotá, Cali and Medellín, but, whenever they returned to the coast, it was to take on their cousins in all-night dance competitions. Their contests weren't about acrobatics or tying their companions in knots, but about the angle of a hat, the slant of the shoulders, the effortlessness of a turn, the coolness of a mask. Lucho and Orlando, the second son, won every time.

The goal of all this activity wasn't technical mastery or the acquisition of a large repertoire of figures, but something altogether harder to define called *sabor*; a good dancer was *sabroso* or *sabrosa* – tasteful, we might say, although what this actually meant wasn't something you could fix in words. It was one of those things you just *knew* when you saw.

So, to Vivi, dance was part of the welter of ordinary undistinguished things she did without ever asking how or why. It let her sense and enact and relate to things in a way spoken language couldn't come close to. It wasn't something she had beliefs or doubts about or framed in too many words.

After meeting her, I spent the week in Medellín and we met two or three times. I left to carry on my interviews elsewhere in Colombia, but I returned a month later to work on both my book and our relationship. At the end of our second week together, we kissed. Then I flew back home to England.

Four months later, back in Medellín, I rented a flat for a couple of months and settled in to write my book. We saw each other every day and, on my next trip to Colombia, a year to the day after we met, we married.

We honeymooned in Cartagena de Indias. One day we boarded a *chiva*, a reconditioned Chevrolet truck with wooden seating for 30 or 40, and toured the attractions. The driver, a huge black man with long hair he wore plaited and beaded, tipped his head rhythmically to music resounding from an immense sound system mounted before him. He collected his passengers' fares with an outstretched arm, without breaking his concentration. His posture suggested a man admirably comfortable in his skin. I imagined he received no more than small change for his services, but he seemed so fully himself that he could take the world as it came, free of the urge to take more from each moment than each moment has to offer. And I imagined that salsa had something to do with it; not just a momentary distraction from his circumstances, but – what? – a set of values, a way of being.

I was reading too much into him, no doubt. All the same, I thought, blessed with his temperament, I would have stayed. I was comfortable in Colombia, whatever I thought I was doing there. Instead, after our week in the sun, we returned to reality. Meaning, of course, reality for me.

We flew into winter, landing at Heathrow one morning in January. On the flight, British Airways had upgraded us, so, for the first and perhaps the last time in our lives, we had boarded an airliner, turned left and ordered champagne. When we disembarked, the first impact of Vivi's new life hit her. She had never thought of leaving Medellín, her family and the merging of identities that united her to her mother. Her lungs had never taken in air this cold. And she was suddenly embroiled in one of those fractured families that are no less typically English for being scattered halfway around the globe.

Days after arriving in London, we were on the move again, to meet the rest of my dispersed family at my father's home in Australia. After that second leg of our honeymoon, we returned to my family home in Harwich, on the east coast, to settle. To call another country home must have jarred with her. So must confronting the persistent idea, held with great warmth and well meaning, that difference is surface deep and that beneath it lies universality, and that universality, basically, means England and the English, whose values and way of life were not merely the expression of a set of commonly held desires and preferences but in some larger sense the obvious and necessary values of humankind.

I don't know how much I helped. Coping with my own culture shock in Vivi's country was incomparably easier than responding to hers in mine. I lacked the skills and probably the sensitivity too, when what to Vivi was almost opaquely alien was to me so familiar I could hardly see it was there. There were friends who, with the best of intentions, commiserated with her for her Third World upbringing, failing to understand that Vivi had left behind a bustling modern city with a bustling modern city's cultural life, and that the outlook from England on the North Sea didn't look like Colombia with more options. Good people, caring people, they failed to understand quite how much difference these differences made.

There were the adjustments every new couple has to make, but there was also a good deal of cross-cultural tweaking. At one point I realised there were things I couldn't find. 'If you don't use it for six months, you don't need it,' she told me.

It was good reasoning in tropical Colombia where people don't have entire wardrobes that disappear for seasons on end. I convinced her to make it 12.

Vivi's English was already excellent: all she needed now was to learn how the English used it. In Colombia, for instance, she fired out telephone numbers in volleys of seven or eight digits. Since taking them down right first time was a sign of elementary social competence, people made sure they did. In Britain she had to train herself in the local habit of trying to do at least half of everyone else's thinking for them: so, to forestall potential transcription errors, she learned to over-pronounce sequences of no more than three digits at a time, or to spell out email addresses using foxtrots and sierras and bravos.

She had never driven in Colombia, so she went through a succession of ageing driving instructors to acquire the

'Mirror-Signal-Manoeuvre' approach. She learned to indicate hundreds of yards in advance, and to select not the obvious but the stipulated lane. She mastered the courtesy code of smiles, nods, hand signals and flashes of headlights that was utterly irrelevant anywhere else on earth, but which the British observe scrupulously until the moment they leap out of their cars and set about each other with screwdrivers.

Soon after our arrival, a school accordion orchestra performed in the church. In Colombian music, the accordion is as sexy and flamboyant as a wailing lead guitar and its exponents have included men of semi-mythical status, some of whom took on the devil in musical duels, like Paganini or the early bluesmen did. Before we bought the tickets, we knew the devil wouldn't be welcome – the setting and the child-abuse laws made sure of that – but the evening was entertaining enough.

Soon afterwards, my mother invited us to a Ceilidh. Vivi had been looking forward to seeing the British dance. I tried to forewarn her it wasn't exactly dancing, more a sort of burlesque performed with enthusiastic ineptitude and a few redeeming smidgeons of irony, in collective acknowledgement of the merits of not taking oneself too seriously. But there are no words to prepare the unsuspecting for this philosophy's more forceful expressions, so we bought our tickets at the door with conflicting expectations.

It was an evening of laughter and Vivi was warmly welcomed. Yet to someone brought up not to prize the lovably crankish but to build harmonious movement into one's ordinary unglamorous interactions with others, the erratic shudders, the repeated mistaking of left and right, clockwise and its opposite, the infantile reversion to guileless abandon and the hilarity all this provoked must have looked deeply alien, like a convention of the deranged. Visitors to Colombia comment on its highly formal culture, and on the local penchant for official speeches. A certain physical grace has great social value. We were worlds away here.

The upper reaches of local society were there. A city banker, various professional ladies, the vet, an assortment of customs officers, a couple of farmers and a number of retirees: the sort of people on whom you could build a solid, dependable social order. Yet they all seized the opportunity to display bumbling physical idiocy in public with a degree of elation. Whatever the cultural origins of the individual routines – Scottish, Irish, French, American – they were assimilated into a very English pushing of the matter to its inexorable limit. A similar spectacle attributed by a Victorian anthropologist to jungle-dwelling tribesmen would have beggared belief. These were, after all, physically functional and intellectually competent people of some social standing, whose forebears were the collectors and classifiers with a fascination for things that slot and whir who had given the world the industrial revolution.

Half in and half out of both camps, in on the joke yet deeply uncomfortable with it, and struggling with the feeling of familiar realities under the scrutiny of distant assumptions, I might have been the most deranged of all. I had become the sort of cultural go-between who encourages each side to believe he is more loyal to it than to the other. Made in Britain, mind down, not body up, I felt disengaged not just from the surrounding world but from my own emotions and inclinations and all the other contingencies of my otherwise creaturely point of view, even if I also had to *be* the creature I had subjected to such detached examination, and to live in this extremely distilled fraction of myself. The sense I had of having grown up not exactly to be incapable of feeling but to be capable of it only through the medium of thought suddenly seemed very strange, and very different from Colombia. It wasn't that minds didn't matter there: on the contrary, Vivi's father was a university maths lecturer and her brother an IT expert. The difference was that their minds seemed to be comfortable in their bodies, where ours looked badly installed in the wrong housings by a ham-fisted mechanic.

2

FIRST CONTACT

Una mañana dormía y corriendo me tiré
por un grito que decía hay fuego en el 23.
One day when I was sleeping, I leapt
    up to my feet
Because of people shouting, 'Fire at 23!'
        'Hay Fuego en el 23', composed by
        Arsenio Rodríguez, performed by
                Sonora Ponceña

My perceptions of Medellín's mind–body connectedness
were very different from those of Colombians who came
from elsewhere in the country. They thought of Medellín as
a serious, even staid city, populated by conservative,
industrious, buttoned-up Catholics. It wasn't considered a
salsa city at all. It certainly couldn't compare with Cali.

Founded on a fertile plain irrigated by the Cauca River,
Santiago de Cali is set among sugar plantations once
worked by captive Africans. Slavery was abolished in 1851,
but its victims and their descendants mostly stayed in the
countryside and Cali was still a modest outpost of 20,000 as
the twentieth century began. Today's heaving metropolis
was born in the 1940s and '50s, when political violence and
the mechanisation of the sugar industry drove columns of

peasant farmers off the land and transformed Cali into the blackest of Colombia's big cities.

Refugees arrived with little but the clothes they stood up in and their bodies, which were fluent in dances blending the African, the European and the indigenous, many of which were compatible with the Cuban music that the new technologies of the age – radio, records and the cinema – were spreading throughout the Spanish-speaking world. These languages of movement and dance mingled in the city, and, even though Cali was 500 miles south of the Caribbean coast, Cuban radio had better reception than the local stations and, since the music of the early gramophone industry was Cuban, even the local stations played little else. So Afro-Caribbean songs became the soundtrack to the migrants' new lives, describing realities the Caleños knew first-hand: the legacy of the slave plantation, the landscape turned over to sugarcane and the history of violence that had strangely begotten a culture not of fear but of music, dance and laughter.

Each wave of migrants moved onto land that had been cleared for building but otherwise unprepared. The roads were unpaved and the poorest founded homesteads in little more than wooden shacks. To raise money for improvements, a citywide tradition of subscription dances emerged, and another for teenagers of alcohol-free, afternoon parties in which the main drink served was water and the juice of the citrus fruit *naranjilla*: to the locals, '*agua y lulo*' or, said quickly, *agüelulo*, which was what the parties were called. The *agüelulo* became the conduit through which each generation's identification with Afro-Cuban music and dance was passed on to the next.

And there was something else: the dancing at the *agüelulos* was competitive. Contests became a regular feature, and the prospect of prizes powered an elaboration of the underlying Afro-Colombian dance moves that continues to this day.

In this extraordinary cauldron of movement and passion lie the origins of British salsa.

*

'The only place where we could have a drink and listen to our music was in the basement of a restaurant called La Pérgola in West London, managed by a Canary Islander. Our friends back home would record cassettes of the latest music and send them to us. We'd take them to La Pérgola and spend the afternoon listening, singing and dancing.'

Lubín Reyes, born in Cali, was part of the first wave of Colombian immigrants to reach London. His first job was washing dishes. Seeking an alternative, he rented a room behind a bar and began to hold dances every Sunday afternoon: '*Agüelulos*! Caleño *agüelulos* in London!'

A record collector who had also managed a dance club called El Balcón de las Nieves ('The Snow Balcony') in central Cali, Reyes opened Britain's first salsa clubs. They weren't salsa clubs at all in the sense we mean today, but social events for Colombian immigrants, no-fixed-abode affairs in rented warehouses, restaurant basements, church halls and community centres, temporary spaces where they could listen to the music that represented home and move unselfconsciously in their native body language. They were important refuges, means of staying sane.

Reyes had arrived in 1974 to find a nation that wasn't a colonial power any more, and was much less the workshop of the world. Britain had begun repositioning itself in the world even before the Immigration Act 1971 recognised, in the words of the *Modern Law Review*, that 'Britain is no longer the metropolitan centre of the Commonwealth.'

'The Act,' it said, 'will probably not be the final stage in the process of shedding the vestiges of Empire.'

By removing the distinction between Commonwealth and non-Commonwealth entrants and allowing work permits and temporary residency to people from countries which were not former colonies, the Act led to an influx of Latin Americans. The most numerous among them were Colombians, convinced by government-contracted employment agencies to accept an alien language and an even more alien approach to life in exchange for jobs in hotels, factories and restaurants, or as au pairs and domestic employees. To enjoy in their spare time and remind themselves who they were, they brought music and the dance forms they had grown up with.

Soon after Lubín Reyes arrived, four more young men from Cali reached London. Two of them would work with him as salsa DJs, and one of *them* would, like Reyes, become a pioneering dance-club manager. Together, they would begin the transfer of salsa music and dance from its Colombian carrier community to their indigenous hosts.

Carlos Piedrahita, Alfredo Chalá, Camilo Pereira and Hernán Vargas, also known as El Flaco ('Skinny'), hailed from Cali's Barrio Panamericano, built in 1959, during the thick of the population flight from the countryside to Cali. Barrio Panamericano started out as an illegal occupation but soon became the home of dance clubs and street parties that were famous all over the city, the best of them Guanchito, a dance hall where the city's dancers put on shows.

Carlos, Alfredo, Camilo and El Flaco Hernán were among the first Colombians to enter the country through a recruitment programme approved by the Department of Employment on behalf of the British Hotels, Restaurants and Caterers Association. The scheme allowed recruits a one-year work permit renewable for three further years, after which the workers could ask for permanent residency. It was all done with no public announcements or fanfare in the UK.

The four found lodgings on the third and fourth floors of a six-storey brick townhouse at 21 Gledhow Gardens, off Old Brompton Road in West London, a traditional Polish area. One of their neighbours was Tomasz Zaleski, the London-born son of Polish parents, better known as Tomek. 'In the '50s when I was growing up, the conductors on the number 30 bus would sing out "Polish Corridor" as it swung into Old Brompton Road.'

Despite living in the next-door apartment, Tomek only met his neighbours months after they had arrived, when he returned home after a two-year journey around South America, nine months of which he had spent in Colombia, where he had developed a passion for Afro-Cuban music. Listening to his old record player, he threw open the window, allowing salsa rhythms to drift into the street below. Presently, he became aware of a face staring up at him. It was Carlos Piedrahita.

'I stared back at him, and he sort of motioned: "Are you the one playing the music?"

'I said, "I'll come down."

'Unbelievably, to me, a group of Colombians was living in the next-door flat. It was the first time I'd heard of Colombians in London.'

At the door downstairs, a turning point in the history of British popular culture took place: Tomek and Carlos shook hands. First contact had been made. A future salsa DJ at the Bass Clef and elsewhere, and a broadcaster with Jazz FM and countless pirate stations, Tomek would listen to music for hundreds of hours with his neighbours, and one day help salsa cross over from London's nascent Colombian community into the margins of the national culture.

Tomek was soon hanging out in the next-door flat, which quickly became a meeting point for new arrivals from Colombia who brought the latest records with them. 'There'd be loads of people sitting around, crammed in together in their small living spaces, and some music would be playing and there'd be, you know, two square metres of space for people to dance in. They'd dance outside the rooms, in the corridors.'

Tomek would describe songs he'd heard travelling in their homeland, and Hernán would try to identify them, honing Tomek's taste in modern salsa and its precursors, and directing him towards the old bands.

Playing football with other Colombians, the friends met Lubín Reyes and began to socialise at La Pérgola until Reyes rented his first room and launched the first of his Sunday-afternoon *agüelulos*.

Polite British society didn't take much notice. We didn't even know they were there. What news there was of salsa was coming out of New York through connoisseurs like Richard Williams, head of artists and repertoire at Island Records. In 1975 he put on Héctor Lavoe, the foremost vocalist in the genre, at the Nashville Rooms on the corner of North End Road and Talgarth Road, and then the Fania All-Stars, with vocalist Celia Cruz, bandleader Johnny Pacheco and percussionist Ray Barretto, at the Lyceum.

Salsa mostly remained the sanctum of the tiny community of immigrant workers from Latin America. The parties Lubín Reyes arranged were so profitable that in 1978 he found a venue for the Colombian community's first permanent club in London: Club Colombia in Hanway Street, open every day from three to eleven. 'Although, like good Colombians, we closed the doors and carried on until 5 or 6 a.m., especially at the weekend.'

The clients were Colombians, Spaniards and one or two British men with Colombian girlfriends, and the DJ was Tomek's friend Camilo Pereira from 21 Gledhow Gardens.

Another early arrival was a future salsa promoter and nightclub manager named Leoncio Caycedo. 'It must have been 1978 that we began to meet the first British people in the Colombian clubs, people with open minds who came and discovered salsa for the first time. The thing is, Colombians have this tough image, but they're actually very, very hospitable, so, when British people turned up, we'd offer them a drink, make them feel welcome, invite them home afterwards, and it was, like, "Blimey, you've opened up your home to us!"'

However, as Leoncio emphasised, 'Salsa was still underground, community-based. It wasn't out there on the market.'

Leoncio had arrived in 1977 with his parents and siblings and moved into a Stockwell basement with another Colombian family, seven of them sharing a single room. He told me, 'I liked this country; I liked the respect for individual choice and the opportunities, despite the discrimination. But it was hard to adapt.'

The Colombians were part of that great immigrant army that was now feeding, cleaning, tending and watching over the city: the maternal jobs and the lowest paid. Dancing was an important escape from the hardships. Faced every day with indifference if not downright hostility, it was a way of remembering the old continent. 'It didn't matter if you were Colombian, Ecuadorian, Chilean, Bolivian or Peruvian. We were all friends and everyone liked salsa.'

Lubín moved his club to better locations, but the buildings were often run-down and lacked even basic safety facilities. So Club Colombia moved from Hanway Street to Greek Street, where it became El Dorado, and then to an old coach house with a yellow stucco façade in Denmark Place, off Denmark Street, London's Tin Pan Alley.

In Denmark Place, the club became El Dandy. The building that housed it had a concrete parking bay on the ground floor used as a store room for hotdog stands that served the West End, and by 2.30 a.m. each morning 20 or 30 trolleys were standing in the garage.

There were two upper floors made of timber, accessible through a door that opened from Denmark Place on to a flight of wooden stairs up to a landing and the entrance to El Dandy. From there, the wrought-iron fire escape that led up to the second floor had been encased in plywood. The second floor housed a gambling den managed by a Spaniard named Víctor González, who rented the entire building and sublet the lower floors. Both venues were strictly private. Patrons rang the bell and an upstairs window would open. If they were known to the staff, a key would be thrown down. If not, they didn't get in.

The police knew all about the place. In 1978 González had been fined for flouting licensing and gaming laws but the club had remained open. When a dismembered body was found in Epping Forest in May 1980 and identified as Soho prostitute Pat Malone, detectives had pursued their enquiries to the second floor.

Three months later, on Friday, 15 August, González had a problem with a customer who claimed he was being overcharged for his drinks. A fight started. The doormen threw the man out, told him not to come back and watched him drift off into the night.

It was a warm, close night and El Dandy was crowded and throbbing to music chosen by the DJ, Hernán 'Flaco' Vargas, who had moved on from Gledhow Gardens and was keeping his private record collection at the club. A waitress named Elizabeth Mercado was celebrating her imminent return to Colombia with friends. A large party – whose regular haunt, a restaurant in nearby Charlotte Street called El Rodadero, was closed for redecoration – had also come in, together with the restaurant's manager, Eduardo Arbeláez.

Tomek was a regular at El Dandy. 'I used to go on Fridays and just hang out with Flaco, but it was my birthday. I'd been to see both my parents who were divorced and, frankly, I didn't have any weed, so that night I didn't go.'

Approaching half past three in the morning, Lubín Reyes heard a bang and turned to Flaco: 'Did you hear that?'

'I went out and looked down the stairs. They were engulfed in flames. I went back inside and shut the security door behind me but I didn't lock it. A woman came back from the Ladies and left it ajar. I went straight over to close it but it was already like an oven door and I couldn't get near it.'

The bang had been one of the Calor gas cylinders from the hotdog stands exploding. In seconds, the place had become an inferno.

A window behind a slot machine opened from the club onto a low roof in the interior well of the building. Lubín moved the slot machine and ushered his guests through it. The door out of the building's central well was soon too hot to use, so the escapees broke into the back of Rhodes Music Store, hoping to make it out into Denmark Street. With smoke pouring in behind them, they smashed the shop window using electric guitars, only to find that the security grille couldn't be moved. Having escaped the fire, they now faced asphyxiation.

Luis Jaramillo Silva later told the *Sunday Times*, 'People were shouting, "It's a bomb." I ran to the door but flames were coming in. People started smashing windows with their elbows.'

Customers were jumping from the upstairs floor and breaking legs on landing.

Lubín and Hernán were shepherding customers out but the situation was getting hopeless. 'I looked at Flaco and said, "We'd better get out of here."

'He started to climb out of the window with me, then stopped and said, "The music, *loco!*"

'The records in the club were from Flaco's private collection, and he couldn't bear to leave them.

'I said, "Forget it," but he went back in. He got as far as the record stacks, then the lights went out. People started panicking.'

Eduardo Arbeláez, the manager of El Rodadero, told the *Evening Standard*, 'Before I tried to get out of a window I went back to find my two girlfriends. They were clutching each other, completely petrified. As the flames reached them they started calling my name, asking me to help them. But there was nothing I could do. I felt so helpless.'

Flaco found the girls paralysed with fear, and stayed with them.

The alarm was raised at half past three by the manager of a fast-food shop in Charing Cross Road. The fire brigade arrived to find that Denmark Place was too narrow for the fire engines to enter.

A fireman told *The Times*, 'People seem to have died on the spot without even having time to move an inch.'

Another told the *Sunday Times*, 'These people were roasted where they sat.'

As the fire brigade freed the people in Rhodes Music Store, Lubín Reyes went to look for Flaco's car. 'I knew where he'd left it. I thought, "Maybe he got out." But the car was still there. Hernán, the music, everyone else, all gone.'

Many of the bodies were so badly burned it was not known if they were male or female. One witness reported looking at what he thought was a pile of rubble before noticing two hands welded to a table by the heat. A smell of petrol hung over the scene. The final death toll was 37, 13 of them in El Dandy, 24 on the second floor.

A plastic container found by the front door had traces of petrol and, the following day, the front page of the *Sunday Times* noted, 'If it was arson, it could be the worst mass murder in British history.'

Pursuing the arson theory, police suspected a settling of accounts between 'international drug dealers operating in London, a grudge attack or even the intricate web of South American politics'.

Seven days later, police issued an identikit picture and description of the suspect. He was described as 'of Spanish or South American appearance and aged in his late thirties . . . Between 5 ft 2 in. and 5 ft 4 in. tall, with a distinctive Roman nose, pointed chin and receding hairline'.

But the truth was more prosaic: Maria Delaney, the night

manageress of the hotdog trolley park, said she had seen a man crouching in the doorway. 'The next thing we knew there were flames shooting from the first floor.'

She said the person crouching outside the front door had earlier been refused admission a number of times, and there had been an altercation.

John Thompson, 42, a short, thickset man better known as 'Punch' or 'Gypsy', had been thrown out of the British gambling den upstairs. He took a minicab to a petrol station, hooking his thumb at the building and telling the driver he was going to 'fix them'. He filled a bottle with petrol then went back and poured it through the letterbox. Then he set fire to it.

Tomek heard about the fire on a radio bulletin the following morning, shopping in Brixton. 'I could barely make it out. I jumped on my bike, raced up to Charing Cross Road and saw that Denmark Street had been taped off.

'I bumped into Camilo in Earls Court a few months later. When he saw me, his face turned ashen and he said, "Flaco."

'I said, "I know."

'"You know he went back in?"'

Thompson was tried at the Central Criminal Court in April 1981. He was also charged with arson at a flat in Hackney. He pleaded not guilty to all charges, but on 7 May 1981 he was jailed for life.

In the press coverage, the second-floor club was described as Spanish, although its patrons were mostly British, Irish and Jamaican, some of them unsavoury and well known to the police. El Dandy, they said, was full of illegal immigrants, which was an exaggeration. The vast majority were legal and law-abiding. The club was described as a Colombian drinking club: they'd still never heard of salsa.

For many Britons, Latin jazz was the gateway into salsa and, through the 1980s, an underground Latin jazz and salsa scene spread across the country, with regular Latin nights as far afield as Bristol, Birmingham, Liverpool and Newcastle. There were promoters and DJs playing salsa music, and there were even British salsa bands. The first of them was Cayenne, formed in 1979 by guitarist Robert Greenfield, who translated his name, tongue in cheek, to Roberto Campoverde.

The bands quickly reconnected with the story of Colombian migration to the UK. Roberto Pla, born in Barranquilla on the Caribbean coast, was one of eight brothers and sisters, seven of whom became professional musicians, six of *them* percussionists like Roberto. He spent ten years playing for Lucho Bermúdez, the great populariser of folk forms like *porro*, *gaita* and *cumbia* and one of Colombia's most famous artists. Then he fell for a British woman teaching in an English-language school in Bogotá, and in 1978 they moved to New York.

'I'd played with the best groups in my country and I wanted to play with other musicians because I was young and I had a young man's ambition.'

A temporary trip to the UK became permanent and Roberto found himself sewing buttons on overcoats in a sweatshop in the Midlands, earning in a week half of what Lucho Bermúdez used to pay him in Colombia for a one-hour set. If that wasn't bad enough, he was overwhelmed by the culture shock: the disembodiedness, the lack of eye contact, above all, the taciturn nature of the British.

'I was often tempted to phone Lucho Bermúdez and say, "Maestro, can I come back?" He'd have been happy to have me. But I resisted. I had decided to change my life so I stuck with it.'

For five months, Roberto sank into his own, uncharacteristic mutism. 'I went through a period of depression. I'd come from Bogotá, which has a tremendous swing, and New York, which was on fire in those years. I remembered my Maestro telling me, "You can leave, but

41

my music will pursue you wherever you go." And when I was tired of going up and down stairs with rolls of material on my shoulder, I remembered his music and the wonderful times I'd had with the band.'

One Sunday in 1981 a radio programme mentioned a Latin band performing that night in Islington. 'We got lost and we only arrived for the last three numbers that the band played. But I was the happiest man alive.'

The band was Robert Greenfield's Cayenne. Roberto began to go to every performance, without ever speaking to the band members, 'although they noticed me in the crowd sometimes'.

One day, during a Cayenne concert in a bar at the Royal Free Hospital in Hampstead, North London, Roberto vocalised a percussion improvisation to himself. The girlfriend of one of the band members overheard him, and asked him if he could do the same with his hands. Emboldened by a couple of beers, he decided to show her. He pushed through the crowd and reached the stage. The timbales were occupied, so he picked up the maracas.

'The guy on the timbal began to laugh. He realised I could play and said, "Come and play this." I hadn't played for three years but I played the best timbal solo of my life. At the start of it, I didn't have a single friend in the country. By the time I'd finished, I had 20. And the next day, I was officially a member of the band.'

From that day on, Roberto Pla's name and Colombian feeling for rhythm have been inseparable from the sound of British salsa bands. In 1982 Pla founded Valdéz, with a brilliant flautist and multi-instrumentalist named Stan Thewlis, who Pla dubbed Stan Rivera. 'When I heard the kid play, I was left open-mouthed. Wow! This guy is fantastic. I was so happy. And immediately we were the best of friends.'

In 1984 Pla and Thewlis formed El Sonido de Londres – 'The London Sound' – while Pla also played for his own

12-piece band, the Latin Jazz Ensemble, playing jazz, Afro-Cuban and Colombian rhythms, as well as salsa.

Perhaps the key point of contact between London's Colombian community and the British opened in Charlotte Street in 1981: Sol y Sombra, run by Diego Chávez Tashima, born in Palmira, north of Cali, the son of a Japanese mother. The venue had two levels: in the early days the upper floor was a Spanish restaurant during the week that became a Colombian club with live bands at the weekends; and, in the basement, DJs played Colombian music for a Colombian clientele.

One day, a former cinema technician named Dave Hucker walked in and made the Colombian owners an offer. 'I want to hire the place on a Thursday night. I'll pay you £30.'

Hucker had discovered the Sol y Sombra with two friends who managed The Scala Cinema just around the corner. Today, Steve Woolley and Paul Webster are successful film producers, but in the early '80s they ran weekend all-nighters at The Scala. They would knock off at four in the morning and head to Sol y Sombra which, although unlicensed, and despite its position a few hundred yards away from Tottenham Court Road police station, was one of the many all-night gambling and drinking dens in town.

Hucker had been deejaying in Dean Street at a club called Gossips, playing funk and reggae. 'But I wanted to play the whole range of music that I was interested in: African music, and all the Caribbean genres, Haitian *compa*, Trinidadian *soca*, calypso and so on. I described it as "the music of two continents and a few assorted islands"! Salsa was part of it too.'

Hucker's eclectic music nights at the Sol y Sombra caught on. 'The owners were soon making more out of the gringos than they were out of the local Colombians, especially at the weekends. I was soon doing Thursdays and Saturdays, and I let a friend called Paul Murphy have Fridays, and other people moved in from Monday to Wednesday and the Colombians moved upstairs full-time.'

Hucker and Murphy both played music with the rhythms and vibes of 1950s Latin jazz, mambo and *chachachá*. While they were downstairs, Leoncio Caycedo was in the Colombian club upstairs.

'It was unusual, Britons and Colombians enjoying sometimes the same music in spaces separated by a flight of stairs. They didn't have much contact, much less mix together, but a few Britons ventured up the stairs to see the Colombians dance.'

This cultural mix attracted the Nigerian Afro-Beat star Fela Kuti to one of Dave Hucker's nights. 'He had to wait to get in as we were totally full. It was one-out, one-in time! He sent one of his girlfriends over to ask me to play some of his music.'

At Sol y Sombra the Metropolitan Police made their small contribution to the development of British salsa. In the club's early years, police officers were regular patrons. They ate and drank at no charge and left the building with boxes full of liquor. The mural on the back wall, of a beach scene with palm trees, was painted by the wife of one of the station's inspectors. With the manager Diego Chávez driving a gold Mercedes with every possible add-on, all the signs were that the club was the front for an illegal import business and the law enforcers were taking a cut.

The arrangement no doubt financed some of the acts that performed at the club. In June 1984 the legendary salsa singer Héctor Lavoe and his fourteen-piece band played to London's Latin American community in two unlikely venues. One was Sol y Sombra on a Saturday night. The word was that Chávez was later interviewed by the tax authorities and asked how a business with a weekend turnover of £300 could afford to bring a 14-piece band from New York for a night.

The other venue was the Apostle Hall in Pimlico, where Lavoe and his band were the special guests at the awards ceremony of London's Latin American football league, whose president was Lubín Reyes. 'Since the league consisted of Colombians, Peruvians, Ecuadorians and Bolivians, we ended the prize ceremony with a show in which groups from each nationality performed their typical folk dances. Plenty of local people came to see it.

'Then Héctor Lavoe came on.'

The hall was in a residential area, and locals came out wondering what on earth was going on. The hall was full and the 40 or 50 feet between it and the road were crowded.

'There were more than 1,500 people there, Brits included. The police turned up, and I remember one of them asking, "Who is it that's singing? Can I go in and see him?"

'I helped him through and said, "That's him. Héctor Lavoe!"

'He was singing *"Mi gente"*, and the policeman said, "What an amazing voice!"

'They were just keeping public order, but they were happy to be there!'

In 1984 Diego Chávez left Sol y Sombra suddenly. One day Dave Hucker came in and found someone doing a bottle count. 'Whoever owned the venue had sent him to collect the rent.'

Chávez resurfaced in the United States. In February 1986 an undercover agent working for the Drug Enforcement Administration caught wind of a large shipment of cocaine that was coming into New Orleans. The man who came to meet it was described as 'a Colombian of Japanese descent who had lived in London'. In New Orleans, Diego Chávez confirmed to another undercover agent that he had agreed to deliver cocaine to New York.

On the day of the drop, an agent posing as the buyer flashed a payment of $1.5 million. Moments after the first instalment of ten kilograms of cocaine was delivered, Chávez was picked up in Queens. He was convicted of narcotics racketeering, and sentenced to 20 years in prison, although he was released early and deported. In September 2004 he was driving in the north of Cali when two men opened fire on him. Police described the murder as a settling of accounts between drug gangs and said that Chávez was suspected of having links with drugs boss Diego Montoya.

Sol y Sombra carried on under Diego Chávez's nephew Ruben and a Portuguese manager known as 'Believe Me Leo', but the glory years ended in 1986 when the club burned to the ground after one of Dave Hucker's Thursday nights there. Arson was suspected but no one was ever charged.

The Colombian immigrant community was growing, and more nightclubs were opening to serve them. In November 1990 Camilo Pereira, one of the original inhabitants of 21 Gledhow Gardens, hired a former working Thames barge called *Wilfred*, moored at Temple Pier on the Victoria Embankment, and began to hold Sunday-night dances there. A year later, he bought the lease and converted *Wilfred* into a bar-restaurant called El Barco Latino. Three new South London venues followed, but, with rents increasing and licences harder to come by, it was becoming difficult for old-style, community-centred clubs to survive. The last central London nightclub for a Colombian clientele was La Gota Fria, which opened in Margaret Street in 1992.

The immediate future lay in crossover clubs aimed at a mixed crowd of middle-class Latin Americans, Europeans and British enthusiasts. The Bass Clef, where I pitched up in 1986, was one of these, and there were others dotted all over South London. El Barco Latino managed the transition. Then there was the first floor of Ronnie Scott's Jazz Club, where Dave Hucker continued his adventure in the twilight world of London salsa. One day, he lost the current to his DJ box. Trying to reconnect it, he discovered the electricity seemed to be coming from an amusement arcade in Old Compton Street.

'It had always been a place where you could buy weed. The police raided it once then invited Ronnie and Pete King down to the station to discuss things. They were sitting round a table and the police emptied a huge big sack of weed on to the table. They said they had seized it all during the raid.

'"Bollocks," said Ronnie. "Don't try and pull my fucking leg. I was there on the night and I saw exactly how much you found and it was just a few little bags on the floor."

'The police hummed and hawed and eventually agreed he was right.

'Soon after I started, we were cleaning out a cupboard upstairs and found a plastic carrier bag full of ready-bagged £10 deals.'

The bags found their way to satisfied customers.

Police corruption was still rife. 'Opposite Ronnie's was a Maltese social club, from the days when the Maltese ran the vice in Soho. Every week, an inspector from Vine Street nick would go round and collect £40 in a brown envelope from them, though in those days he gave to the Police Benevolent Fund rather than the pockets of the other coppers. It was described as paying respect money.'

*

Salsa's infectious rhythms, which had flowed across the Atlantic with the trade in kidnapped Africans and colonised the Americas, were now reaching British ears. Nightclubs like the Bass Clef attracted a small number of Latin Americans who had grown up dancing. Most of the patrons were European: Italian, Spanish and British, who couldn't dance as such but who listened to the music and translated it into dance using whatever movements they could find.

We longed to respond physically to the music but didn't know how.

Britain was looking for a teacher. It found one in Xihomara ('See-oh-mara') Granados, who never intended to teach salsa, or even take on British students.

Born in the tiny village of Aguachica, close to the Magdalena River in the north Colombian department of César, Xihomara had come to London in June 1986. The daughter of professional dancers in Colombia – her mother directs the Ballet Folklórico de Colombia, one of the country's largest dance companies – she came to learn English after completing her Baccalaureate in Bogotá and three years at the École supérieur des cinéastes in Paris.

'When I first arrived, we had small community places where Colombians got together and danced. A few curious Brits came along too. They were very well treated. I would go over and talk and invite them to dance because I thought it was great they were interested in our culture.'

Xihomara taught folk dance at the Albany Centre in New Cross, South London. 'I just wanted to train a small group of Latin Americans to perform traditional Latin American genres. It was quite difficult to get to and I only ever had about five students, two Mexicans, two Chileans and a Colombian.'

A year later, she moved her lessons to the much more accessible Oval House. 'By 1987 British people were coming in and saying, "I hear you're doing salsa classes."

'I said, "No! We do *cumbia, bambuco, joropo, mapalé, vallenato*, Mexican dances, Peruvian dances, the whole panorama of Latin American folk dance." But salsa was all they wanted.'

The trouble was, Xihomara had never taken formal salsa lessons. For her, it was simply there. But she had had years of training in Colombian folk dance.

'I wasn't a salsa teacher but I thought, "With my training, I could try to explain it to the British," you know?'

Faced with the demand, Xihomara succumbed, and brought the explicitness of the show dancer to her classes. There were other pressures that shaped the format of the classes and the nature of the dance itself. 'Teaching a Latin American to improve their quality of movement is one thing. Teaching people with a total separation of mind and body is something else! I felt I couldn't teach the British students at the same time as the Latin Americans because the British couldn't even understand the basic rhythm.

'I created names for some of the steps because I knew that it would make them easier to remember. Everything had to pass through words. It had to make sense to them intellectually. When it did, they'd say, "OK, now I understand," and start moving their bodies!'

All of this created a new clarity, a distinctness between dance gestures that hadn't been there beforehand. 'It wasn't there in the first place, that's right. But you have to do that to structure a class.'

Soon, Xihomara was joined by a second salsa teacher.

In the summer of 1989 Nelson Batista, a Cuban who had arrived in the UK the previous year, went to the Suave Suave Festival, a week of Cuban art and music, at the Institute of Contemporary Arts (ICA) in London. One of the island's leading *son* bands, the Septeto Nacional, was playing. The septet had been founded in 1927 by Ignacio Piñeiro, a well-known bass player and composer, most famously of the song '*Échale salsita*'. If a Cuban bandleader wanted his musicians to play with more feeling, to swing it, he'd tell them, '*Tócala con salsa!*' But '*Échale salsita*' is sometimes mentioned as the first published use of 'salsa' to refer to music, and therefore it marks the origin of 'salsa' to describe a musical genre.

Also at the ICA Festival were one of Cuba's leading Afro-Cuban rumba bands, Los Muñequitos de Matanzas. For Nelson, it was almost a homecoming. 'It was my first real contact with Cuban music since I'd left a few months earlier. The singer of the Septeto Nacional was Carlos Embale, a national figure in Cuba and a great rumba singer. And I'd seen the Muñequitos play rumba in Matanzas.

'There were lots of British people who were interested in the culture but couldn't dance.'

Nelson was with another Cuban, a male friend, and, having no girls to dance with, they moved solo to the familiar rhythms. 'We danced as if we were in Cuba and had a great time.'

Nelson attracted the attention of the festival organiser, who asked him, 'Where did you learn to dance?'

'At home, with my family.'

'Well, come along for the rest of the week for nothing, and dance away.'

'The next day, I met a Cuban girl who'd only been here a few months, like me. We danced and danced and danced, and then a British woman approached me and said, "If you want to teach people how to dance, I will arrange everything for you. I will find a venue and advertise."

'I thought about it and said, "OK."'

The British woman was a dance teacher and musician called Daniela Rosselson who created a business called The Salsasonic Dance Company, found a venue in the Highbury Roundhouse, a North London community centre, and had leaflets printed and distributed. Together, she and Nelson started teaching three times a week.

'I hadn't yet acquired the concept of punctuality so I strolled in about 15 minutes late. There was a car park in front and a huge queue. I asked the guy at the end of the queue, "What's happening here?"

'And he said, "We're waiting for a dance class, but the teacher's late."

'I thought it was someone else. I went inside and Daniela was there, panicking. She said to me, "There are too many people."

'There was a proper dance studio upstairs and a large hall downstairs, so I said, "Let's use the room downstairs which is bigger."

'We had about 70 or 80 people. And then I kind of began the process of breaking down what was natural to me.'

3

Basic Steps

Amor de mi vida no te vayas pa'l colegio.
Di que estás enferma y quédate un
   ratoconmigo
Love of my life, don't go to school.
Say you're ill and stay with me a while.
   'Nido de Amor', composed by Octavio
   Daza, performed by El Gran Combo

Vivi's favourite film was *Alive*, the story of an air crash deep in the Andes and its aftermath, when its survivors were forced into cannibalism before being rescued many months later. I gave her Piers Paul Read's book and the various memoirs that followed it, and she devoured them so quickly I wondered if they contained a metaphor for life in Britain with me.

I remembered it when Vivi's favourite salsa group, El Gran Combo de Puerto Rico, performed in a North London nightclub. Before the band was announced and the venue filled to standing room only, a happy air of Western mechanical genius filled the place and Vivi was taken on to the floor by a man who looked like he'd learned salsa from a book. He yanked her through a progression of jerks like someone working the levers in a signal box. Each move was as overwrought as it would have been discreet in Colombia. Colombians didn't get too involved in their inner life when they danced: their idea of taste had less to do with personal expression than with issues of social appropriateness and acceptability. His movements reminded me of a soul-destroying moment in *Alive* when one of the marooned survivors tries to reconnect the aircraft radio, sorting through hundreds of tiny, colour-coded wires despite his defective know-how and frostbitten fingers. Trying not to watch from the sidelines, I could feel myself being dragged back into parts of me I had been using Colombia to escape. It was our first taste of what salsa had become in some parts of Britain: a dance form built on empathy and eye contact that was danced with very little of either.

Vivi eventually escaped the succession of ligament wrenchings and skeletal jerks and returned across the dance floor. She told me she felt used. It occurred to me that Vivi was useful to her erstwhile partner to the extent that a genuine Caribbean could serve to authenticate his dance. His salsa, which could so easily have been mine, was, if nothing else, impolite.

I decided that, if I was going to learn, it would have to be in Colombia.

On our next trip, I found the Medellín telephone directory was full of private academies that served up a faintly overemphatic version of family salsa, in classes that were one to one or one to a couple. They didn't advertise these lessons because something like a taboo hung over them. Having to learn salsa in a formal setting was tantamount to acknowledging that your upbringing was deficient in something that really mattered. The need for classes could be seen as an unstated indictment of one's parents, so, although plenty of people took them, few would have openly admitted to doing so. In Colombia, the salsa aesthetic was deeply opposed to dance classes. The division isn't hard and fast, but as a rule the children of the upper reaches of Colombian society grew up dancing a little less than those lower down. The better off people were, the quieter and more private their lives. Upwardly mobile workers who moved out to the suburbs either gave up their partying or ended up dealing with the law, and as a result the minds and bodies of the wealthy were more tenuously connected than those of the poor. When dancing became a necessary part of forming relationships, they turned to the private dance academies.

The academies existed primarily to teach tango, whose ethos and atmosphere had sunk deep roots here. Medellín once thought of itself as the second city of tango: the songwriter and pianist Joaquín Mauricio Mora abandoned Buenos Aires and settled here. Carlos Gardel, the greatest tango singer of all, met his death in an air crash at the Olaya Herrera airport in 1935, and in the *barrio* of Manrique there was a monument to Gardel. Tango was danced with a special intensity there, although dance academies across the city turned this nostalgia to their advantage. A few years from now, Vivi and I might end up there.

The waltz, too, brought in a few pesos, and so, surprisingly, did belly dancing, thanks to generations of immigrants from Turkey, Syria and the Lebanon, and more recently to Shakira, the Colombian artist born in Barranquilla to a father of Lebanese descent.

Salsa was different: the vast majority of Colombians danced it, and that meant the poor, who grew up dancing in street carnivals, family reunions and neighbourhood *parrandas* – loud, long and regular parties – where noise levels were high but so was neighbourly tolerance. Since getting it wrong meant losing the girl or boy, there was no room for clumsiness or unseemly ostentation. And since, in turn, the people who knew, Colombia's *real* dancers, were generally from poorer backgrounds, the academies inverted the social pyramid by giving them the ascendancy over their superiors for an hour at a time.

Vivi's family had made something like the same transition, in theory, at least, when they moved from La Cabañita to El Poblado, an avowedly middle-class area in Medellín where parties are fewer and more moderate. In theory, because in the 1980s El Poblado had become a magnet for nouveaux riches with popular tastes, and the traditional bourgeoisie began to move eastwards and out of town to Rionegro and Llanogrande. In any case, the move coincided with marital breakdown, and, as Lucho had been the instigator of the drinking and dancing, they too more or less ceased.

Two dance academies stood within walking distance of Vivi's family home where she had lived with her mother and two brothers in a corner of El Poblado known as Patio Bonito. I visited the humbler of them, where the board outside read: 'Classical ballet, gymnastics, Pilates, jazz, tap, flamenco, contemporary, ballroom, tango, belly dancing, music (violin/organ), massage, medical consultations.' No mention of salsa. I rolled up for my first class with the determination of a man undertaking a physical trial.

My teacher, a graduate of the school run by Medellín's top dance organisation, the Ballet Folklórico de Antioquia, was slender and erect, with an air of grace and translucence. I saw her recently on television, dancing tango beautifully, still perhaps cursing the day I appeared, leaning over her like a condemned building. But I was entering a realm in which nothing was certain, in which my body was prone to rebel against the most elementary instructions. It was like learning to walk all over again. Or learning to crawl because, when the time came, walking didn't go all that well.

She wanted me to pace around the room naturally. When I came to think about it, there'd always been some artifice to my gait, an unnatural tension in the shoulders, a deliberate turning in or out of the toes, depending on which film star, footballer or father figure I was modelling myself on at any particular moment. Always a leaning towards someone or something. All that night, I heard bandy-legged footsteps: my John Wayne phase, looming out of childhood to haunt me.

When I'd completed that ordeal, I discovered I'd made it across one minefield only to encounter another, because salsa wasn't like walking at all: it was more of an epileptic pacing, going nowhere, and one I enacted for the first time in twenty years in the unpromising company of my own bemused reflection: left foot forward on one, with the slightest lift of the right heel. Right heel down on two, left foot back to its starting position on three. Then, a pause before repeating the same sequence but in reverse: right foot back on five, with the slightest elevation of the left heel. Left heel down on two, right foot back to its starting position on three.

And pause.

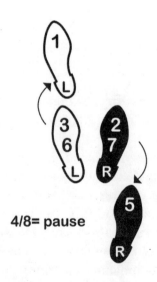

4/8= pause

These first, tentative quaverings were like a private game: I watched in vivid self-appraisal, correcting myself in the glass, disappearing for minutes into the disassembled man in the mirror, only re-emerging to breathe. By looking too hard at all the pieces that made me up, I managed to make it even trickier: a simple, stop-start stagger translated into a full-body malfunction in which unintended interruptions interrupted the intended ones. The moment I stepped away from the mirror, the self-absorbed fantasy of dancing with someone else who was really me was destroyed by the undeniable physical presence of my teacher.

Then we tried dancing together. It was something like patting your head with one hand and circling the other on your stomach, except that it involved my whole body and my whole body wasn't really minded to co-operate. I felt rather giddy. As the music doesn't remain the same, nor can the dance, so we moved on to a variation, throwing our legs sideways. This raised the problem of the phase shift from to and fro to sideways and back again. I limited my ambitions to adding a veneer of amiability to my incompetence.

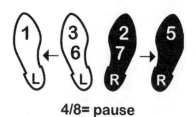

4/8= pause

She taught me other variants: I marched unstoppably forward and retreated as far as the wall. There were sideways excursions. Within my embrace, I turned her through not-quite-full circles, this way then the other, and from time to time the moves even seemed to have worked their way into my rhythm centres, and dancing felt a little less like a dangerous breaking of cover. I felt like one of those lumbering plywood-framed aircraft my grandfather flew during the war: crippled and sightless on the ground, but swift to take off, bank in formation and head purposefully into enemy territory.

My body was roughly the same but the terms of occupancy were radically new. My co-ordination was hesitant; I could no longer take balance for granted but the feeling was far from unpleasant. Here was the simple pleasure of bodies moving together, tenderly embraced – a primer in how to love.

There were moments I might even have achieved a sort of qualified grace, stepping out of the narrative sequence of everyday life and into a state of temporary timelessness, as if a forgotten knowledge was seeping into me through the soles of my feet, propelling me through two worlds at once, because, skipping over the squares on a dance floor in a building somewhere in southern Medellín, I confronted spaces inside myself so vast and unexpected they left me light-headed. Those first steps may have been only the simplest of salsas, but salsa they were, and, from then on, when the air vibrated to the music of the Spanish-speaking Caribbean, I could vibrate with it.

My days in Medellín began with ice-cold water spilling from a naked pipe. The impact on my morning skin shattered the fragile truce between mind and body until breakfast and beyond, and it was only on the basis of a number of possibly fictitious revitalising properties I hoped it might confer – enhanced energy, fertility and vascularisation of the muscles, and perhaps even a rejuvenated scalp and thickened hair – that I could bring myself to submit to this daily torture. In any case, not even the weak-willed actually *need* hot water, I told myself. My body wasn't convinced. The matter demanded consideration because Vivi's family rarely switched the boiler on: hardly unusual in a town in which proximity to the equator kept the heat constant and altitude kept it more or less bearable, earning Medellín the soubriquet of 'The City of Eternal Spring'. Far from a sign of under-development, a cold shower in such a climate is a consumer preference, and if there was no shower rose it wasn't because there were no shower roses in town – Medellín has the same gargantuan DIY emporiums as any other Western city – but because the shock of bracing water from the pipe is more energising. It takes a while to adapt to, of course, but you can get used to anything.

I was even getting used to dancing. There were setbacks; there were bound to be. I'd learned the elementary mechanics, but they were still far from natural. My shoulders were still tense, my head bowed, my arms at a loss. There were uncontrollable asymmetries. I'd still lose the beat or look in the mirror and see a pair of enormous feet and a pale face on a rhubarb stick of a neck, and recognise that my old aim of melting into the music, of becoming a little less conspicuously tall, white and foreign was doomed. As long as no one was watching, my movements were relatively uninhibited, although they fell apart in the glare of other people's eyes. Being watched scrambled my mind's links with my body. But that first intensive course had given me a selection of basic movements and there was no longer that sense of the music seeing me coming and saying each time, 'Not you. Not now.'

The Ballet Folklórico de Antioquia mixed folklore with classical, modern and contemporary dance, so the salsa my first instructor taught me wasn't family salsa. It had rigour and structure and maze-like preparatory moves that were more ballroom than family salsa. I probably had more than I needed already, but the bit was between my teeth now, so, when that first intensive course was over, I looked for another.

I had learned that the owner of the school opposite had a reputation. He was a tango connoisseur and the preferred teacher of many of the city's wealthiest, most benevolent matriarchs, with their bourgeois traditions of philanthropy and elegance. These ladies were the sponsors of the network of parenting centres Vivi's mother had been instrumental in setting up all over the city during the previous 20 years. So, with Marlen's introduction, we went over and met him.

José Fernando González had learned his vast array of Colombian folk and tropical dances, plus his beloved tango, not in classes but through the time-honoured method of just doing it, from a very early age. Caribbean styles of music and dance had been part of Medellín life since the 1950s, and José Fernando drew on them all.

The building he presided over was a rambling structure with many rooms in unexpected places. On the way to our lessons, we'd pass a group *chachachá* on one side, a geriatric *paso doble* on the other, and, through the next door, kids working up a threatening hip hop. As often as not, we'd arrive to find José Fernando dancing a seductive tango with his sister, an eye-catching, statuesque beauty whose striking glamour contrasted with and perhaps went some way to explaining José Fernando's detached temperament. Like his sister, his every movement was beautifully precise and delicate. Whenever business allowed, they would disappear off to Buenos Aires to spend hours learning alongside the masters.

José Fernando danced with both of us, swapping easily between leading and following. With Vivi, José Fernando's loose-limbed, improvisational style, saying 17 things at once and marvellously adaptable to the passing thought, was a wonder. Then I would take over, sticking doggedly to the point. Mislaid in my own physicality, still learning basic motor control, it felt like a midlife return to primary school, although I rather enjoyed primary school and I rather enjoyed this too.

Most of all, we worked on leading. As the male, I had to dictate the dance, while my brain focused on other things: listening to the music for cues that made a change of movement appropriate and signalling the change to my partner. Physically, it was straightforward, like walking hand in hand and changing direction with a gentle but decisive pressure, but that's not easy when you're in full body-spasm. Besides, I could just about follow the beat: registering the music as anything more than that was utterly beyond me. I had little spare mental capacity, so, when I danced, my tongue could well have been hanging out in my absorption. I could have been drooling or wearing pyjamas or even dancing stark naked.

José Fernando reframed the problem. It was not so much an incessant bargaining over what to do next, as a matter of learning to interpret the music's exhortation to move; of being responsive to the changes in timbre and intensity. Mind-reading, yes, but also co-authoring, in bodily movement, a common feeling for the music.

José Fernando was instinctively hard on the fancy stuff. Dance, he said, was more than a series of lyric highs, exciting enough in themselves but with no cumulative sense. It had as much to do with overall structure as with individual sequences. Each movement should rehearse in miniature the more complex orchestrations of the dance. It had to be sustained, integrated: between the moves, there had to be a self-igniting spark.

He asked us to perform an exercise, leaning into each other, eyes closed, moving blindly and uncertainly through space. There was a degree of progress. I centred my dance within our embrace; I learned what it was not to dance for the eyes of others. This planned disorientation, to sensitise me to the strangeness of two attempting to act as one, seemed to work. It certainly took immense patience on Vivi's part: I was new-born into these movements, although not like a foal or fawn because they don't tower over you as I did over Vivi, unleashing heavy blows wherever our bodies meshed, which was everywhere. If Vivi was antelope graceful, I was moose-calf clumsy. I justified this with mathematical proofs that the larger the body, the thicker the limbs and bulkier the skeleton. Then we'd see a portly Colombian couple dancing and my self-justifications would collapse.

Or we'd watch Vivi's uncle Edgar dance with Marlen, his sister, in Vivi's 15th-birthday video. He weighed three stone more than me but moved effortlessly. The other men were in suits, but Edgar wore jeans and a blue shirt: he'd driven 12 hours to be there. A powerful, two-footed centre-forward with a good head, he was a rhythmic, fluid dancer, and I modelled my salsa on his.

The video had been made a decade and a half before in the house in La Cabañita, a tiny corner not of Medellín but of Bello to the north, poorer and less prestigious than the metropolis but the perfect location for the all-night parties that followed Lucho's weekend games of softball. He was the team's star player: a stylish batter and the author of a slow, looping curve-ball that had its victims tying themselves in knots. After the games, a section of Medellín's Costeño community – the section centred on the university where Lucho worked – reconvened in the big old family home with Lucho, Marlen, Vivi and her brothers to talk, drink, listen to music and dance the night away.

Lucho drove the festivities, although Marlen matched him in conversation and on the dance floor. Whisky, rum and aguardiente flowed, but this was the respectable, university-educated middle class so there was no question of marijuana doing the rounds, for instance. And, as salsa throughout the Caribbean is primarily a family dance, there was no cutting in or using it as a device for making approaches.

For girls in Colombia and elsewhere in the Caribbean, their 15th birthday marks a coming of age, and the celebrant, partnered in turn by her male relatives and friends, dances a ritual waltz. It's the height of exoticism. Just think: music and dance with no Afro-Caribbean rhythms or indigenous colour! After the long round of waltzes, normality resumes and salsa takes over for the rest of the party. But that, of course, goes without saying.

The tape was ageing, and the reds and blues leaking

across the picture made the birthday girl's eyes and cheeks, made up by an over-zealous neighbour, shine like hummingbird wings. The camera lingered over the cake, the champagne glasses, the guestbook, the pen fitted inside a long quill and the guests at the door in saturated pinks and greens.

Vivi is dancing her birthday waltz to *Tales of the Vienna Woods*. Lucho is her first partner, before a succession of uncles, then someone's best friend and someone else's, a classmate or two, and then her six-year-old brother Luis Fernando. There are cheers as each partner gives way to the next, although someone is missing: Vivi's elder brother Nestor, upstairs with a foot in plaster that he's broken playing football. Nestor's dancing days are over anyway: he learned to dance the way Vivi did in Cartagena but he prefers rock music, and at the party they tell him he's only broken it to avoid dancing with his sister. All the same, she poses for photographs with both brothers.

Downstairs, the music has changed: Joe Arroyo, Cartagena's most famous vocalist, sings of brutality meted out to slave girls; the Grupo Niche croons a dream of love; Eddie Santiago has a song of distinctly erotic content; and there is the occasional *merengue* and *vallenato* by Jorge Oñate: perhaps '*Nido de Amor*' ('Love Nest'), about the way a drop of rain in Colombia brings everything to a halt.

Then, more exoticism: 'Happy Birthday' in broken English. Vivi cuts the cake, there are more photos and the dancing resumes with strong hands and floating hips, a minimum of everything, conversations continuing over the rippling movements, the quality of movement exquisite. The demands of social style press down on every fibre.

4

BODIES, THE EXHIBITION

Ricardo viene de frente, con su sonido
bestial,
. . . Como bestia tocando tumbao.
Ricardo's coming, head on, with his
bestial sound,
. . . like a beast playing *tumbao.*

'*Sonido bestial*', composed and
performed by Richie Ray
and Bobby Cruz

New York was my fault. Without meaning to, I had begun to think of salsa in a way Vivi never could: as a sort of hobby or personal project. I wanted to understand the whole salsa story and, since New York City was one of the key staging posts, I had to go there. So when, after three years in England, Vivi received her UK passport, we decided to start routing our journeys to Colombia via the United States.

An hour or so before arrival the landing cards came out. The A-side was for flight numbers and passport details. The flip side started with questions about communicable diseases and offences involving moral turpitude. It culminated in: 'Have you ever been denied a U.S. visa?'

Vivi was looking at me.

'What?'

She and her mother had wanted to visit a family friend in New Jersey in 1999. They had paid the cash fee to the US Embassy in Bogotá for an appointment and travelled to the capital for the interview. They were turned down, no reason given. Disappointing but hardly surprising: rejection was probably the norm there. But in this new context, on the flight from London, it set her apart as some sort of criminal.

Worse, the card specified:

> **IMPORTANT:** If you answered "Yes" to any of the above, please contact the American Embassy **BEFORE** you travel to the U.S. since you may be refused admission into the United States.

We didn't really know what to do. Pretend it had never happened and hope for the best? Neither of us was much use at lying. Vivi ticked the 'Yes' box and we began to divide the contents of our hand luggage so that I could carry on with our suitcases if she was turned back. We disembarked with churning stomachs and joined the queue for passport control.

The officer greeted us carefully, thetn glanced at both sides of our landing cards. He picked up his rubber stamp, brought it down decisively twice and wished us a pleasant stay. Our fears had been misplaced. When the tension had passed, it even seemed appropriate that our salsa tourism trip should have started with a bout of deportation anxiety. After all, for salsa's carrier communities, being refused entry to and being deported from the United States were everyday topics. Along with violence and racist marginalisation, they were among the life experiences condensed in the salsa sound. Listen carefully and you can probably hear them in Willie Colón's trombone on '*El Malo*': nervous, edgy, never clean, never quite in tune, always either forcing the beat or dragging behind it.

It was easy to imagine this adrenalin-driven musical

SALSA FOR PEOPLE WHO PROBABLY SHOULDN'T

impetus giving rise to a dance powered by something centripetal, full of forceful, slingshot forms that hurled partners into distant disjunction then returned them to each other with all the risk of painful collision. I wanted to see it. But first I had a record shop to visit.

New York forces the old truism on you: it's America but it's a lot more. You're always somewhere else as well, slipping between worlds, turning corners and emerging in a small town on the outskirts of Naples or a Chinese border settlement. It has Arab islands, Japanese atolls, Russian archipelagos. 786 Prospect Avenue in the South Bronx was one of these portals. Its owner, a quietly spoken Puerto Rican named Miguel Ángel Amadeo, was an important salsa songwriter. He wrote the title track of Héctor Lavoe's second album *De Ti Depende* ('It's up to you'). He wrote '*Que me lo den en vida*' ('Give it to me while I'm still alive'), one of El Gran Combo's biggest hits, and many other songs in the band's repertoire. Celia Cruz and Cheo Feliciano, two of salsa's greatest vocalists, recorded his tunes, and another, his nephew Tito Nieves, recorded an album of his songs called *Entre Familia* ('In the Family').

The longest continuously operating Latin music store in New York City, it was listed on the State and National Registers of Historic Places in 2001, in recognition of its significance to the Latin music scene and its role in the Puerto Rican experience of New York City. It became a pilgrimage for us, and every time we were there we would drink rum with Mike Amadeo and he would tell us more about his life or introduce us to other hidden treasures of Latino New York. One day he walked us two blocks from the elevated train station at Prospect Avenue to a truck called Mama Isabel's, parked off-road on the corner of 156th Street and Prospect Avenue. It was the sort of place you wouldn't look twice at unless you knew beforehand that the best *pastelillos* in New York City were there.

786 Prospect Avenue and its proprietors have been at the

heart of New York's Latin music scene since 1941, when Rafael Hernández and his sister Victoria opened it for business as the Casa Hernández. By then, Rafael was recognised as one of Puerto Rico's finest songwriters, although he had composed many of his most enduring pieces in New York, including perhaps the most beautiful bolero of all, the exile's *'Lamento Borincano'*, which serenades Borinquen, the indigenous Taíno name for Puerto Rico:

Borinquen, la tierra del Eden	Borinquen, the garden of Eden,
y que al cantar el gran Gautier	that, when he sang, the great Gautier,
llamó la perla de los mares.	proclaimed 'the pearl of the oceans'.
Ahora que te mueres con tus pesares	Now that you're dying of grief,
Déjame que te cante yo también.	Allow me, too, to sing to you.

He was, above all, a master of the bolero, that genre of lilting ballads in which all the symbols of the early shifts from country to city and then abroad were condensed: lyrics that sang of love and loss, a guitar accompaniment suggesting the countryside, and a gentle, Afro-Caribbean cadence, all packaged into a short format that suited the early gramophone industry.

The songs of Rafael Hernández took on national sentiments in a number of countries: *'Linda Quisqueya'* ('Beautiful Quisqueya') is a Dominican favourite; Cubans think of *'El Cambunchero'* and *'Cachita'* as national songs; and among Puerto Ricans *'Preciosa'* is a national hymn. More than one country laid claim to his guitar trio too. With two Puerto Ricans and a Dominican, they were known as the Trío Borinquen in New York and Puerto Rico, but in the Dominican Republic, known to its inhabitants as Quisqueya, they became the Trío Quisqueya. By this sleight of hand, the bolero, in the hands of Rafael Hernández, became the first musical genre to be cherished by the entire immigrant community, wherever their origins in Latin America. Between the world wars it contributed to the emergence of the Latino, that New York creation that made a single, composite entity of the disparate community of Puerto Ricans, Cubans, Mexicans, Dominicans, Colombians and Venezuelans.

The story of Rafael Hernández connected with salsa in other ways. Before 786 Prospect Avenue, he and his sister had owned a store at 1735 Madison Avenue called Almacenes Hernández. It had opened in 1927 and is thought to have been the first Puerto Rican-owned music store in Spanish Harlem. In a room behind the tiny shop, Victoria gave piano lessons to a generation of musicians who included the young Tito Puente.

Rafael and Victoria sold the Madison Avenue store on to an impresario named Luis Cueva who owned a record company called Discos Bernay and recorded some of the pioneers in a new musical form that, in the years after the bolero boom of the 1940s and early '50s, took over as the most popular form of musical expression among Latin American migrants.

The mambo was the closing section of a long-established Cuban genre called *danzón*. It had its own orchestration and rhythmic feel, with the horns playing syncopated figures. In 1938 a Cuban musician named Orestes López had had the idea of flouting the conventional rules of arranging and setting the main theme of a new *danzón* to the rhythm and instrumentation of the mambo. It worked well enough to inspire a Cuban bandleader, Dámaso Pérez Prado, who took up the idea and had a dance choreographed to go with it. He first presented the mambo dance at Havana's Tropicana nightclub in 1943. The sound was percussion-led with a big band-style horn section. It could be joyous, arch or ironic, and Pérez Prado made a career of it, performing on film in Mexican movies and on stage around the world. In 1951 his song 'Rico Mambo' became an international hit, and mambo music and dance spread internationally.

In New York, as well as Pérez Prado, groups like Machito and his Afro-Cuban Orchestra and the ensembles led by two Puerto Rican percussionists, Tito Puente and Tito Rodríguez, performed mambo at the great Palladium ballroom at Broadway and 52nd Street. It became a phenomenon: in the 1950s and early '60s there were mambo nights three times a week, and a Sunday-matinee session that attracted movie stars like Marlon Brando and Sammy Davis Jr. Film footage of the Palladium shows dancers in outrageous costumes, full of creativity and spontaneity.

These were also the years of the most intense Puerto Rican influx to New York, and mambo was the music the immigrants and their children grew up with. In a memoir of life in Spanish Harlem called *When the Spirits Dance Mambo*, the academic Marta Moreno Vega describes huddling under the bedclothes to stop her parents hearing the telephone when her elder brother called from the Palladium and held the receiver high to let the sound of Tito Puente flood down the line.

In due course, mambo became the most important New York precursor to the salsa movement.

Rafael Hernández died in 1965. Four years later Victoria sold the shop at 786 Prospect Avenue to its current owner. Miguel Ángel Amadeo and his mother Gloria Vicente Rodríguez had come to New York on the last voyage of a US warship called *Marine Tiger*, which had brought in thousands of Puerto Ricans after the Second World War. It was 12 June 1947 and Miguel Ángel, who was soon known as Mike, was still a child. Their journey took them, not to the Puerto Rican stronghold of the Barrio Latino – Spanish Harlem – that stretched from 96th to 156th Street between Third and Fifth Avenue, but to the Italian quarter that extended from Third Avenue to the river, in the days when a Puerto Rican couldn't live in the Italian neighbourhood.

'The school was straight across the street,' he told me, 'but I had to run to get there.'

They had come to join Mike's father, Alberto Amadeo, a musician and songwriter who played with the Cuban bandleader Desi Arnaz on NBC's Latin America service. It would have been a prestigious gig for any musician: thanks to *I Love Lucy*, the TV show he produced and appeared in, Desi Arnaz was a household name in the United States. He played a Cuban bandleader called Ricky Ricardo, and his real-life wife Lucille Ball played Ricardo's wife Lucy.

One December day in 1948 Mike Amadeo and his mother took the subway to Prospect Avenue in the Bronx to make a family visit. As they descended the steps from the elevated train, Mike heard the sound of Christmas music – the song was '*Aires de Navidad*' by Los Romanceros – that transported him back to Bayamón, Puerto Rico, the place of his birth. The music was coming from the record shop at 786. Mike went in and bought the record.

'Who could have imagined I would one day own the establishment?'

Mike's story and the story of Latin American music, of bolero, *son* and salsa, would be forever entwined. He followed his father into the music industry, taking up the guitar and founding his own bolero trio, The Three Kings. He was also writing songs, and by the mid-1950s some of the best acts in New York City were playing his compositions. His fame as a songwriter spread to Puerto Rico, and in 1954 he visited the island and was introduced to a well-known bandleader called Rafael Cortijo, whose new, small-band format – he called it a 'combo' – was taking the Spanish-speaking world by storm. Amadeo became friends with Cortijo's pianist Rafael Ithier, whose uncle Salvador played in Rafael Hernández's guitar trio. In 1962, after Cortijo's vocalist was arrested for drugs possession, the band fell apart, and Ithier created El Gran Combo de Puerto Rico from the ruins. Mike Amadeo began to contribute songs to the new group.

He also found steady work in the record industry, first with ABC Paramount, and then with Alegre Records, where he was reunited with kids he had grown up with in the South Bronx. 'The Palmieri brothers Charlie and Eddie, Orlando Marín, Joe Quijano, Ray Barretto, Willie Rosario, Johnny Pacheco: they grew up here in the neighbourhood. We played stickball in Longward Avenue. I played in the street with all those people, without knowing the future.'

Johnny Pacheco was Alegre's biggest artist. He had created a band in the style of the Sonora Matancera, the great Cuban ensemble that Pacheco loved and whose arrangements he shamelessly plagiarised. It was one of the key influences on the salsa sound.

Pacheco generated most of the money for the label, and, when he realised his financial clout, he decided to create his own record company, and in 1964 he founded Fania. But he found it impossible to run the record company and have a band, so he invited his divorce lawyer, Jerry Masucci, to join him in the business. Even so, he continued to visit Mike Amadeo at Alegre. 'We'd sit down together and he'd say, "Do you know any songs?", and I'd play him the music I liked.'

By then, the first generation of Puerto Rican youth born and raised in New York City was coming of age – the Nuyoricans. To them, the mambo big bands sounded distant, especially compared with the generational rebellion of rock music. They began to experiment with new hybrid genres, modifying the combo format that Cortijo had popularised in Puerto Rico. African-American and Caribbean forms of music and dance began to cross-fertilise each other. In 1965 Detroit R&B duo Tom and Jerrio had a hit with a song called 'Boo-Ga-Loo', starting a short-lived fad in the tradition of ephemeral dances like the pony, the chicken, the madison, the alligator, the fly, the jerk, the yo-yo, the sweet pea, the slop, the fish, the Popeye and the locomotion. King Coleman, who had created his own fleeting craze with the mashed potato in 1960, followed it with a series of novelty dances including the shimmy, the hully gully, and then took up what he called the Booga Lou.

The Nuyoricans combined it with Afro-Cuban percussion styles and created Latin boogaloo. 1966 saw the recording of the best-known song in the genre, Joe Cuba's 'Bang, Bang'. Three years after it appeared, Latin boogaloo was, if not replaced, absorbed into a new musical movement, soon known around the world, that consciously reflected the life of New York's immigrant underclass.

This was salsa.

A disturbing 1967 memoir of growing up Puerto Rican in New York called *Down These Mean Streets*, by an addict and mambo dancer called Piri Thomas, evokes the reality expressed in salsa, in which the poverty and brutality of the *barrio* in East Harlem created a kind of creative energy. He describes the convergence of drug taking, music, dance and violence:

> Then it comes – the tight feeling, like a rubber band being squeezed around your forehead . . . You like the sharpness of your ears as they dig the mambo music coming up the stairs. You hear every note clear. You have the power to pick out one instrument from another. Bongos, congas, flute, piano, maracas, marimba. You keep in time with your whole body and swinging soul, and all of a sudden you're in the middle, hung up with a chick; and the music is soft and she's softer, and you make the most of grinding against her warmth. *Viva, viva, viva!*

> Then the Jolly Rogers walk in and everybody starts

dealing. Your boys are fighting and you fall in with them. Bottles are hitting everything but the walls. You feel somebody put his damn fist square in your damn mouth and split your damn lip and you taste your own sweet blood – and all of a sudden you're really glad you came. You're glad you smoked pot, you're glad somebody punched you in the mouth; you're glad for another chance to prove how much heart you've got. You scream mad and your mouth is full of 'motherfuckers!' and you swing out hard, Ah, *chévere!* That broke his fuckin' nose.

Salsa began to celebrate this inner-city, streetwise spirit in the music of Willie Colón, who grew up on 139th Street in the South Bronx. Colón was a trombone player who had found a job early in the 1960s selling records for Alegre when Mike Amadeo was working there. Alegre introduced Colón to a singer called Héctor Lavoe and released their first record, *El Malo*, in 1967. The album cover established Willie's identity as a bad street *guapo* and Lavoe as a brash wise guy. Forty years before gangsta rap, their violent lyrics and driving rhythms managed to be both shocking and compelling.

No hay un problema en el barrio	It's peaceful in the hood
A quien se llama El Malo	if they call you a mean mother.
Si dicen que no soy yo	If you say I'm not,
Le doy un puño de regalo	I'll knife you as a gift.
. . . El malo de aquí soy yo.	. . . The mean one around here is me.

Willie Colón, 'El Malo' (1967)

Or:

Mete la mano en el bolsillo	Put your fingers in your pocket,

Saca y abre tu cuchillo	Take your knife out and unlock it
y ten cuidado.	and beware.
Póngame oído	There are hoodlums in the ghetto
En este barrio muchos guapos	who are killers.
han matado.	Are you listening with care?

Willie Colón, 'Calle Luna, Calle Sol' ('Sun Street, Moon Street') (1973)

Calle Luna and Calle Sol are narrow streets in San Juan, but the world they describe could have been anywhere in the Spanish-speaking Caribbean. Piri Thomas expressed the same intuition, in which the *barrio*'s essential criminality was the symptom of a kind of rhythmic vitality:

> In the daytime Harlem looks kinda dirty and the people a little drab and down. But at night, man, it's a swinging place, especially Spanish Harlem. The lights transform everything into life and movement and blend the different colors into a magic cover-all that makes the drabness and garbage, wailing kids and tired people invisible. Shoes and clothes that by day look beat and worn out, at night take on a reflected splendor that the blazing multicolored lights burn on them. Everything seems to develop a sense of urgent rhythm and you get the impression that you have to walk with a sense of timing.

Tito Puente called Willie Colón's group a kiddie band and musicians scorned Willie's playing, but his rasping trombone, with split notes and faulty intonation, caught the attitudes and gestures of a way of life. The first few seconds of their signature tune, '*Che Che Colé*', illustrates the point: the piano intro is fumbled, and then Willie splits a note in each of the

74

first two trombone riffs. It would have been easy to re-record them but, with astonishing conviction, Colón left them exactly as they were. He knew they couldn't be improved on.

Richie Ray and Bobby Cruz, from Brooklyn, began putting old songs to new arrangements. Their 1968 album *Los Durísimos* took up a Cuban classic called '*Yo Soy Babalú*' ('I am Babalú'), by Celina González and Reutilio Domínguez, who were regarded as the most authentic interpreters of Cuban rural music. The contrast in styles was glaring. Celina and Reutilio's version had a rural jangle thanks to the *tres*, a guitar-like instrument with three double strings, and the rattle of lighter, subtler percussion instruments. Richie and Bobby's version was brutish and jarring. It starts with a hammering of piano keys followed by a blaring trumpet motif before the percussion enters and the piano states a simple chord sequence with block voicings. Bobby Cruz's voice is booming, uncontrolled, hypnotic: it was rural music made urban for a public that was going through the same transition.

And, knowing that the old, gentle rural dance styles no longer suited their super-charged new sound, Richie and Bobby contracted a well-known New York street dancer called Louie Flóres, nicknamed La Máquina ('the Machine'), to invent something more appropriate.

But it was Fania Records, through stars like Celia Cruz, Cheo Feliciano, Pete 'El Conde' Rodríguez and Rubén Blades, that defined the new sound and marketed it under the term 'salsa'. In the new, cosmopolitan sound, there was perhaps a loss of the distinctions between the many, once clearly defined types of Cuban and Puerto Rican music. Tito Puente, who was punctilious about his genres, even had a song called '*Pachanga Si, Charanga No*' that mocked the confusion among the young between the *pachanga*, which was a dance, and the *charanga*, which was a type of band. To musicians who had been educated on the islands before they migrated to New York, the many varieties of

Cuban rumba, for instance, or the different dance crazes, from *danzón* to *chachachá* and mambo, were distinct forms that were not to be confused. To their New York-born sons and daughters, they were so many ingredients to be blended and experimented with.

The driving beat, rasping trombone riffs, simmering improvised sections and sometimes menacing lyrics gave salsa an identifiably urban edge and made it the escapist option for working-class Latinos. Salsa – gritty, rebellious and new – was associated with a new generation who nonetheless preferred ancestral bongos and congas to the electric guitar and drum set. At the same time, in basements and apartments across the city, Cubans, Puerto Ricans and Haitians were keeping their identities intact by attending rituals with drumming and dancing at their heart. Marta Moreno Vega describes her cigar-smoking grandmother tending to the nine clean glasses on her ancestral shrine or *bóveda* in the altar room in her apartment, and being possessed by spirits who sang in African tongues and moved to their own rhythms. Salsa perhaps signalled the way back to less inhibited, more magical ways of being.

Although they were fusing and confusing the genres, the Nuyoricans were purists in terms of language. Even youngsters brought up in New York who spoke English among themselves wrote their songs emphatically in Spanish. It was a form of resistance, a deliberate way of distancing themselves from mainstream America. The second-generation Puerto Rican Willie Colón made it a matter of principle: 'The language was all we have left,' he said. 'Why should we give in on that one?'

The New York singer Ismael Miranda had to spend a year working on his Spanish before he could embark on a solo career.

Many of New York's salsa musicians grew up in the sort of economically depressed, inner-city neighbourhoods that

Piri Thomas describes, in which disempowerment, alienation and violence were familiar experiences. The night-time economy in these areas, where the threat of violence was constant, may even have shaped the sound texture of salsa and the dynamism of the dancers' response to it.

The trombonist Chris Washburne remembers an incident that took place in 1995 but comes straight out of the world Piri Thomas was describing in the 1960s. Washburne was queuing up with the rest of Pete 'El Conde' Rodríguez's band outside Fuego Fuego, a club at 157th Street and Broadway. Fuego Fuego was a notorious hotspot, and the musicians' entrance was in a dark side-street where a drug deal was going off. But an argument flared up and the dealers pulled guns on each other, with the musicians sandwiched between them, pressing themselves into the wall. The side door opened in the nick of time and the band darted out of harm's way, but the experience had a noticeable effect on their performance that night.

> . . . the band seemed to play slightly louder than usual; the percussion section pushed many of the tempos; the horn players responded with more intense solos, emphasizing their higher registers; the piano solos included more fast and dissonant runs than usual; and virtuosic flurries permeated the percussion fills. The overall timbre choices the musicians made were brash and raw, at times pushing their volumes to distortion and even mimicking cries, yells, hollers, growls, howls, and screams within solo passages.

After another fight-marred night, one of his colleagues asked him, 'Did you notice how the whole vibe changed after the fight? Everything got real intense. It was so dark.'

Over time, this shell-shocked, adrenalin-fuelled vibe evolved into a performance style in which violence has left a definite sound texture in New York music. Washburne spoke to professional musicians so traumatised by witnessing violence in New York salsa clubs, in one case seeing a man shot in the face in front of the stage, that they had stopped performing salsa and moved to other genres of music. When percussionist Ralph Figueroa left New York for Florida, local musicians wanted to hear his tales of the murders and shootings he had experienced. But, he says, they didn't believe him. 'They want to play like New York musicians, but they can't since they have not experienced what we did.'

*

Responding in movement to the fury of the music, New York salsa dancers in the mid-1970s began to fuse the merriment of mambo with grittier street-style elements that reflected the new vibe. This was the basis for the famous New York style. I wanted to be part of it so we took the 1-train to Houston Street and exited through one of those two-way New York turnstiles where you stake a claim to right of way with timing, posture and, if need be, pig-headed aggression. The trombonist Jimmy Bosch and his band were performing at SOB's, a venue set in a rare enclave where the Manhattan grid system gives way to improvisation as the lots hug the East River and street names replace numbers.

We went along to enjoy the music of one of contemporary salsa's most famous bandleaders, and to dance. But the evening didn't turn out quite as we expected.

'Introduce yourself. "Where are you from?" Aaaaand rotate to your next partner . . .'

The publicity hadn't mentioned that the event would start with an hour of something combining salsa, line dancing and speed-dating for people who'd never danced before and might next week go paint-balling or go-karting.

By the time the class was over, the place was full. Women were removing items of clothing and donning dancing shoes. Their faces bore the serious mien of people who were about to set other people categorically straight on issues of some importance.

Then the band came on. Jimmy Bosch blasted out his fabulous 'Descargarana':

Aquí tengo descargarana	I've got an improvisation for you:
Bailen como les dé la gana.	Dance any way it grabs you.

. . . and the dancing began.

Immediately the activity was frenetic. Like the night-time feeding frenzy of hundreds of giant squid, tentacles coiled behind heads and around bodies. Some used arms and stiletto heels to thrash and stab and clear a space in which to prosecute their battle for survival. Others, self-contained enough to keep to their tiny patch, writhed meekly before the massacre.

The fact was, for ethnic mix, SOB's probably matched or surpassed those nineteenth-century sugar plantations where workers from China, Japan and Portugal lived and worked with Koreans, Filipinos and Puerto Ricans, except that we weren't the soulful, disenfranchised poor: we were a cross-section of modern, restless, rootless, super-enfranchised travellers.

There were no doubt many different ideas of what cosmopolitanism means, being knotted together in the dance floor's many mixed partnerships. There was liberation and restriction, a sharing and denying of meanings. Maps and histories temporarily merged. Contours and divisions of culture and country were reinforced in some parts of the room and obliterated in others.

The dizzying variety of intricate figures, convoluted

turns and expensively schooled complexities, acquired in visits to New York's famous dance teachers, sat strangely with the rasping, high-energy, unpolished style of Jimmy Bosch and his band. I was stunned. This was the body language of people for whom salsa represented an escape from low-paid jobs in a hostile world into a night-time world where the possibility of encounters with real violence only added to the experience. But the forces that had infused early salsa with its special intensity – poverty, racism, immigration anxiety – were little felt here.

| *Luisito Lozón, Les toca el bongó.* | Luisito Lozón's playing the bongo for you. |
| *Mauricio toca la flauta!* | Mauricio, play the flute! |

I pushed through the revellers towards the cloakroom, saying my excuse-mes in Spanish and garnering puzzled looks. There was more Korean and Japanese, perhaps more Bulgarian, than Spanish being spoken, even if the music was in Spanish, the dance was Latin American, and the dancers mentioned in the song had Spanish names. It was clear that many, perhaps most, of those present had little or no Spanish and had no access to the lyrics of the songs and their surrounding culture.

Not that there is ever a cohesive, uncomplicated language that speaks for a straightforward, single culture. José Fernando, my teacher in Medellín, was always flitting off to Buenos Aires or here to New York, and people like me were always flying in to see him – but New York's salsa clubs belonged to a wider, global world in which salsa was quite differently connected. The dance floor here was a place of dispersion and disassembly, the Wild West resurrected in battles for the floor by supporters of different styles and schools. No consensus over fundamentals seemed possible. The only common idiom seemed to be a language of the eyes, dozens of pairs of which, strangely oblivious to the energy of the music and the generalised frenzy it had provoked, were casting outwardly directed glances around the room. There were couples in which both partners were gazing outward, forgoing all eye contact with each other. I wasn't sure what was going on. The interlinking of gazes in this insistent visual messaging wove a fabric that seemed more real than the dancing. There were no doubt people looking for someone better to dance with, but I thought I recognised something else: a petition to be admired as original and imaginative, a New York appeal to an audience, a self-infatuation.

Much of the feverish commotion on the dance floor was being pursued with wilful conviction. Each couple seemed to have their own terrifying sense of purpose, as if the appearance of deeply felt sincerity proved that it was genuine. Perhaps that was the meaning of these ceaseless, insistent turns and spins.

Baila, baila, baila, baila sabroso	Dance, dance, dance, dance, with taste:
(Bailen como les de la gana)	(Dance any way it grabs you)
Venga y apresúrese mi pana	Come on, get moving, my friend!

Vivi and I embraced beside one Oriental woman armed with both the aggression and the footwear to defend an extensive territory. Her extravagant spins and extensions suggested that physical contact with her partner was something she would prefer to avoid, although her skills didn't stretch to the quiet art of dancing in a crowded room.

I had started the evening with the intention of immersing myself in the atmosphere, becoming one with the spirit of New York salsa, grasping its idiosyncrasies from the inside. Instead, my appetite for self-display diminished, Vivi and I kept strictly to basic steps. In New York, it seemed, the making of one person's dance was the unmaking of another's.

There was a couple closer to the bar, marginal to the dance floor. They were older and more self-contained. They provided a counterpoint to the hyperactive madness around them by doing almost nothing. They told me they were Dominicans. They looked out of place in this transit lounge of recent arrivals and imminent departures. As Jimmy Bosch soloed between choruses of '*Toca como sólo tu tocas*' ('Play the way only you can'), they seemed to be blissfully unconcerned about self-display.

The intrusive game of looking and being looked at, not to mention the sheer belligerence of some of the dancers, threatened Vivi in ways I barely understood. Salsa had been etched into the grain of her life early on. It had probably given shape to many of the mind-structuring, identity-forming interactions of her childhood: her first attempts to stand, for instance, at that stage of development when we start to organise our sense of who we are through the body and its postures. This is the time when we acquire our intuitions about being in step with the world, what it is to put a foot wrong, where we stand with others and how we should hold ourselves in their presence. They aren't things we carry with us in clearly formulated language. Perhaps they can't be brought to consciousness even in principle. They certainly aren't matters of individual choice.

If Vivi had been with another Colombian, I was sure she would have simply tuned into the music and enjoyed the evening like the Dominican couple I'd been talking to. But I could see, on the dance floor and in my own inner forum, salsa being used as a device for loosening the grip of lineage. For dancers who have learned salsa through choice, inheritance has little to do with it. I was one of them, of course, and Vivi wasn't, and our intertwined lives gave each of us an uncomfortable insight into the other's predicament.

We hadn't lasted much more than an hour and a half when, leaving our contestations unfinished, we grabbed our things, left the building and wandered into the night.

*

I didn't really relate the hellish time we had at SOB's with New York salsa as such. I thought I could cut through the posing by going straight to the source. So the following day I took Vivi to a dance class. We walked five blocks and ducked out of the freezing air into number 244 West 54th Street. We took the lift to the 11th floor and there found the Nola Studio. According to the publicity, we would find in Studio Four an open class in 'Shine and Partner Work' with the most famous salsa instructor on earth.

Like other New Yorkers, Eddie Torres had learned to dance in the 1960s and '70s, soaking up steps from films, musicals and other dancers, and shaping them into his own style. What made him different was that he codified his moves into a syllabus of some 300 named figures and turns that he called 'shines'.

Until the mid-1970s only two styles of Latin dance had been common in New York, mambo and *chachachá*. Then, in symbiosis with the new, hard-edged salsa music, a street-style dance emerged that changed the emphasis of the steps to the music's second beat, now known as 'On-2'. I'd been reading up on it before our visit. Louie 'Máquina' Flóres, the dancer who had worked with Richie Ray and Bobby Cruz, said it followed the *clave*. Eddie Torres said it followed the congas.

The basic step was the same as ours but began on the second beat in the bar, which meant you started each bar with a rest: 'pause-two-three-four, pause-six-seven-eight'. There was talk of dancing 'on *clave*', referring to a rhythm used in salsa that came from Cuban *son*.

Clave is sometimes spoken of as a two-part rhythm consisting of a three-beat pattern with notes on beats one, two-and-a-half and four, and a two-beat pattern with notes on beats two and three.

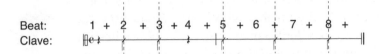

In terminology invented in the 1950s by Mario Bauzá, the musical director of Machito and his Afro-Cubans, *clave* can be either three-two or two-three. Dancing 'on clave' meant starting the basic step or, as they say, 'breaking' on two, like the two-three version of *clave*.

As far as I could see, whether you started on beat one or two or, for that matter, on beat three or four, the basic step coincided with three of the *clave* accents, paused on one of them and walked straight past the syncopated second note of the three-beat cell.

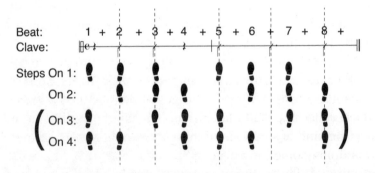

It seemed to me to be perfectly possible to step on the beats of the *clave* and no others, although no one was suggesting that. There was a phoney sophistication about the right and proper interpretation of *clave*.

In any event, whatever On-2 meant, we were here to learn it with the master, Eddie Torres, who had started teaching the On-2 style in 1987.

It all went wrong from the start. At least 20 students had got there before us. As we removed our heavy coats, a couple of Korean girls appeared in leotards, leggings and high heels. One of them was in New York for three weeks; the other was here for ten days. Then our instructor came in: not Eddie but his wife Maria. I had no doubt that she was an excellent dancer but you can't orchestrate a cult of the personality and then send the wife along to cover.

We started stepping on the second beat, but, instead of counting with the movements of our feet, '(pause)-two-three-four, (pause)-six-seven-eight', Maria gave the count that we were used to of 'One-two-three-(pause), five-six-seven-(pause)', which didn't correspond to what our feet were doing. To my mind, our feet were On-2 but we were thinking On-1. I was used to José Fernando's lessons, which he always started with a gentle *cumbia* to allow the rhythms and body language of Colombian dance to sink into my bones. Here, incredibly, there was no music at all. To make sense of it all, I withdrew most of my consciousness from my body, and shrank back into my head. We moved forward and back in regular rows and columns, enjoying all the gentle warmth of a surprise algebra lesson.

As we practised these unfamiliar perambulations, another dozen students arrived. Soon, there were 30 or 35 of us in the class. After the basic step, we learned a shine Maria called the Half Flare. It looked like hopscotch, and it was the kind of step you might perform while your partner was doing something else, or the two of you might repeat in parallel, facing the same direction: in other words, it presupposed an audience. I couldn't see myself using it with Vivi. Then we learned another, similar move, equally devoid of any practical use. This was how we passed an hour or more, shuffling about without physical contact, without music, fixed in rows and columns.

The second half of the class was conducted to music. There was no closing of the eyes, no mention of improvisation. No dancing for ourselves. We spent a fruitless hour wrestling turns we could usually perform without a second glance into the unfamiliar logic of the New York style. In two hours, no period of continuous movement lasted more than ten seconds. After each collective manoeuvre the class stopped and we returned to our starting point. Between each turn we were instructed to slap hands, high-five style, as we passed each other. We did so in order not to disrupt the class. Vivi, forced to dance without music and to numbers for the first time in her life, was giving me 'What-have-you-got-us-into?' looks.

At the end of the class, I recognised Eddie Torres himself in the corridor. I introduced myself, hoping he would have a moment during our stay to talk. He asked me where I was from.

'England, but I've been in Colombia with my wife's family for the past three months.'

'You survived three months in Colombia?'

I expected more than the thoughtless equation of Colombia with danger and violence. What I found unforgivable was that he had said it in front of Vivi.

We left the building and walked out in the New York winter. I'd intended to take several classes but I was no longer sure of my plans. Still, although Vivi had no enthusiasm, I thought I should at least see a class taken by the man himself. We had, after all, come a long way. So we slept on it and, the following day, we went back for more.

*

The class started with another sequence I knew I'd never be able to use. Tap, heel, toe, double kick, step. Chimeras and fragments. It had started late, and slowly, with 20 minutes of repetition until we were tapping, heeling, toeing, kicking and stepping like automatons. Then Eddie turned on the music and began to dance, one set piece after another, pincer movements and cavalry charges set to the beat. I tried to follow but I was forced to give up almost immediately so I stood there and counted and watched. There were 75 of them. Of *us*, I mean: I counted while I was waiting. The dropout rate was colossal. The dancers who knew the steps formed a group around Eddie Torres so that the rest could barely make him out in the wall-to-wall mirror. They performed the long sequence of moves together, until, one by one, dancers dropped off, their knowledge exhausted. It was salsa as long division or the periodic table, and by the end of the sequence perhaps only eight of us – *them* – were doing anything at all.

The truth was, I could have got into it too. I had my obsessive tendencies, an aptitude for narrowing my focus of attention to small details and losing sight of the bigger picture, trusting blindly that when it comes back into view everything will make sense. I had it in me to dedicate myself with samurai austerity to the pursuit of technical mastery and learn my 300 steps, and I could no doubt have manufactured some peculiar personal sense of my own authenticity in doing so. But I had Vivi, thank God, keeping things in perspective.

Trying to remain calm and composed among all these strange devices, I sat down, took out my notebook, and started to jot down some thoughts. At that moment, Eddie's wife Maria came over and confiscated my pen. It was a claim to copyright – and that was when I understood this salsa wasn't an indistinct image that would, in time, grow in focus and detail, but a jigsaw, the pieces of which you purchased one at a time. The edginess of immigrant life in New York City had, it seemed to me, been commodified into something new: salsa with world-making intent. Like an exotic designer handbag, you could find the Eddie Torres style in London, Paris, Milan, Tokyo and Singapore, where it belonged to the cosmopolitan rich, prepared to invest large sums in classes and competitions.

I realised the interview I'd arranged with Eddie after the class was probably not going to happen. We walked out into the street, no longer sure that we could dance at all.

*

The following day we went to an exhibition of corpses.

> BODIES . . . THE EXHIBITION is organized by Premier
> Exhibitions, Inc. of Atlanta, Georgia. Premier
> Exhibitions, Inc. is not affiliated with any other
> organizer of human anatomy exhibitions, including Mr
> Gunther von Hagens, Mr Gerhard Perner, or Genlife
> Biomedical. BODIES . . . THE EXHIBITION should not
> be confused with 'Body Worlds,' 'Body Exploration,'
> 'The Universe Within,' or any other human anatomy
> exhibition.

We had dared each other to go in. To face down a taboo,
probably, in a world where people feel they have no further
use for them. In any case, it was a boundary we easily
crossed. There was no pallor or putrefaction here. The
bodies on display at the South Street Seaport by Brooklyn
Bridge were rigid and sanitary. In a sort of over-evolution
of the modern deodorised armpit and the shaven urban
pudendum, the carcasses had been cleaned and treated
until, part-flesh, part-plastic, they were inoffensive enough
to bring crowds streaming into this and nine other versions
of the show in cities across America, without counting three
rival 'Body Worlds' exhibitions and heaven knows how
many other productions, all keen not to be confused with
the others but all utterly interchangeable and flitting
restlessly across the nation.

The sanitised cadavers were presented on educational
grounds, as if by learning no longer to avert our gaze before
the dead we could learn to do the same before the living.
But display here was used as the subtlest form of
concealment: the flaying of skin and the exposure of internal
organs served to mask, not reveal, the essential facts. Rigor
mortis had been harnessed to convey the illusion of
movement, often on a sporting theme. One body had been
twisted into a frozen slam-dunk, another into a petrified

dive for a volleyball, a third into a pitcher hurling a baseball. Even the information plaques served to obscure what we were looking at. If the Latin and Greek terms had been replaced with their Anglo-Saxon equivalents, there would have been a stampede for the door.

Faced with this diorama of deceased people, I was surprised how easy it was to stand unmoved in the presence of dozens of human carcasses. I realised how even the most physical of emotions – horror, anger, sexual desire – had been dimmed in us, damped down to nothing more than momentary sensations. We lived at an astonishing distance from our bodies compared with the people of pre-modern times, for whom body and identity were the same and you were sanguine or phlegmatic or choleric because of an excess of blood or phlegm or yellow choler in the balance of your humours, and melancholy wasn't merely caused by black bile, it *was* black bile.

Elsewhere and in the past, then, people *were* their bodies. We thought of our hormones, for instance, as drugs on which we could become pathologically dependent: we could become adrenalin junkies or testosterone addicts. For us, identity was more or less independent of the body, except during illness when the body could influence mood and we said things like, 'I'm not really myself.' Knowing it was just body chemistry got us off the hook.

But the ability to be unmoved can also be an inability to be moved, an involuntary dissociation from reality, and 'Bodies . . . The Exhibition' seemed to me a study in dissociation. There was no mingling of sweat or odour or body heat, no interaction between corpses, or between the living and the dead. We had grown impervious to their uncanny, supernatural presence.

In fact, spectators seemed to spend a lot of the time looking at each other's reactions to the skinned carcasses, which at times seemed nothing more than a pretext for this close-knit crisscrossing of looks.

I realised I'd seen the same thing at SOB's. The real me is what I choose to display to the world. Our bodies, we inherit; our body displays are a matter of individual choice. So, magazines, TV shows and products promise 'a new you' and generally mean the old one plus or minus a few pounds and a little abdominal muscle definition, with a new wardrobe or hairstyle, the claim being that, by changing the display, you change the inner person. It is all a matter of style.

By becoming bodily spectacles, the cadavers had been liberated from all identity. For the duration of the exhibition they became whatever their disposition in space made them. At SOB's, the wealthy and the rootless could spend the evening in a nightclub in Manhattan pretending to be Latin. I understood why Eddie Torres called his flourishes 'shines': they were intended to catch the eye.

But in either case was there really anything to see? The intricate and permanent postures of the cadavers seemed to me to suggest a tender back-reference to former lives. If Babe Ruth had been among them, I was sure we would have been told, but I hoped at least to find Perspex-covered cards telling the world that those whose husks stood before us had, for example, played Thursday-night games with old school friends or enjoyed part-time careers in the minor leagues. But although I looked, there was no information to hand about the identities of the dead.

The exhibition website reported that the bodies came from the Dalian Medical University in the People's Republic of China. The question of consent was fobbed off among the FAQs by this statement: 'Human specimens in medical schools in China, the United States and other countries throughout the world are donated or unidentified bodies.' It wasn't at all clear that these were not the bodies of China's tired and poor, its huddled masses, sent tempest-tossed to New York, treated with formaldehyde and set in see-through plastic.

At SOB's, to the musicians, the Dominican couple and to

Vivi, salsa represented an inheritance. The rest of us on the crowded dance floor, or so it appeared to me, were doubles, substitutes, fictional versions of ourselves, dressed, made up and exhibited to the world. Our disparate approaches to life, our intricately arranged dissimilarities, were scrambled and pressed together in a bizarre game of *as if*: we danced as if we were Spanish-speaking Caribbeans, as if we'd been born into salsa, as if we belonged to another time and place and therefore to different lives. As if our bodily displays, too, referred to the lives we had led up to now, when of course they didn't.

*

After a few days in New York, I was utterly confused. Even Vivi was losing her interest in dancing. But, on our last night, we took the subway to Queens, where we found a Colombian club called Extravaganza. There, for a few hours, we left one version of New York behind us and stepped into another, and, by a miracle, embracing on the dance floor, we remembered how to move and danced into the night.

Then it was time to go. We boarded the Bogotá plane, never the pride of the fleet but an ancient 737 for which no museum could be found. As often as not, it has a problem with a fuel valve or a heated window so you wait an hour or so for an engineer, then an hour or so more when it is decided you have to change planes. But at least no one's being singled out for special surveillance: given your destination, everyone by definition is under suspicion. So you can stop behaving for the benefit of people who are looking at you and start behaving like yourself. And when the ground finally rises to meet you and the landing gear touches Colombian soil, a round of unsophisticated applause ripples through the plane. Far from thinking it silly, you feel your face creasing as if you could burst into tears and you put your hands together, glad at last to have arrived.

5

THE WORLD SALSA CAPITAL

Del puente para acá está Cali
On this side of the bridge is Cali
    'Del puente para allá', composed by
    Jairo Varela, performed by El Grupo
              Niche

News had spread around the family that I was writing about salsa and one of Vivi's uncles invited us to Salomé Pagana, Bogotá's most famous Afro-Cuban club. It was a venue for the literati and the highest echelons of the Colombian political classes. Salomé was the only dancer named in both the Bible and El Gran Combo's fabulous *'Falsária'*. The pagan was César Pagano, the club owner and one of Colombia's leading music writers: his books, mostly biographical studies of the classic salsa vocalists, were displayed behind glass in the entrance hall. César himself presented me with a great sheaf of interviews and obituaries he had written for the newspaper *El Tiempo*, and a number of small books. I thanked him for his generosity and, lacking even the knowledge that would have allowed me to ask him an intelligent question, I kept our conversation to a minimum.

Then I was introduced to two scholars of Colombian folk music and dance: Rosni Portaccio, a composer and singer, and his brother José. They were from Barranquilla on the Caribbean coast, and between them they brought me a small library of books, videos and CDs to draw me further into the turbulent waters of Afro-Colombian music. I didn't know how to tell them I was interested not in expertise and explicit knowledge but in stillness and silence and the failure of all articulacy. I was afraid I'd be misunderstood – I wasn't sure I understood it myself – but I needn't have worried. Salomé Pagana also had a dance floor, and after a performance by a *gaita* ensemble from Sincelejo – a *gaita* is a traditional instrument resembling an oboe – the room was cleared for dancing.

On the far side of the dance floor, a well-known Colombian soap star was soon groping a voluptuous model in a public display of marital infidelity. Next to them, a large, smiling bank manager flung his tiny wife around the floor in a series of turns so perfectly executed they seemed hardly to have happened at all.

But the heart and soul of the dance floor was Rosni. The main feature of his face was a magnificent set of jowls organised around a broad smile, framed by a silver goatee and dark, smiling eyes below a smooth, bald head. He had a weightlifter's build and, when he took to the dance floor, he moved like a Costeño: strong, upright, the rhythm flowing through every inch of him. There was hardly a turn to send a ripple across his coolness, yet he danced deep in attentive conversation with his partner, periodically singing along with the music in a magnificent baritone voice. He was *sabor* personified. I wanted to move like Rosni.

But dance didn't come naturally to me. It dressed my face in an expression of either childlike over-enthusiasm or puzzled ineptitude. To achieve the illusion of spontaneity, I had to paste one false item after another on to it, and hope for a generalised suspension of disbelief. However, lubricated by whisky and mojitos, I began to sink slowly into the evening. Vivi and I danced close. Music melted into motion, and each subtle variation refreshed the rhythmic flow; the simplest turn broke the pattern of our breathing like a sigh. As the alcohol seeped into my nervous system, a gentle drunkenness softened the jet lag to give me something like the skin-comfort of a sober Colombian. I felt embraced not just by Vivi but by Salomé Pagana, by Colombia's high-altitude capital and by the music itself. My salsa, said Rosni, was *sabrosa*: the word had been used. It wasn't a street-corner rumba in the Chocó but for me it was a big step into salsa, and by the time we left I was drunk on dance, as well as simply drunk. But I was left with two questions: was Rosni just being kind? And could I dance when I was sober?

Vivi's aunts in Bogotá shared family stories with me, and I learned more about life in San José del Palmar. The village founded by Vivi's great-grandfather was isolated from the rest of the Chocó. In any case, the arrivals from Antioquia had a strong sense of regional identity and, whether they were peasants, farmers, shopkeepers or big businessmen, they liked to work among their own, forming, in black areas like the Chocó, entrepreneurial groupings in what became effectively ethnic enclaves. They tended, over the generations, to whiten the community, so Palmar was mainly light-skinned and its musical tastes were generally limited to a music known onomatopoeically as *chucu-chucu* in which the Caribbean tang was highly diluted.

Palmar's dance hall, the Pisagua, was managed by Marlen's brother Edgar, a powerful, robust man who was also quiet and infinitely patient. Their sister Luz Dary selected the music. This meant that, when Marlen brought Lucho to town, and Lucho brought his salsa LPs, they got to try them out on Palmar's public. El Gran Combo, Joe Cuba and Guillermo Portabales didn't go down well.

And since Palmar was a village of farmers who generally carried machetes, minor disagreements over the music could always flare up into serious trouble. One day, such a quarrel broke out. It blew up into a physical confrontation, and one of the parties pulled out a revolver. Edgar the peacemaker stepped in. He wrapped his huge hands around the pistol but, as he wrestled it away, the gun went off, leaving Edgar's hands with a permanent gunpowder burn. It only happened once, and no one was hurt, but the family still talk about it as 'the salsa war'.

Edgar, one of my models when I danced, was Sigi and Colomba's eighth child and the youngest of the boys. He finally left San José del Palmar to study at agricultural college, then went into the transport business, driving yucca and other farm produce to the Pacific port of Buenaventura, and returning with cargoes of timber or glass. He lived with his wife and two children, not in San José but in another Palmar midway between Cali and Buenaventura. One Friday in August 1993 he stopped at a village called Atunzelas to buy food, then set off home. He never arrived.

Two days later his brothers went to look for him. They had stumbled on Edgar's driving licence near an access ramp beside the river, clean of fingerprints, as if someone had intended it to be found. They climbed through the forest to a place known as Tragedias, and found a group of young men playing football in a clearing. They claimed no knowledge of their brother or his truck but, when they got back to the road, the locals said that the footballers were guerrillas. After ten days of fruitless searching, they gave up.

A year passed. Then, an engineer contacted the family with word of Edgar. He'd been working on a farm set back from the Cali–Buenaventura road. On the night of Edgar's disappearance, the farm owner had heard a truck and a car, and gone out, quietly, to see what was going on. Two men shorter than the truck driver had forced him out of the cab, walked him three hundred yards along the river bank, then murdered him with a single gunshot. The truck was never found and, as far as anyone could tell, Edgar had been executed after refusing to drive a cargo of drugs to the port.

There has been little truth and reconciliation in Colombia. Edgar's children will most likely never know their father's fate. When I watched him dance with Marlen on Vivi's birthday video, it struck me how much remembrance there is in movement. We embrace, and we turn away from each other, call and response, love and play, life and death.

*

In Bogotá we always stayed with Marlen's oldest friend, Ana. She brought out a box kept high in a closet. It contained letters they had exchanged through the years of their friendship. Dancing had always been part of it. 'Tell me about your life,' the 19-year-old Marlen wrote on 20 December 1965. 'I want to see you getting in trouble like me, through loving too much. I search here and there but in the end I come back to the same place . . . PS. Dance a lot.'

Marlen's letters were full of these brief, undeveloped allusions to dancing. Salsa was part of the inheritance that had come down to Vivi without leaving an inventory, and her mother's letters went some way towards compiling it.

In August 1966 Marlen wrote to Ana:

> I won't give you more details about my visit to Cali because it was so delicious I feel lost in a labyrinth when I try to start the story. What I can promise you is that, if enjoying life leads to damnation, Cali is the anteroom to Hell.

In February 1967 soon after she had met her future husband, Marlen told Ana:

On the thirty-first we didn't sleep, we danced until 7.30 in the morning. I'm telling you, after the Cali Festival, nothing else counts. It's much better than any carnival.

We decided to follow Marlen to Cali. With 24-hour music and dance all week, and the greatest salsa bands performing, no other festival in the world comes close to Cali's annual Sugarcane Fair. But, just when I'd decided salsa should be unconscious, inarticulate, unelaborated, I discovered a city where it is none of these things.

The evening after we arrived, we were spoiled for choice. At the football stadium, the 'Super-concert' had enough live music to sate a salsa fan for a lifetime. It started at seven o'clock with Carlos Vives, a Colombian folk-rock singer. At nine, Cheo Feliciano, one of the great salsa vocalists, came on. Johnny Pacheco, the flautist, bandleader and founder of Fania Records, started at 10.30. The *merengue* star Sergio Vargas was due on at midnight, followed by the *vallenato* performer Jorge Celedón at 1.30 a.m. and then the evening's biggest draw, the salsa band Son de Cali, at 3 a.m.

But there were plenty of other options. There were open-air concerts in the car parks of the city's biggest shopping centres and they had some of the most popular bands, including Richie Ray and Bobby Cruz. At the Parque de la Música in town, four groups were appearing to accompany the feverish trade among the vinyl collectors, and there were seven stages set up in squares across the city offering free live music and dancing until dawn. There were private concerts in theatres and hotels, the entire array of Cali's nightclubs, and there was local television coverage of some of the live performances, so that anyone who couldn't be there in person could enjoy the music at home. It would be impossible to quantify with any accuracy, but the Cali

Sugarcane Fair must have been catering for a million customers, perhaps tens of thousands, hundreds of thousands more.

We made for the old aguardiente distillery known as the Citadel. Inside, the place was heaving. We headed past two enormous dance halls, full to bursting, and took a crowded corridor which led me to what I was looking for: the national salsa competition. The place was a riot of shiny suits, porkpie hats, two-tone shoes, extreme haircuts and glitter. This was just the audience. The performers were put together from their eyelashes down to their shoes. In the competition area, everything was made up and polished, costumed and propped, masked in paraphernalia. Every seat, every available space to stand was taken. Dancers from all of Cali's 48 dance companies, who between them managed 145 troupes, had come along either to compete or to cheer on their colleagues. The atmosphere was fantastic.

Deafening announcements squelched out of antiquated loudspeakers and echoed indistinctly around a high-roofed hall above already delirious crowds. I could make out little. The music that followed lost all definition and you could choose which beat you wanted to dance to: the one leaving or the one coming back from the wall opposite. The cacophony was everywhere.

The youngest dancers can have been no more than seven or eight. They came on, one pair at a time, tiny figures with toothpaste-selling smiles, the boys in baggy suits, the girls in scant costumes. As props, they used wigs, parasols, mirrors, a clothes stand, a football.

A number of routines started with a snatch of movie soundtrack or recorded dialogue. The kids mimed the words, gesturing theatrically, before the music began and they burst into dance. The choreography, even for the youngest entrants, had all the artifice of a West End musical. In the worst cases, it looked less like a salsa competition for kids than a choreography contest between adults for whom the children were merely instrumental. A little girl – ten? eleven? – in knee-length boots caressed a jointed wooden snake, before stripping off her yellow cape to reveal a skimpy dress. At one point in the routine, she dropped into a full splits and held it as her partner performed a solo sequence. It was pre-pubescent camp, at times reminiscent of *Bugsy Malone*: custard-firing splurge guns would have fitted in perfectly.

The music was mostly frenetically over the top, the enemy of shape and definition. Even so, the dancing was astonishing. These children seemed to suck the music in and metabolise it into ecstatic, contagious movement that passed through them and out into the very air through which they span.

Enough kids forgot sequences and fell out of sync with their partners for the showbiz veneer to fall away and the authentic magnetism of childhood to shine through. In any case, the mistakes mostly occurred during extremely acrobatic tumbles that looked decidedly unchildlike to me. The audience greeted errors with sympathetic applause and the conclusion of each performance with near-hysteria.

Then a pair of dark-skinned kids stepped up and, after a few brilliant close steps, started throwing themselves around in just the way I usually didn't like. They circled and recoiled with moves that were distinct and immediate, performed with drastic clarity and dazzling vitality, and in the end there was something about them, something I couldn't define, perhaps just the way the light fell on them, that suddenly I had the translation for *sabor*: charm.

It was also pure show business. You wouldn't have been able to use much of this on a nightclub floor. Much of the time, the dancers separated and performed in parallel. You couldn't do that in a social dance. Anyway, it's all very well for kids to be beguiling. Cuteness isn't a sensible goal for a 45 year old.

Nor are acrobatics; nor, indeed, is public exhibitionism, but both were conspicuous when the adult pairs got going. There were holds, throws, handstands, circus-style spins and body-juggling, but also grinding, looking, licking and the occasional rhythmic spanking of an exposed female arse. The national salsa championships were war, and sex, like athleticism, was a weapon with which to win over the public and the judges.

I wasn't sure about it all. Competitive dance seemed to me to miss the point. It smacked of questionable judging and publicly shed tears. But my discovery of dance was recent, and I'd made of it an oddly inward, philosophical matter, a question of self-transformation, self-revelation, according to criteria I was only borrowing from other people. In any case, historically speaking, I was wrong: dance duels in clubs and discos, large and small, had been central to Cali tradition and style since the 1930s. Which meant that the national salsa championships in Cali were more than just a dance contest. They were social history performed before our eyes.

*

A tale is told in the city about a kid in the 1950s who danced barefoot in the streets of Buenaventura. Sailors from the US steamships moored in the harbour threw him coins or chewing gum. Heading up to the brothels on La Pilota, one of the city's three hills, the dancers among the sailors – black and white Americans, Puerto Ricans – would stop and laugh with him and show him jitterbug twirls or steps from Fred Astaire or Gene Kelly films. He copied their moves and fused them into a style that needed quick feet and elastic limbs like his to follow the music's many rhythms. He danced the Charleston and the foxtrot, and, when the time came, twist, boogaloo and *pachanga*. Someone must have taught him the moves that went with 'The Wah-Watusi', The Orlons' hit which reached number two in the

Billboard Hot 100 in the summer of '62, and the street kid must have danced it well because someone, not knowing his real name, decided to call him Watusi and the nickname stuck.

Watusi eventually joined the great move to Cali. He danced in a nightclub named Picapiedra ('Flintstones') in the *barrio* of San Nicolás, where his astonishing displays rivalled the girls as the main attraction. And then he grew up and found a dance partner called María. In 1974 the first major dance competition was held in the city, and Watusi and María won it. It was a key moment in the city's history; for the first time, the skills of its poor, dark-skinned dancers were recognised by wider society.

Watusi and María are legends in Cali but they are nowhere to be found. There were black and white photographs but I never saw them dance on film, much less in the flesh. Someone thought Watusi was living in Miami. Someone else said he must be dead. But everyone agreed from that ragbag of gesture and movement, given coherence and shape in the street kid's gift of movement, was born the Cali style.

All the elements are there: talent, poverty, blackness, the whole, vast range of influences. And Watusi certainly existed. It's just that the tale told about him is more a genesis story than strict history. In reality, there were at least two generations of dancers before he appeared. Alejandro Ulloa, who teaches at the School of Journalism at the Universidad del Valle and hosts a weekly radio programme about the city's dance culture, has compiled a remarkable *War and Peace*-sized historical account of salsa in Cali, in which he explains how the classic Cali style was created.

In working-class areas, he says, dances had been held in family homes with wide verandas as early as the 1930s. They danced foxtrot, bolero and *paso doble*, Colombian folk steps like creole rumba and *porro*, and Cuban genres like conga, *son*, *bote* and *guaracha*. Already dance in Cali belonged to the black or mixed-race working classes, in part due to the absence of opportunities in other, perhaps more lucrative sectors.

That first generation of show dancers included Alberto Insuasti from Tumaco, known as 'the Colombian Fred Astaire', and Benigno Holguín and his four brothers, who grew up with parties in their family home, sharing their moves with friends in their living room, and later on taught at the first working-class dance academy of which any memory remains, La Cumparsita, in 1949.

The early dancers performed at bars in the working-class part of urban Cali or in the red-light district in Barrio Obrero. This was a sector built in 1916 to provide housing for black railway labourers from the Pacific coast, and for families who had been living by the Cauquita River on the site of what had once been a *palenque*, a refuge for escaped slaves. In the history of salsa in Cali, Barrio Obrero is key.

Umberto Valverde, a novelist whose books are set in Cali's salsa scene, grew up there. 'There were more than 200 bars, all of them playing Cuban music. I remember them because I was a boy in the 1950s and I used to see my brother, who was seven years older than me, and the other neighbourhood kids, go out to dance there. They created the dance movement.'

With the advent of mambo after 1950, the syncopated rhythms widened the scope for improvisation. A catalogue of new steps began to appear with names like *tijereta* ('the snip'), *caída de hoja* ('leaf fall'), *aguja de reloj* ('clock hand') and *caída de muerto* ('dying fall'). Dance became a spectacle.

The generation of the 1950s incorporated movements from the *chachachás* they danced in the cabarets and brothels, and they would watch the Mexican mambo movies two or three times at the cinema, then go home and practise the steps. And those weren't their only influences. Carlos Valencia, who danced in the 1950s with a trio called the Three Pachucos – the name came from a Mexican film – remembers how they adapted movements from football, basketball and boxing into dance steps.

Watusi and his partner María belonged to a third generation that grew up in the 1960s when Cali style was transformed by Cuban *pachanga*, the boogaloo, the improvisation of the *guaguancó*, the smoothness of the *guajira* and the feeling of the *son montuno*, all grouped under the generic name of salsa. And, as Watusi was working his magical synthesis, a group of musicians came to Cali and accelerated the metamorphosis.

In 1968 the promoters of the Sugarcane Fair brought the pianist Richie Ray, his singer Bobby Cruz and the rest of the band to Cali. Their debut album, *Richie Ray Arrives*, recorded in 1964, had been a huge success. In 1966 they'd played promotional gigs for Pepsi Cola in Caracas, Venezuela and Barranquilla, on Colombia's Caribbean coast, where such crowds turned out that, on safety grounds, they were moved out of the coliseum and on to its rooftop so that they could perform to the heaving streets.

By the time they reached Cali in December 1968, Richie and Bobby were among the biggest stars of the Spanish-speaking Caribbean. They brought with them the virtues and the vices of the New York music business, as Bobby Cruz recalled:

> When we got to the airport, police officers come into the plane. 'Everybody but Richie Ray and his band, leave the plane.'
>
> The musicians I worked with were all drug users, so I said to my guys, 'Empty your pockets, we're going to get arrested here and we'll never leave this country.'
>
> After a long time, the police officers announce, 'OK,

the Richie Ray band, come to the front of the plane.'

They didn't take us into the airport terminal, they took us around the back, and I figured, 'This is it, they're taking us to prison.'

I said, 'What about the luggage?'

'Don't worry about the luggage, it'll go straight to the hotel.'

They put us in open cars. There were banners everywhere: 'Welcome Richie Ray and Bobby Cruz'. As we came into the city, there was an overpass with a figure of Richie so big that the cars had to drive between his legs. I was over the lanes in the opposite direction. Everywhere it was: 'Welcome Richie Ray and Bobby Cruz'.

They decided to take us to a restaurant to eat. The fans started to push against the outside wall and knocked it down.

In New York Richie Ray and Bobby Cruz hired professional dancers who would pull people out of the audience and show them how to dance. There was no need in Cali. The city had its own dance celebrities: Evelio Carabalí, who created the first large stage shows involving 20 or more dancers, and virtuosos with showbiz monikers like Jimmy Boogaloo and, most famously of all, Watusi himself.

Then there was Amparo Arrebato. An *arrebato* is a sudden fit or spasm: the term caught the astonishing foot speed and rippling movement of the Cali dancers, which had implications for the music. To accommodate the style Watusi and the rest had created, Caleños had begun to play 33 rpm LPs at 45 rpm. As time went by, musicians began to adapt to the dancing.

Richie and Bobby started playing their music their own way, and ended up playing it Cali's, faster and faster still. For Umberto Valverde, the music of Richie Ray and Bobby Cruz is inseparable from classic Cali-style salsa: 'Our affinity with Richie Ray is so thorough that the Cali dancer dances to Richie Ray's piano. He doesn't dance to the musical structure of the record; he dances according to the structure of Richie Ray's piano.'

On 29 December 1968 Richie and Bobby were performing at a Cali venue called the Caseta Matecaña when Amparo Arrebato took to the floor. Bobby Cruz complimented her on her dancing and her legs. She invited him and Richie to eat *tamales* at her home the following day. There they learned her real name. Amparo Ramos Correa was a former national sprint champion who'd represented Colombia internationally, and was Jimmy Boogaloo's dance partner. As a young woman, she had lived in San Nicolás, two blocks from Picapiedra, the bar where Watusi danced. She'd become a regular there and built a reputation: when the great Cuban bandleader Dámaso Pérez Prado came to Cali, he saw her dance and invited her to join his dance group, although she turned him down.

Richie and Bobby came back the following year with a suitably up-tempo song named after her:

Amparo Arrebato le llaman	Amparo Arrebato, they call her,
siempre que la ven pasar	every time they see her pass.
Esa negra tiene fama	That black woman is a star
de Colombia a Panamá.	from Colombia to Panamá.
Amparo enreda a los hombres	Amparo ensnares her partners
y los sabe controlar . . .	and she knows how to control them . . .

The trouble was, there was more than one Amparo Arrebato in Cali. Another brilliant dancer used the name: a smaller, darker-skinned woman called Amparo Caicedo. She has left little trace; she left Cali for New York and nothing more is known about her. But she too had a claim to the song, and the story Bobby Cruz tells these days includes them both: 'There were two girls: one golden, the other white, and both of them called themselves Amparo Arrebato. They were dancers, and they danced salsa in the Cali style, fast! At the time Richie and I had struggled hard to make it, and when we saw them struggling the same way, we wanted to give them a hand, so we wrote the song, which caught on and made their lives easier.'

In the greater scheme, the identity of the real Amparo Arrebato was irrelevant: the *idea* of her was a more potent part of Cali's identity than any historical reality. She belongs to the same part of the Colombian imagination as María Varilla, a local washerwoman who was also a wonderful dancer and is celebrated in a famous early-twentieth-century *porro* of the same name. In any case, Amparo Arrebato, Watusi and the other seminal figures, by dancing their dance, did something else too: their brusque new steps, jumps and figures shattered the old rhythms, the old synchronies and, to the music of Richie Ray and Bobby Cruz, opened an imaginative space that generations of characters in search of a song rushed in to occupy.

Richie and Bobby, like Willie Colón and Héctor Lavoe, were part of the first wave of salsa music that rippled back from New York towards the cultures that had supplied it, triggering the same creative processes in the swollen cities of the Spanish-speaking Caribbean. Despite its identification with blackness and, hence, in the prejudiced terms of their national cultures, backwardness, salsa brought echoes of modernity through its connections with New York. Afro-Caribbean folk genres met commercial music and dance, and the results could be read as Spanish-Caribbean folklore or as metropolitan culture.

Either way, the opportunities that salsa-mad Cali offered musicians drew Colombia's top bands to the city. Grupo

Niche play some of the most infectiously melodic but also creatively avant-garde salsa, and, although they weren't founded in Cali and neither of their co-founders was a Caleño, they are intimately associated with the city.

The group was formed in Bogotá in 1978 by two musicians from the Chocó, singer and songwriter Jairo Varela and trombonist Alexis Lozano, who had both grown up in Quibdó, and learned to read and write music from a Spanish priest named Fr Isaac Rodríguez, who ran the city's first choir. Varela and Lozano relocated to Cali in 1982 and never left, although the band subdivided into other classic groups. When Alexis Lozano left in 1984, he formed a band called Guayacán. In 2000, after many years of singing with Grupo Niche, singers Willie Garcia and Javier Vasquez left and started their own group, Son de Cali.

Several times I had approached the city in the entourage of the Tour of Colombia, a Tour de France-style cycle race, to the sound of Grupo Niche's 'Cali Ají', the unofficial theme tune of the Cali Sugarcane Fair. It always made my eyes moisten. Another song adopted by the city as its unofficial anthem is 'Cali Pachanguero' (1984). This song became the focus of a bitter dispute between Cali and New York over the use and abuse of clave.

In son and its derivatives, including New York salsa, clave was not just a rhythmic ornament, it was an organising principle. It followed African tradition in this: the Yoruba and the Ibo shared in a greater culture of two- and three-beat rhythms that structured music all the way across sub-Saharan Africa. For arrangers schooled in the New York tradition, the clave is taken to be implicit even when no part in the arrangement is actually playing it, and the stress patterns of the vocals and horn lines are expected to coincide with its rhythm. If they do not, the clave is said to be cruzada, or crossed, and the arrangement is considered defective. The clave rhythm is two bars in length. This means that any bridge section with an odd number of bars cuts off in the middle of the *clave* and 'switches it' from two-three to three-two or vice versa. Composers have always played with this: Mario Bauzá's arrangements for Machito and his Afro-Cubans often switch *clave*. Bauzá taught Tito Puente to do the same. Rafael Ithier of El Gran Combo does this in the glorious *'Son de Santurce'*. However, as far as the New York power base was concerned, Jairo Varela pushed the practice too far.

In the introduction to *'Cali Pachanguero'*, the trumpets announce the theme, while the trombone repeats a five-note, three-against-two polyrhythmic accompaniment that cuts across the *clave*. Then the trombone moves to the centre of the sound with a descending figure that lasts three beats, and is superimposed on the four-beat rhythm of the song. After four repetitions, the *clave* is turned and, as the trumpets join in, the motif lines up with the *clave* rhythm.

It was all typical Jairo Varela. He loved to play with repeated figures that cut across the rhythm only to rejoin it a few bars later. At the start of his 1981 arrangement of *'Mi mamá me ha dicho'*, a traditional song from the Chocó, the trombones and trumpets execute a cascading three-beat call-and-response motif that throws you gloriously out of rhythm if you let it. But when *'Cali Pachanguero'* became a massive salsa hit, it was derided in New York, and even now, according to Chris Washburne, older dancers and musicians refuse to dance to it.

The criticism seemed unfair. Varela, who was neither Cuban nor a New Yorker, was being judged by the standards of cultures that were not his own. Indeed, by fusing the Afro-Colombian music of his own background with a New York influence, Varela was both creating his own musical identity and expressing reverence to a style he knew and admired. The disparagement his music was subjected to in some quarters was an almost risibly misplaced pulling of rank, given that the song was written in and about Cali, where there is no question of a crossed *clave* putting a dancer out of his stride because the dance steps of classic Cali salsa make no pretence of corresponding to the *clave*. And the middle section, which was singled out for criticism, was a quotation from '*Pachito Eché*', a song that had become famous when it was arranged to the *clave* and recorded in Cuba, but it was actually a *bambuco* composed by a Colombian.

In 1987 Varela invited Afro-Venezuelan trombonist and arranger César Monge to join Grupo Niche. One of Monge's first tasks was to write new arrangements of '*Cali Pachanguero*' and other songs, straightening out the *clave*. In local nightclubs and at parties, the original *cruzado* recordings are usually played, but Grupo Niche perform the rectified versions in their live shows. Varela wished to broadcast a new, improved image of Grupo Niche as a polished band on a par with the best of Puerto Rico and New York. But the outcome of the dispute was a bald statement of where the power lay.

*

As '*Cali Pachanguero*' comes to an end, the vocalist Tito Gómez sings, '*Oye, Cañandonga, sepárame una mesa*': 'Listen, Cañandonga, put a table aside for me'.

The *cañandonga* is a tree called the coral shower tree that grows to fifty feet and flowers in large red-pink panicles, each of which has an outer envelope of five large, lavender sepals around the same number of rounded, peach-coloured petals, three large male organs – the stamina – and a long, curved female organ or pistil. The flowers, of course, fade and the petals drop away, but after fecundation the pistil elongates, dries and hardens into a long woody sheath containing tan-coloured seeds and a thick, dark, strong-smelling honey. The word *cañandonga* comes from Kimbundu, an Angolan language. Herbalists use its sap to treat anaemia.

Whether because of the prominent genitalia or the life-giving honey, Cañandonga has been adopted as a name for nightclubs all over the Spanish-speaking Caribbean, as well as in New York, where the famous Queens Cañandonga club hosted Tito Puente, Eddie Palmieri and other legends in the 1970s.

Cali's Cañandonga opened on December 1982, one of a number of new clubs – including The Apple, The Patio, The Green Worm, The Red Giraffe, The Calipso – that started up in the wake of a pioneering venue called El Escondite ('The Hide'). At its height, no small club on earth could match El Escondite: the Puerto Rican bolero singer and film star Daniel Santos appeared there. So did Rubén Blades, Grupo Niche, Fruko y sus Tesos and the Cuban violinist Alfredo de la Fé, who played solos on the tabletops. El Escondite's clientele danced Nuyorican style, based on the couple rotating, and in double spins by both partners. It was a style imported from New York. But times change and, when the new, romantic, ballad-based salsa arrived from Puerto Rico in the 1980s, Cañandonga became one of the city's most important salsa venues.

The drugs trade was at its height and the flood of cash brought in the best bands and kept the new clubs full of patrons. Cañandonga's owner, a well-known dancer named Jairo Obando, invented a dance step that caught on with his patrons, in which the couple didn't embrace but danced side by side. The basic sequence lasted four beats: on one and two, the partners turned inwards, towards each other, and kept turning until they had completed a 180-degree about face. On three, they tapped the floor ahead of them with the inside foot, the one closest to the partner, and, on four, they made a proper, weight-shifting step on to the same foot, on the same spot, which became the axis of the next 180-degree turn. Many variations follow, but this is the basic *Cañandonga* step, or *Pasito Cañandonga*.

These were the years Grupo Niche, along with El Gran Combo, the *merengue* band Rikarena and the brilliant Venezuelan performer Óscar D'León appeared at private parties hosted by the Rodríguez Orejuela brothers who headed the Cali drugs cartel.

In 1995 Grupo Niche's inspirational leader Jairo Varela was imprisoned for fraud, conspiracy and money laundering, to be released later and cleared of all charges. The Cañandonga was destroyed during a shoot-out between rival gangs in January 1996, although Jairo Obando's dance style is still danced in Bogotá, Miami and New York. Back in Cali, the *Cañandonga* style is considered a relic of the 1980s and 1990s, the years of the Cali cartel.

Vivi and I learned the *Pasito Cañandonga* from William and Myriam, two of Cali's pioneering dancers of the 1970s and '80s. I had met Myriam at the national dance competition, where she was one of the judges. Around the corner was the house where Amparo Ramos Correa, one of the Arrebatos, lived until her death in March 2004.

William and Myriam introduced us to the Cali interpretations of *pachanga* and boogaloo, which are still danced in Cali. William's salsa hinted at what the great Watusi must have looked like: quick feet, great balance, with something crudely systematic about his dancing. It was more a montage of steps and moves than a unified dance. Cali was sweltering and each two-hour session left me drenched in sweat.

*

The national dance competition had been dominated by members of an academy called Swing Latino, where the latest transformation of salsa in Cali was taking place. Swing Latino, like all of the city's best academies and dance troupes, was a charitable foundation.

Luis Eduardo Hernández, known as El Mulato, is Swing Latino's founder and leader. With his first partner, Liliana Salinas, he represented Cali at an international salsa competition in 1998 in Puerto Rico, where he encountered the face-to-face embrace and square geometries of cross-body salsa, and began to work these influences into his own quick-footed, side-by-side salsa.

For the historian Alejandro Ulloa, Hernández is the guardian of the classic Cali style and the bridge between past and present, the local and the global: 'He spans two traditions, one from the *barrios* and dance floors in the city, and the other that comes from outside through video, world festivals and international dance competitions. He brought them together, integrated them, and invented his own elements, because he's wonderfully creative. He has fused both currents, but he conserves certain features, those basic cells: the tendency to centre the dance on the feet and to dance very quickly.'

El Mulato describes his style as 'a fusion of Los Angeles and Puerto Rico with the original Cali style and a touch of my own'.

'We're the mother of all the schools here, in almost all of Colombia, and most of the directors in Cali studied with me. We rehearse for seven long days a week. I think Swing Latino is where it is today because we work so hard. No other company works the way we work. If we have to work from 9 a.m. to midnight, we do, if it's the only way of getting to the top and staying there, which is the hardest thing of all.'

He works with ballet instructors, gymnastics coaches and fitness trainers.

The city's tendency to absorb movement from every possible source has meant that, since about 2005, the classic Cali style has been strengthened by gestures coming from classical dance and ballet, including outstretched arms and the turning of the hands, quite apart from a variety of salsa developed by Javier Leudo and his group Súper Ballet de la Salsa, who dance *pointé*.

El Mulato started the group as a project to help young people: 'I began with 30 couples in Barrio El Diamante, all young people, because my work has always had been social work.'

El Diamante was one of Cali's most deprived areas, built on the flood plain of the Cauca River known as Aguablanca. Its history is one of shambolic occupations. Wave after wave of refugees swept in, displaced by a long series of natural and man-made disasters. The *barrio* was first occupied in 1974 by immigrants to the city fleeing violence in the mountainous regions of Tolima and Huila. In 1979 three new neighbouring areas were occupied by survivors of an earthquake that hit the city of Tumaco, on the Pacific coast, and the subsequent tsunami. In 1983 two more new *barrios* sprang up, filled with refugees after an earthquake that destroyed the city of Popayán. In 1985 after a volcanic eruption killed 22,000 and wiped out the village of Armero, yet more refugees marched into Aguablanca.

Luis Eduardo and his family were among the displaced people who had poured into Aguablanca in the 1970s. Born in the high mountains of Colombia's coffee fields, he was the son of peasant farmers who migrated to Cali in 1978 after being forced off the land by armed groups known as the *chusma*. His father found work on the Pacific railway and took his family to Cali, settling in Barrio El Diamante.

In 1982 Luis Eduardo formed his first dance group, Los Pibes de la Salsa ('the Salsa Kids'). In 1994 he opened his own school of dance, initially called Los Inquietos de la Salsa ('Salsa's Restless'). In 1995 he changed the name to Swing Latino.

Today, the school is in the Cali suburb of El Cedro but El Mulato says he has never left El Diamante: 'I still go there every week, I recruit young dancers there, I still do social work in El Diamante and in other parts of Aguablanca. When I was young, just starting adolescence, I was a gang member too. I never took drugs, but I committed robberies. So I know how that world is. We go to the most vulnerable *barrios*, we pull youngsters out of drugs and gangs. That's the fundamental work of Swing Latino.'

In 2004 the journal *Social Science & Medicine* reported the results of a major investigation that covered part of El Mulato's catchment area. Early in 2002 a team of fifty researchers had descended on two of Cali's poorest and most violent Comunas to investigate the prevalence of mental illness. One of them was Comuna 13, El Diamante. In the course of nearly 1,200 interviews, the researchers found evidence that 24 per cent of the people sampled were probably suffering some form of mental illness.

One in four sounded astonishingly high, even if it was the worst economic crisis in Cali's history and the proportion roughly matched both the local unemployment rate and the figure for residents living below the official poverty line of $3.20 a day. But one in four was also the corresponding figure for the United Kingdom. Either the poor of El Diamante were admirably robust, or we in Britain were terribly fragile.

The researchers mentioned music and dance as attenuating factors there, important local resources of what they called 'social capital', the 'stock of investments, resources and networks that produce social cohesion, trust and a willingness to engage in community activities'. Social capital, they said, had several dimensions. One was structural, providing access to formal and informal institutions which could help reduce the impact of negative life events by providing additional support. The other was cognitive, promoting a sense of belonging, shared values and trust.

Weaving a strong social fabric was part of El Mulato's plan: 'We are constantly trying to connect with the community around us, building relationships with other community leaders and other sectors like sport and culture.'

And in Cali's impoverished margins, salsa demanded of its students a life of order and discipline that helped them resist the temptations of drink and drugs. In this respect, it had something in common with those evangelical movements that ask for a similar level of commitment of addicts and help them turn their lives around. This partly explains the sheer speed and difficulty of Cali-style salsa, with the intense dedication and the physical demands it makes of its exponents.

Swing Latino's greatest rivals in Cali and the wider world were Pioneros del Ritmo, working in the poor and sometimes violent Comuna 16 and La Unión, which, like El Diamante, were founded by refugees from the countryside in the early 1960s.

La Nueva Dimensión ('New Dimension'), a dance school for children from across the city, was founded to keep children entertained and safe from the dangers of gang culture and substance abuse. They have more than 300 pupils aged between 4 and 24.

Meanwhile, dancers from a company called Combinación Rumbera were giving free lessons in salsa, *merengue* and *bachata* to 6–15 year olds in Barrio Panamericano. They, and many other dance foundations in the city, were offering neighbourhood kids activities for their free time, and a form of training that's fun and, for the best of them, a living. No matter how complicated it became, no matter how many influences it absorbed from abroad, salsa in Cali still belonged to the people.

All the same, the language of social capital, with its financial imagery and its derivation from the Latin word for the head (*caput, capitis*), sought to contain or even deny the body and its soulfulness, and to confine lineage and inheritance to a carefully delimited analytical slot. These are the ways the disembodied think about themselves. They hardly reflect the experiences of Caleños, Chocoanos and Cubans whose descriptions overflow the sober terminology of social scientists: in their lives dance becomes a bodily means of accessing the ancestral flow of wisdom, flooded with memories and their attachments. They exemplify that ancient recognition that history seeps into everything. Not a step, not a note is uncontaminated.

I had always found it very difficult to get close to musicians in London or New York. In Cali, it couldn't have been easier. So, on our last day, we took a taxi to the Dan Carlton hotel for a meeting with El Gran Combo de Puerto Rico. No musician or group of musicians has deeper or more authentic roots, or is closer to salsa's essence.

We met the band's agent, Mario Rodríguez, in the hallway. These had been Vivi's favourite musicians all her life but she didn't want to tag along: it offended her sense of discretion. So Mario took me up to Rafael Ithier's room. Rafael was there with Jerry Rivas, one of the band's two lead vocalists, and Papo Rosario, the backing singer who also choreographs the band. We shook hands, sat down and began to talk. For once, Rafael took centre-stage. The two singers both deferred to their bandleader, who, despite his eighty years, was full of anecdotes and laughter.

'We think of ourselves,' Rafael told me, 'as working men, musical labourers. This is how we chose to earn our living; we go up on stage to entertain the people. That's how we began and that's how we'll die.'

Mario asked them to give me 20 minutes or so. We talked for over an hour, until I reminded them they were playing later on. Rafael spoke about the Palladium era, when the evening started with a dance lesson, followed by a show that featured the professional dance troupe.

'When we first played it, we called it Tropical music or Antillean music or Caribbean music. Salsa didn't exist. Or rather, they didn't call it salsa because the term didn't exist yet. In the old days, we played *son montuno* or *guaguancó* or conga, and now all that's called salsa, although it was the same music. It was only when they started adding trombones to the horn section and playing timbal solos after the theme that they started calling it salsa.'

Like Richie Ray and Bobby Cruz, El Gran Combo had adapted their playing style to changes in dance styles over the years. They play more slowly today than they did in the early '60s, when the dance in vogue was the *pachanga*. The Palladium was on a second floor above a car showroom and, when everyone started doing the *pachanga*, the entire building began to shake so violently the fire brigade sent inspectors round.

'They didn't close it down but they imposed restrictions. They more or less banned the *pachanga*. There were so many people, they said it was dangerous.'

Rafael smiled. He was quoting one of El Gran Combo's most popular songs, 'No hay cama pa tanta gente' ('There aren't enough beds to go round', a witty way of saying, 'There's not enough room for so many people'), by Puerto Rican composer Florencio Morales Ramos, and sung, these days, by Jerry Rivas:

> Pa' fuera! Pa' la calle!
> Tírenlos pa' bajo que son un peligro arriba!
> Outside! Into the street!
> Throw them down, they're dangerous upstairs!

The song tells a funny story about a party where all the great stars of salsa and Afro-Cuban music are playing:

> Willie Rosario y su orquesta la salsa quería empezar
> y Héctor Lavoe al llegar tarde encontró que La Selecta
> ya se encontraba dispuesta para alegrar el ambiente
> y en una esquina Tito Puente empezaba a pestañear
> y volvió Celia a gritar: '¡Azúca'! No hay cama pa' tanta
>   gente.'
> Willie Rosario and his band wanted to start the salsa,
> Héctor Lavoe, arriving late, found that La Selecta
> Was already set up to cheer the place up,
> And in a corner, Tito Puente was starting to nod off,
> When Celia Cruz again shouted, 'Azúcar! There's no
>   room for all these people.'

A line-up like that, you could only find in Cali.

In New York, they discovered bands with conservatory-trained musicians, unlike the Puerto Ricans, but without fixed line-ups, and, as Rafael's primary concern was showmanship, he turned this to his advantage: 'We were born at a time when television was starting in Puerto Rico, and we understood that, as well as playing, we had to

118

entertain because television has the visual element. So we began to choreograph dance routines so that people would see us as we were. That smile is part of El Gran Combo. They couldn't choreograph their performances because they changed personnel every couple of months. We had different uniforms and routines for each show.'

The dance routines of their three singers in the 1960s helped spread salsa dance movements. Roberto Roena, the bongo player, was also a wonderful dancer and Ithier asked him to choreograph the band's stage act. The early television performances featured routines that illustrated the stories told in the songs. Roena left in 1969 to form his own band, Roberto Roena y Su Apollo Sound.

In 1977 El Gran Combo's lead vocalist Andy Montañez also left. Replacing him was as much about finding a great dancer as it was about finding a great singer, because Andy was both. Jerry Rivas didn't imagine it could be him. El Gran Combo were an all-black band; he was white and blue-eyed. And he was too young; he had gone to school with Rafael Ithier's daughters. Worse than any of that, he couldn't dance. All the same, Quique Lucca, the leader of another of Puerto Rico's long-lived bands, the Sonora Ponceña (founded in 1954), recommended him to Ithier.

'When the call came, I thought it was a practical joke. But it turned out to be true. It wasn't easy. Andy's fans told me to my face, "You're a good singer but you're not right."

'I couldn't dance, so I had to learn.'

The dance routines had to be simplified but, far from losing their fascination, they stripped salsa down to the bare minimum. The new, toned-down stage show probably also made it possible for the band to age with a degree of elegance, which, given that Rafael Ithier was born in 1926, served a purpose.

El Gran Combo de Puerto Rico were a rare example of a salsa band that had handled their finances and record deals well, and had never lost control of their management or artistic integrity. One of the secrets of El Gran Combo's remarkable longevity was a decision taken in 1970. They'd parted company with Gema Records, who had recorded Cortijo y su Combo in the 1950s, and all of El Gran Combo's records so far.

Fania came in with an offer. Rafael Ithier discussed it with the band members: 'We understood that Fania had too many artists, all of them very good ones, and they couldn't dedicate much time to one or two groups. They had to be thinking of all their artists. I talked to the boys and we came to the conclusion that it was better to do our own thing, to concentrate on ourselves, and not to fall into Fania's hands.'

Subsequent events proved them right. Fania's main objective had always been to convert the music emerging from New York's *barrios* into a profitable commodity. To do so, it had adopted ruthless business practices, taking over smaller labels that offered competition, buying radio airtime and monopolising club bookings. Much of the repertoire recorded by the label had been written by known Cuban composers, but, under cover of the US trade embargo on the island, Fania began omitting composers' names and replacing them with the initials D.R. for *Derechos Reservados* or 'Rights Reserved'.

Fania soon had troubles of its own. Its founder, Johnny Pacheco, eventually lost his share of Fania after his arrest in the mid-1970s on suspicion of drug dealing. His erstwhile partner Jerry Masucci put together an expensive legal team, then forced him to sell his Fania shares to pay the legal fees. Pacheco reflected in 2006, 'I should have seen it coming.'

By 1979, however, Fania's sales had slumped. When musicians, promoters, composers and producers realised the extent of the royalty payments that had been withheld, they began a campaign to win full payment. Masucci responded by ceasing further productions and, the following year, he sold the company to a group of South American investors.

Rubén Blades later recalled, 'Masucci was clever enough to understand the potential of the music and he made it big . . . he facilitated the talent's opportunity, but he ended up keeping all of the money. He ripped everybody off, but there was nowhere else to go. Fania was the only game in town.'

Rafael Ithier told me, 'Instead of going with Fania, we decided to create our own label and record for ourselves. So we set up a label called EGC.'

The first record El Gran Combo recorded for their new label was called *Estamos Primeros*, which roughly translates as 'We come first'.

I thanked my interviewees and left, and in the lobby I met up with Vivi. But before we could leave, Jerry Rivas – a man as famous as Mick Jagger in the Spanish-speaking world – bounded into the lobby and intercepted us. I introduced him to Vivi and we sat down, amazed: like probably everyone else in Cali, we would have gladly shined his shoes and pressed his trousers if he'd asked. But Jerry wanted to ask a favour: he wanted to give us some CDs and DVDs of some young Puerto Rican acts.

Young musicians were going into rap music, not salsa, he told me. The music scene was in crisis and, if the situation continued, salsa would soon cease to exist.

The problem lay in the turn taken by the recording industry after Fania's crisis in 1980 had left a vacuum at the heart of salsa. In 1987 a concert promoter and manager called Ralph Mercado, who had worked with Jerry Masucci when he ran the Cheetah nightclub and was well schooled in his business practices, created RMM records. Just like Fania, who in 1971 had brought its main vocalists, bandleaders and session musicians together as the Fania All-Stars, Mercado formed the RMM All-Stars in 1994, with an incredible generational mix from Marc Anthony, who was in his twenties, to Celia Cruz, in her seventies.

In the 1990s a struggling salsa artist told Chris Washburne, 'If you are not signed with Ralph, you are nowhere. He's got the market locked up.'

In the mid-1990s when RMM entered agreements with Sony and BMG to expand its distribution network, it received a full audit by the Internal Revenue Service, and artists, publishers and composers realised the extent of the rights payments that had been withheld. After dominating the salsa industry for a decade and a half, RMM was brought down by disputes over unpaid royalties. After threatening to expose the company's practices, some artists were released from their contracts. Marc Anthony was one; he left and joined Sony.

But when Puerto Rican composer Glenn Monroig sued for breach of copyright and was awarded $7.7 million in damages, Mercado was forced into bankruptcy. In November 2000 the company ceased to exist. No new label had appeared to fill the gap, so opportunities were limited for acts who were yet to make a name for themselves on the scene.

Meanwhile, the established stars were either dead, like Celia Cruz, Ray Barretto and Héctor Lavoe, or ageing: Rafael Ithier was in his eighties and Cheo Feliciano was not much younger. Jairo Varela and Willie Colón, the best of the next generation, were born in 1949 and 1950 respectively, and even the young guns of *salsa romántica* were well into their middle years: Marc Anthony, born in 1969, was younger than Gilberto Santa Rosa, Rey Ruiz or Víctor Manuelle.

So, salsa music largely existed as a closed corpus of recorded work. We were dancing to music recorded long ago by artists now in their autumn years. As a newcomer to salsa, I was in the same predicament as the narrator of Kafka's story 'The Great Wall of China', who comes to realise that, because his village is so unimaginably isolated, the dispatches they take to be the latest news from the capital take hundreds of years to reach them:

> Long-dead emperors are set on the throne in our villages . . . Battles that are old history are new to us, and one's neighbour rushes in with a jubilant face to tell the news . . . With a loud cry of woe our village eventually hears how an Empress drank her husband's blood in long draughts thousands of years ago.

That night, we met up with the band again at Cali's Rumbadrome for the final concert of the festival. They were the headline act, coming on at 3 a.m. at the end of yet another excessive programme that included two of Colombia's top *vallenato* groups, *merengue* star Sergio Vargas and Cuban salsa vocalist Rey Ruiz.

We were too tightly packed on the dance floor to move so there was more watching than dancing. It wasn't, to tell the truth, the best concert experience I'd ever had: everyone seemed to know all the lyrics to every song and sang them with, or over, the artists. But we were there, which was magical enough.

We left for the airport at 4.30 a.m. and arrived in Medellín so tired we didn't care where we slept, or if we'd ever wake up.

6

Sexy Salsa

Ella era una chica plástica . . .
De esas que . . . sudan Chanel Number
Three.
She was a plastic girl . . .
Like the ones who sweat Chanel No. 3 . . .
    '*Plástico*', composed and performed by
                                        Rubén Blades

British salsa had begun to develop in the late 1980s. It was very quickly severed from its historical associations with the Colombian immigrant community and reconnected to Cuba. At the heart of it was a fashion-industry innovator who had made a career from setting trends or catching them early on. At the end of the 1960s David Shimeld had opened a fashion store in Kensington, London, called Che Guevara, which he claims was the first use of the Argentine revolutionary as a fashion icon. Shimeld had a passion for meticulously designed interiors and contracted fashion designer Anthony Price, the man who styled Roxy Music's album covers, to design his shop. The solution put the hero of the Cuban revolutionary war into the luxurious setting of the *Titanic*.

'The interior was wonderful: it had black walls, and the

carpets were black and lime green and lay crosswise as you walked into the shop to give you a sense of depth. There was a big fountain in the middle that made it one of the first air-conditioned shops. And we put lilies everywhere, which were very visual and gave out an intoxicating smell. The lights were like the funnels of the *Titanic*, in the same black and green, and in the changing room we had the original old *Titanic*-style wall lights. It was really quite an amazing shop for the time.'

With Biba down the road and Mr Freedom and Lee Bender's Bus Stop around the corner, Che Guevara was at the heart of London's fashion scene for the moneyed and style-conscious. Angie Bowie and Twiggy were regulars.

Shimeld's next project was a fashion outlet on the Fulham Road called Plaza, also designed by Anthony Price and as innovative as their earlier venture. Then he turned his eye for a meticulously styled interior to the night-time economy and pioneered some of Britain's first wine bars. First came three venues branded Cork's Wine Bars, then he established another line known as The Pheasant Tree group.

By 1988 Shimeld was exploring new avenues. It was the time of the first tapas bars and Shimeld caught the trend early, opening three of his own in London: Bar Madrid in Wentworth Street, just off Oxford Street, Bar Seville in Old Compton Street and Rey Camino on the site of the original Pheasant Tree wine bar on the King's Road.

'I did my research and I found there was a lot of Spanish people in England, as there are a lot of English people in Spain, so Bar Madrid was basically made for the Latin community. It took off instantly.'

Shimeld asked Chris Greenwood, a DJ who had been hosting Latin-style parties in a club called Pachanga, to manage theme nights at his tapas bars.

'I said, "I think you need a dance class followed by a band followed by a DJ." If every Latin night starts with a salsa class now, it's probably my fault.'

125

It was an old formula, used at the Palladium in New York during the mambo years, for instance. But it was new to London, and had profound consequences for future perceptions of salsa in Britain. Greenwood brought in the Cuban dance teacher Nelson Batista, who took the same template to Rocket, a club on the premises of the Polytechnic of North London in Holloway Road. Over the coming years, it spread all over Britain.

Shimeld's tapas bars had opened in uncertain times, after Black Monday in October 1987. Eventually they ran into difficulty and Shimeld sold them on. But the salsa nights had been a huge success and Shimeld harnessed their potential in his next project.

After his *Titanic*-themed fashion outlet and his chain of bars designed around British perceptions of Spanishness, he turned to the Caribbean: 'Puerto Rico reflects fairly violent images. I did not want that sort of image; I wanted a mysterious image of the Caribbean. Cuba's always got that mystique about it, but I didn't want what Cuba has now because they don't have the resources, so I went to see what the Cubans have done in America.'

Shimeld went to Miami to clarify his ideas. He took his menus from a restaurant in Key West and came up with Bar Cuba in Kensington High Street which opened in January 1992. He aimed to use the ethos of pre-Revolutionary Havana to attract casual smart, upmarket punters aged between 20 and 40. His target clientele consisted of Spaniards and local English people attracted because, as he said, 'It was different.'

This sense of the exotic was mixed with alcohol-fuelled silliness: 'We used to sit at the door and when people came in we used to cut off their ties and give them a free glass of champagne. It was mad.'

Eighteen months after Shimeld had opened Bar Cuba, his

former accountant Eric Yu and a group of investors who called themselves the Breakfast Group opened another themed venue in the Trocadero in Piccadilly. Founded on the site of a failed Irish theme pub, Bar Rumba was a cultural cacophony, named after a Cuban dance but selling Spanish tapas and Mexican food. Yu said the idea behind the club was to create 'a modern and trendy place for people who like Soho and Covent Garden'.

Bar Rumba was intended to be a Latin-styled club, but, as the accent shifted from music to dance, investors were beginning to notice that the dance-class clientele didn't drink and were hard to make a profit out of. Yu brought Chris Greenwood in to do what he'd been doing at Bar Cuba. Greenwood saw an opportunity for more lucrative promotions.

'The West End was trendier than it is today and I thought we could do something a bit more cutting edge, so we did drum and bass and house nights and promotions with Juice FM. It was much more contemporary, although we always had a Latin night.'

Greenwood's memories reveal some of the bizarre experimentation with identities and dress codes that Bar Rumba's early salsa nights encouraged: 'One guy used to come in and take his jacket off, revealing a holster underneath. He must have felt like Al Pacino. Then his jacket would go back on and he'd pick up his briefcase and off he'd go.'

The old Sol y Sombra DJ Dave Hucker remembered him too: 'He kept his keys in there. These days it would be a mobile phone.'

For the serious learners, the concentration needed to master movements meant alcohol consumption was minimal. For the rest, the exotic theme nights offered a little welcome identity loss.

Jim le Messurier, a British conga player, often played at

these new theme bars in the early '90s before an audience that wasn't particularly interested in Latin music. 'They were mainly young professionals, yuppies, really, out after work in the week nights. The distributors of bottled beers like Sol, Corona, San Miguel and Havana Club were trying to get a piece of the market, so there were cheap deals on drinks. It was more of a theme-type experience, really.

'People used to get quite pissed and that was probably a good thing from our point of view, as the live music, given the budget, was never going to be that good. But it was an opportunity for us musos to make £50 on an otherwise dead night.'

And this was salsa's attraction to nightclub investors. Salsa, as they marketed it, occupied early-evening, midweek niches that were otherwise hard to fill. It usually guaranteed a good crowd, it didn't necessarily run late into the night, and very little was required in the way of security.

Dave Hucker deejayed at Bar Cuba on Wednesdays with his Sol y Sombra night and at Bar Rumba on a Sunday. The Sunday event, which he called Sunday School, eventually moved to Villa Stefano in High Holborn.

Chris Greenwood was also involved in Sunday School at Villa Stefano, and booked an ex-drill sergeant with the Colombian Air Force named Elder Sánchez as a dance instructor. Elder, from Palmira, north of Cali, had gone absent without leave, entered the UK illegally and spent a year cleaning floors before meeting Nelson. He was no show dancer.

'I always danced socially, although, in Colombia, people who dance socially don't dance with many movements. So, when I started to teach, I saw Nelson and Xihomara and said to myself, "How am I going to teach this?"'

At a small club in Covent Garden called Bar Sol, Elder met Nelson Batista and the two became firm friends. 'Nelson taught me technique and inspired me to create my

Dramatis personae, *c.*1965: Vivi's mother, Marlen, and father, Lucho.

The first contact sheet:
Cuban Nelson Batista
and Londoner Daniela
Rosselson *c.*1989, with
accompanying poster.

Xihomara Granados and the London Salsa School distribute
a little non-specific exoticism (early '90s).

The *Sunday Times*, 17 August 1980: salsa didn't exist yet, so the press called Lubín Reyes' venue a 'drinking club'. (© *Sunday Times*/NI Syndication)

(Below and overleaf) A selection of Dave Hucker's fliers for the Sol y Sombra, where many British revellers first encountered Colombian salsa.

'Rooftop, University Heights, Bronx, 1979', by David González, captures salsa's urban setting and its role as a form of cultural resistance.

Authenticity personified: Miguel Ángel 'Mike' Amadeo at 786 Prospect Avenue in the South Bronx. (Portrait by David González)

The glitter of Cali: the children's section of the Colombian salsa championship, 2005.

In the heat of Quibdó, 2006: Mi Sangre Candente and leader Milciades Rentería (right); and Emilia Caicedo's Grupo Papitú (below).

The university of salsa: Jerry Rivas, Charlie Aponte and Papo Rosario front El Gran Combo de Puerto Rico.

Jerry with Vivi, Cali, 2005.

own movements. I didn't want to copy his style so I adapted it to my way of dancing.'

Soon Elder was teaching in six or seven different places a week. His dance classes at Villa Stefano attracted 80 to 100 people.

Chris Greenwood remembers him playing on his macho, Air Force background. 'Elder was very funny. I'll never forget the description of salsa dancing. He'd say things like, "The man must be hard and the woman must be soft."'

The theme bars benefited from other branches of the English-speaking culture industry that used a similar mystique to tempt the paying customer, some of them making for profitable cross-promotions. There were fajitas, and tacos and tortillas. There was Bacardi and bottled beers with slices of lime in the neck. Chris Greenwood became involved with Sony and organised promotions of Gloria Estefan and Ricky Martin albums. There was also a rash of films that depicted Latin America, and especially Colombia, as a wild, scenic, sometimes sexualised backdrop to an adventure, although they had no real interest in life there. Most of the Latin American characters, regardless of their provenance, had Mexican accents, like the actors who played them. This divided audiences into several camps: non-Latin Americans, who could enjoy a hundred or so minutes of what they thought of as harmless entertainment; Latin Americans in general, who found them rather silly; and Colombians, in particular, who found themselves relentlessly stereotyped and given accents they considered ridiculous. It was like watching a film in which all the white Londoners had the character traits of Stephen Lawrence's murderers and were played with Texas accents.

The other side of the stereotyping coin worked in favour of the male salsa teachers who were happily surprised to find their female British learners open to a little Latin love. Some instructors bedded their students in large numbers, while second-generation Colombian males discovered that the theme bars were guaranteed pick-up joints. Salsa, the family dance of Spanish-speakers from the sometimes rather Catholic and sexually repressed countries of Central America, began to reflect the sexualised nature of this encounter, and took on an erotic hue. Elder Sánchez played along and called his brand of dance 'Sexy Salsa'.

In truth, all of the early salsa teachers – the Colombians Xihomara Granados, Elder Sánchez and their colleague José Polanco, and the Cuban Nelson Batista – were adapting themselves and their body language to meet the hopes and fantasies of their British pupils. Of Elder Sánchez's 'Sexy Salsa', Nelson Batista said, 'It was very mellow, not a lot of combinations, very controlled. I think it was a mixture between old Cuban *son* and Colombian dance. But it was his own creation.'

But Nelson had developed his own style too. He taught his students to tap the floor with one or other foot on every beat: 'The Cubans do not tap, they hold the step and then they go. I thought people would understand the tap on every beat, and it made it easier for me to explain the steps.'

In turn, the first British-schooled students of these hybrid styles began to give classes themselves. Elder Sánchez's Turkish dance partner Mina Elliot was teaching at La Finca on Pentonville Road, near Angel. At Bar Cuba, Londoner Elli Galvani, who had been taught by Nelson Batista, was running early-evening classes.

British salsa was beginning to configure itself. The classes at Bar Cuba, Bar Rumba, Salsa!, Fiesta Havana and the other theme bars allowed their customers to position themselves somewhere exotic but non-specific and, in any case, outside the received conventions and geography of traditional Britain. The steps and moves offered membership of a sort of symbolic micro-community, in which constant effort and continual reworking and upgrading was required to maintain one's status, so different levels of salsa dance, from beginner to advanced, had to be invented. The very nature of salsa was being transformed. The dance floor was turning into an extension of the adult-education sector. The good students might become better ones and then experts and instructors. It was also taking on the traits of a new-age, self-help, self-improvement therapy. It was quickly unrecognisable to the Colombians who had brought it to London.

And the British interpretation of the body as, among other things, the object of the health and fitness industry created a problem for the clubs. British dancers, as a rule, drank non-alcoholic drinks, which severely restricted revenues at salsa venues. Instead of alcohol, profits had to come from classes. That meant a continuous expansion in the repertoire of dance moves.

*

Until the mid-1990s, British events were generally small and organised by Spanish-speaking Caribbeans with community roots. Then the business community discovered salsa. It took time to discover how difficult it can be to turn someone else's cultural practice into a profitable concern. The fate of the salsa theme bars illustrated the point.

David Shimeld's Bar Cuba was doing well. 'We used to take fantastic figures. It was an amazing success. And then I got a good offer from My Kinda Town.'

My Kinda Town, which called itself 'a branded destination restaurant group' operating 53 units in 16 countries, was the creation of Bob Payton, a marketing expert first sent to London to promote Kraft products.

A working-class Jewish kid from Miami with parents of Russian extraction, Payton fell in love with England and Englishness and was soon buying his shirts in Jermyn Street and riding with the Cottesmore Hunt. When he moved into the fast-food industry, he played on Britain's wildly ambivalent attitude towards US culture. He told *Inc. Magazine*, 'America is what's happening to these people, and they have a love-hate relationship with us. They watch American TV, listen to American music. America is their fantasy, and they come to my restaurants to live it out.'

In 1977 he opened his first Chicago Pizza Pie Factory in central London. This was followed by a series of theme restaurants: Rib Shacks, Chicago Meatpackers, Henry J. Bean's and a fish restaurant called Payton Place.

In February 1995 Payton added Bar Cuba to an earlier acquisition in London's Charing Cross Road called Salsa!. David Shimeld received £1.3 million, which he used to open a beach resort in St Lucia.

Chris Greenwood, who had stayed on at Bar Cuba after the acquisition, came to know and admire Payton. 'He saw potential in the Latin thing. It was becoming a High Street commodity, something that could be rolled out. The clubs were open every night, there was volume, and it was an older demographic so, if you were clever about it, you could get them to spend money.'

Payton made the underperforming Salsa! a huge financial success by completely ignoring salsa's Caribbean, Spanish-language ethos.

Greenwood saw it happen. 'They kind of jumped on the 1994 World Cup. They said, "We're gonna become the home of Brazilian football," and that totally transformed it. Television crews came down and they made sure there were lots of sexy Brazilian girls around. There weren't as many Brazilians as there were Colombians but the community was growing and all of a sudden they had a home. Salsa! just completely took off.'

Payton then combined aspects of Salsa! with the more sophisticated design concept of Bar Cuba in a venue called Havana, which he opened on the site of failing Chicago Pizza Pie Factory in Hanover Square. Another Havana opened in Fulham, although, when the owners realised they couldn't trademark a city's name, they rebranded them Fiesta Havana.

Chris Greenwood became a consultant. 'They asked me to programme it, and all of a sudden I was programming seven or eight Latin venues. I had engineers and a whole network of bands that were working. I could give one band twenty gigs and pay them less.'

Until now, the theme bars, however spurious their identity, and however focused they were on a British and European clientele, could always fall back on the large Latin community. Bar Rumba wasn't aimed at the Colombian population, although Eric Yu recognised that having Latin Americans in the club added to the atmosphere. They brought a quality he called 'authenticity'.

My Kinda Town began to look outside the capital. The Rib Shacks in Manchester and Glasgow were failing, so they closed down and reopened as Fiesta Havanas.

Chris Greenwood was involved in this expansion. 'It was tough when you moved out of London because there was no Latin community. We had plans to open one in Liverpool, too, but by then the recession had hit.'

In June 1995 My Kinda Town went public, valued at £33 million. The following month Bob Payton rolled his Range Rover and was killed. In November 1996 Capital Radio PLC bought My Kinda Town. Capital Radio had had experience rolling out Harry Ramsden-branded fish and chip restaurants but had no expertise in the new Latin theme-bar sector, so the acquisition sent its share price plummeting. In 1999 the company sold the bars to the Surrey Free Inns Group (SFI), the pub company behind the Slug and Lettuce and Litten Tree chain. It was an unhappy cross-cultural encounter. SFI's all-white head office faced allegations of racism, and Chris Greenwood and Dave Hucker both walked away, citing unpleasantness and incompetence.

SFI went into administration in 2005. The Latin bars were sold off piecemeal and the company was wound up. But by then there were salsa nights in pubs, clubs and village halls all over Britain, run by and for Britons who had no links with the Latin American immigrant community and saw salsa not as a piece of someone else's way of life but as part of British exercise culture, something to add to the aerobics schedule.

As well as the fixed theme-bar venues, much larger, one-off events began to appear. Cressida Childs, a PE teacher trained in Exercise to Music, had got involved in contemporary dance before a fellow teacher introduced her to salsa. They started giving classes in Bristol in 1993, and Childs was one of the first teachers in Britain to push hers one stage further. The history of salsa suddenly converged with the British holiday-camp tradition.

'I wanted to do more than just teach my students their one-hour class so I thought I'd offer them a mini-break. Butlin's in Minehead kindly let me have use of a room. Somehow people from around the country got wind of it and before I knew it we had 50 people booked.'

Childs approached the other big holiday-camp company, Pontin's at Brean Sands in Burnham-on-Sea, which ran themed dance breaks. Pontin's agreed to finance a salsa weekend, and the first Pontin's Salsa Weekender, which took place in February 1998, attracted 250 dancers. Another one was held in December the same year and brought in five hundred customers. Soon, they were bringing in crowds of 2,000 from every part of the country.

The Salsa Weekenders were owned by Pontin's, whose ambitions were limited and finances tightly controlled, but they inspired an independent promoter to organise a big new salsa event in 2002, hosted by Butlin's.

The organiser was Paul Young, a marketing expert and a salsa dancer who had attended the second Pontin's Weekender in 1998 and had been inspired. Young had taken lessons with Elder Sánchez, Ramiro Zapata, Xihomara

Granados, Robert Charlemagne and Nelson Batista. He was a regular visitor to Bar Rumba and Villa Stefano and knew Tomek, the DJ from Gledhow Gardens in West London who had helped salsa cross over from the Colombian community to white Britain.

'Tomek worked for me for a while. Back when I first started, he tutored me in the history of salsa in the UK.'

Young promoted his first salsa night in Croydon in 1999 and lost money, but by 2002 he and his then wife Imogen Moore were ready to move into the big time.

The first World Salsa Congress had been held in Puerto Rico in 1997, organised by a promoter called Eli Irizarri. The formula has been fine-tuned over the years but remains largely unchanged: five or six hours of dance workshops during the day, performances by the show dancers in the evening, followed by all-night parties hosted by the top DJs. At the same time, dancers can visit a trade show where exhibitors offer all conceivable salsa-related goods and services, from post-dance massage and protective braces to two-tone shoes and salsa headgear.

The Puerto Rican event inspired imitation. There was a salsa congress in Haarlem, the Netherlands, in 1998, and another in Los Angeles in 1999. The congress movement was in full expansion, and Young wanted to organise the first British one.

'Pontin's was a congress, really. Cressida Childs was slow in claiming that ground. She opened up the idea in the first place, it was like, "This can be done," but she made the mistake of allowing Pontin's to own and brand it. I didn't want to make the same mistake.'

In 2002 Young and Moore rented half of the Butlin's holiday camp in Bognor Regis. Eventually, Butlin's insisted they take the entire venue. The Bognor Regis congress ran from 2002 to 2006, growing bigger each year. Live music was always part of it, along with the best teachers, performers and DJs available.

'We attracted 3,000–4,000 dancers from 30 different countries.'

Young was a risk-taker who got involved in some of the most successful salsa productions in Britain, and some of the most disastrous. He was on the steering committee for Latin Splash, a one-day summer festival in Clapham Common, South London between 2003 and 2005. 'We got 10,000 people. It was the biggest [salsa] event ever in the UK. We brought over Óscar D'León and the Buena Vista Social Club: superstars!'

But he was also involved in the debacle that surrounded a West End production entitled *Murderous Instincts*, a 'salsa-comedy-murder-mystery' that had had a successful run in Puerto Rico two years before, but in Britain soon became a laughing stock. During its pre-West End run in Norwich, the leading lady, Nichola McAuliffe, had revealed to the press lurid accounts of backstage affairs and details of endless rewrites, characters that didn't fit the plot, actors unable to dance salsa, a poster that looked as though it had been designed by a sixth-former and, above all, the American producer's 'habit of sacking everyone'.

'This show has had, to date, eight directors, four PR companies and innumerable general managers,' she told the *Daily Mail*. 'But for the past week we've had the same team, and if they last another couple of days, I might even start to learn their names.'

When the show hit the West End, the reviews were appalling: Lyn Gardner described the show as 'pure poison' in *The Guardian*: 'Thoughts turn not to murder but to suicide.'

The £2m production closed less than a week after it had opened. Salsa came out of it looking faintly ridiculous.

In 2007 Paul Young moved his British salsa congress to the Bournemouth International Centre, although he was already eyeing a bigger move. 'I wanted to take the UK congress from south to north because it was getting too expensive to hold it in the south. You couldn't house it in a small venue and retain the concept, so you had to go to bigger venues and there aren't many in the UK. I was looking to take the UK congress to the Winter Gardens in Blackpool.'

In 2006 Young joined forces with a Manchester-based company called Salsology to organise a new event called the Brit SalsaFest. In February 2006 the first SalsaFest attracted about 2,000 customers. A second one in February 2007 was just as successful, although by then relations between Young and his northern partners were breaking down. At the end of October 2007 the partnership fell apart. There was a court case over the use of assets and Young lost. The 2008 SalsaFest was cancelled at short notice, and Young, the biggest and most successful salsa promoter in the UK, withdrew from the scene completely.

There were, he says, personal reasons for moving on, but also a business logic. 'In salsa, it's very difficult because of the lack of alcohol. Every time I got a decent venue, I'd lose it because the alcohol sales were rubbish. You could get the numbers – I filled the Ministry of Sound [nightclub in London] with 1,200 people but they only took £800 behind the bar. With those numbers, they would normally take 30 or 40 grand. It just wasn't a business where you could make any money.'

7

Cobao in Cartagena

Yamulemasese . . .
'*Yamulemau*', performed by Joe Arroyo,
composed as '*Diamoule Mawu*' by Laba
Sosseh

In October 1965, writing to Ana, Marlen joked, 'Marriage is a shady deal and worse with a man from the coast.' The Costeño in question wasn't Vivi's father Lucho. They hadn't yet met. It was an earlier suitor who had tried to use music to break into her heart: 'On St Valentine's Day he gave me a ring with his name, an LP and a pretty diary with a key.'

But Colombian highlanders have always considered Caribbean men lazy and morally remiss. Caribbean men know this and play up to it. One of them, a Puerto Rican singer and songwriter of rural folk music called Chiquitín García, even wrote a song about it, one that almost every Colombian can sing along to: '*Y no hago más na*' ('And not another thing').

Yo me levanto por la mañana,	I get up in the morning,
me doy un baño y me perfumo,	I wash, put on some aftershave,
me como un buen desayuno	I eat a hearty breakfast
y no hago más na', más na'.	and I don't do another thing.

138

And so he goes on through the day, reading the paper, watching television, eating, sleeping, singing, chatting with his wife. In the version recorded by El Gran Combo, the backing vocalists call, *'Qué bueno vivir así, durmiendo sin trabajar,'* ('It's great to live like this, sleeping without working,') and the lead singer, Jerry Rivas, responds,

Señores, si yo estoy declarado en huelga, ¡sí!,	Gentlemen, I'm on strike.
¡mi mujer que me mantenga! *¿Oíste?*	My wife can take care of me, you hear?!

The humour is beautifully crafted, the arrangement flawless, El Gran Combo's swing compulsive. Everyone involved is a Caribbean male, and that is the point: the craftsmanship should be achieved while conveying the impression of absolute nonchalance. In Cali I'd asked Rafael Ithier what sort of man the composer Chiquitín García was, and he'd said, 'Just like the man in the song!'

Grace without effort, the song seems to imply, should be achieved in the simple details of everyday life, and in things as demanding as producing the perfect song.

Seen from the Colombian hinterland, then, the Caribbean was a place of humour and peace, despite the heat. It was also a place of languid sensuality. Marlen went on a university trip there in June 1965 and wrote to Ana,

> I still haven't told you how happy I was on the coast. I fell in love with the parts I visited: Barranquilla, Cartagena, Santa Marta, Cienaga, Fundación, Valledupar, Fonseca (Guajira), San Juan, Maicao, Riohacha, El Pájaro, Manaure. Before you ask, I didn't see Señor Díaz.

'I came back black,' she added. 'I sunbathed by the sea, I danced a lot.'

There were overnight parties: 'My excursion to the coast doesn't feel as though it really happened any more. I wouldn't survive a climate like La Costa's now, with all those sleepless nights.'

Formal marriage was perhaps less common on La Costa than in Antioquia, which was one of the most religious regions in the country. Costeño men often kept a wife or main partner, while raising socially recognised children with one or more other women. These sexual mores were regarded as quite improper by people in the interior who sometimes attributed them to African influences. The Caribbean males in Medellín brought from the coast the close dance style that the girls were desperate to learn and their parents were equally desperate to stop them learning.

Marlen was one of the girls in question, although she didn't betray anything in the letter she wrote to Ana in February 1966, as she prepared for her exams:

> You can't imagine how happy I am in sixth grade, the study is hard but I don't care. The lessons are given by two men, there are only two nuns who say almost everything in English.

This is the first time she mentioned Vivi's future father to her best friend. Six months later, something was in the air:

> I have a boyfriend from Cartagena and it's none other than my physics teacher, the subject I hate more than any other. . . . You can't imagine the difficulties we've had because in class we can't speak, which means he tries to show me his affection with looks which won't give us away, knowing how my classmates talk. It could be it'll come to nothing but I want to tell you about every step of my life. His name's Luis Miguel García and he's nice.

A few weeks later, she wrote:

> I'll tell you about my new conquest who left twenty
> minutes before your present arrived on Saturday. He
> came round from 2.30 in the afternoon until seven in
> the evening and never has time gone so quickly . . . he
> looks at me as if I was very grand; I won't start a long
> list of qualities because I'd never finish, although I
> think this sums it up: he is a sort of second heaven in
> which I've been living since February, even if our
> condition as pupil and teacher has allowed us only
> looks and simple conversations.

Marlen's mother Colomba had been told she should not
have children, but she had ten, and died, aged forty, in April
1970. In August that year, Marlen and Lucho married. There
followed the birth of three children, the death of her father,
various comings of age, the end of her own marriage and
the beginning of her daughter's. There was the acquisition
of forms of wisdom, and the discovery of their uselessness.
There was her work: she travelled to Medellín's most
troubled areas to open parenting centres and deliver courses
that perhaps contributed as much to the city's survival of
the violence of the 1980s and 1990s as any institution.

By the time I met Vivi's father, he had been living in Medellín
longer than I'd been alive. The Spanish spoken in Medellín
and the local customs and way of life were markedly
different from those of Cartagena, but Lucho was so settled
in his identity that he had never stopped speaking and
thinking like a Costeño. He couldn't be angered or
frustrated, and he responded to the most fraught situation
with words that raised a smile.

We once waited outside a bank in Medellín while he went
in to discuss a loan. The clerk told him categorically he
didn't have the income to justify any credit. But he charmed

her into letting him see the manager and disappeared into his office. Minutes later, the two men emerged in fits of laughter. Lucho, it transpired, had sweet-talked himself into twice the loan he'd wanted.

Another day, waiting at some traffic lights, he rolled very slowly backwards into the car behind. Listening to music, as he almost always was, he didn't notice, and, when the driver made an angry gesture, Lucho thought it was because the lights had changed, so he drove off. A few hundred yards later, the aggrieved motorist headed him off, leapt out of the car and prepared to set about Lucho, who was in his late sixties, with his fists. Within a matter of seconds, the two men were sharing a joke at the side of the road.

Even approaching 70, there wasn't a grey hair on Lucho's head or a wrinkle of stress on his brow. I had no idea how Lucho did it, but it clearly had something to do with an attitude to life that seemed to come straight out of Chiquitín García's songs.

Cartagena de Indias has become Colombia's biggest, perhaps its only real tourist attraction. Modern Cartagena was founded in 1533 and soon became the capital of the Spanish conquest. In 1984, the walled city and the castle were designated UNESCO World Heritage Sites, and these days it is a regular stop-off point for luxury liners cruising the Caribbean. I had seen the Cartagena of the tourists during my honeymoon with Vivi. But beyond the walls, kept brilliantly clean for the tourists, and Bocagrande to the south, where high-rise hotels towered over the town's most popular beach, Cartagena languished in poverty.

Raised by his grandmother because of his parents' financial difficulties, Lucho had grown up in this other Cartagena. He remembered the days when the Hotel del Caribe, famous for its beauty pageants, was the only hotel on Bocagrande. One day, he skipped school and went to the beach at Laguito, next to the hotel. A schoolmate had pushed him off the breakwater and he had sunk to the sandy bottom. Whatever he went through on his panicked struggle back to the surface prevented him from ever learning to swim.

I wanted to see Cartagena through Lucho's eyes, so the whole family went, Lucho and his partner, Vivi and her two brothers, and me. Since Lucho lived in the countryside and needed a rugged vehicle, he drove an enormous, indestructible 4x4. He rattled around at not much more than walking pace but the car was too worn with age and solidly built to mess with, so other drivers kept well clear.

Vivi and I met him at the University of Antioquia. The traffic was horrific and Calle Barranquilla, just outside, was blocked. The lights changed periodically but the drivers ignored them and were ignored in turn by three cops who recognised absolute deadlock when they saw it. A little altruism might have eased the blockage but no one was surrendering an inch, so Lucho edged the car out into the road. His sidling into the fray elicited horns and the occasional shout, but he seemed genuinely not to notice. Suddenly, inexplicably, we lurched out of the snarl-up and on to open road. The gridlock disappeared into the distance behind us, like a twisted relic from the age of heavy industry, enveloped in exhaust fumes. It was like emerging from a rainstorm into brilliant sunshine. I wondered if I'd witnessed some sort of miracle, but it was simply that Lucho drove the way he danced.

We left the city and reached the open roads, but Lucho, like a good Costeño, was in no hurry. He had to be coaxed above 50. His son Nestor was Medellín-born and liked to put his foot down, but somehow we stayed together through the night and reached Cartagena mid-morning. Lucho had rented a flat for us all, so we parked the cars in the basement and took taxis around town.

One night we visited Lucho's cousin Julio, a former weightlifter who had travelled the Caribbean with the

Colombian national team. Julio, then 76, was talking about dancing *serrucho*, tight against the body of a girl he liked, during the 48-hour party that followed his graduation in accountancy, but then his stories veered off into childhood experiences, most of them other-worldly: a headless horse that ran down the street, scaring him half to death and sending him into a fever, and a ghostly figure that appeared behind him like a man draped in a sheet, only floating over the table.

In Cuba, sufficient numbers of slaves with common origins had been able to stay together to retain some semblance of their African language, religion, music and dance. Not so in Colombia. Although at its peak the slave trade delivered 12,000 Africans a year to Cartagena, the majority of them were 10 years old or younger. They were often sold on several times and dispersed in small groups over vast expanses of territory along the Magdalena and Cauca Rivers. As a result, many of their African memories were lost and the impulses that had survived were flooded by European fantasies. All the same, I wondered if the reality Julio spoke of, in which people were not yet buffered against the spirit world, was itself, at root, an African survival.

Much later that night, when we were all rather drunk and the music was very loud, Lucho told an inconsequential tale about a dance contest between himself and a mechanic called Carmelo. The judge had fallen asleep during the competition. Everyone laughed.

Lucho said, 'I don't know why people complicate their lives.'

At various moments during the evening, he took his daughter in his arms and danced. They hardly needed to move to be exquisite. As a result, we were all drawn into their dance. The slightest change of gait or emphasis, the smallest leaning in or away, had us nodding our heads in agreement. There was, I recall, the occasional, slow turn. But nothing demonstrative. Nothing of note in the way of technique, just minute adjustments of weight and balance, the slightest of swaying to and fro and from side to side, movements that fall into synchrony the way pendulums do, hips, legs and feet making almost imperceptible accommodations. I was fascinated by their nothingness of a dance. At times, it took a moment to realise they were moving at all.

Our time in Cartagena was filled with family stories.

Another night Lucho fell into conversation with a taxi driver about the open-air parties around which Cartagena nightlife revolves, when huge sound systems known as *picós* (a Spanish garbling of 'pick-ups') are erected on the beach or on an expanse of wasteland and blast out music for the dancers.

'Which is the best *picó*?'

'El Guajiro.'

'That's my cousin's.'

He was talking about a boxer and racing cyclist called Carlos Arturo Pájaro, who was also a wonderful dancer.

'They called him Puerto Rico, and his *picó* was called El Guajiro. When he died, it went to another cousin. His children run it these days. What else?'

'El Fidel.'

'Another cousin.'

Before he could explain, we reached Barrio Bruselas and pulled up outside La Charanga de Jhosep Black, a bar owned by yet another cousin, José Carmona. José was also a community leader and was under pressure from some quarters to stand for mayor in Cartagena. Everything that went on in the *barrio* went through José.

His father had run a small *picó* at the start of the 1960s. 'They used to send me to bed at 8 p.m. My father arrived at ten. He brought the sound system home with him. They put the music on and I would lie there listening to the music. And there are records I remember hearing, *"La Mecedora"* by Silvia De Grasse. *"Mece la mecedora . . ."* I heard it recently and it took me back 50 years, lying in bed as a child with my father downstairs.'

At José's bar we drank beer while he and Lucho talked about the family. They spoke of an uncle who had fathered 23 children with several different women, and collected them all once a month on a flatbed truck to make sure they knew each other and wouldn't intermarry. Another worked on the trains and had 54 children with 13 different women, each of them at a different railway station. Yet another, a teetotaller who sang Afro-Cuban music for Cartagena's Orquesta Número Uno, ended up leading the band because he was the only one sober enough to collect the music at the end of the evening.

Lucho had wanted to be a musician too. 'But my grandmother stopped me. It was the only frustration of my life.'

José wanted to know what had set me off on my travels. I told him the story of Tom Evans, a great-great-uncle of mine who sailed steerage to New York each April and back to Liverpool each September. Tom was a boxer and a carpenter. He survived the San Francisco earthquake and worked on the Empire State Building, helping to create the preposterous verticality that Manhattan passed on to salsa, with that strong male hand at the top of the turn, although, whether it was the boxing, the earthquake or the vertigo, Tom felt the fragility of his mental health and checked himself into a lunatic asylum between trips.

I thought I might have had something of Tom Evans in me, although the truth was I had known nothing of his existence until my father, researching the family tree, had discovered him. My parents, who were both compiling family histories, used databases documenting births, unions and deaths to reconstruct our provenance. But we were, in fact, utterly disconnected from the vast collection of individuals they had uncovered. So, whereas in Colombia, everyday life was enmeshed in vast and very real extended family networks, the people whose memories my parents had resurrected were as distant to me as the old song that transported José Carmona back to childhood.

Lucho had once warned Vivi never to go out with a man from Cartagena. They could be cousins. Instead, she had married me and moved to a very different type of world based on the sociability of strangers, with a husband who was very comfortable living in a society rich in its resources of anonymity.

José had a vast collection of vinyl discs, some of them brought to Cartagena from Havana and New York more than 50 years before by sailors with the merchant fleet of *La Gran Colombiana*. 'When salsa became popular in the 1970s, they could sell the records at ten times the price they'd paid for them.'

At the same time as the New York salsa boom, Cartageneros had begun to listen to African music too. The *picós* mixed salsa with music from Ghana and Nigeria, the Congo and Cameroon, Angola and South Africa. This combination of styles has continued to the present day and, as a result, songs that have been largely forgotten in Africa are still well known on the Colombian coast which acts as a vast reservoir of African musical memory.

The titles of popular African songs were garbled into phonetic versions of the original, or were given the names of the *picó* that played them, or acquired new titles in Spanish. Over time, local musicians who grew up playing them began to add new Spanish lyrics, or compose songs mixing African influences with elements from other parts of the Caribbean – Haitian *compas*, Antilles' *cadence* and *zouk*, and Jamaican reggae. This led to a new, hybrid genre known as *champeta*, which retained and reworked old African music into current memory.

At Uncle José's bar they didn't play Chiquitín García's '*Y no hago más na*" but they did play El Gran Combo's salsa version of '*El Jíbaro listo*' by another singer of Puerto Rican rural folk songs called Victor Lluveras. It is a wonderfully funny, warm song about a country boy or *jíbaro* who makes it in the city:

Ya no camino descalzo	I no longer walk with my feet bare.
Ahora mis pies yo los calzo	These days, I make sure they wear
Con zapatos de glacé	patent leather polished shoes.
Doy ese lujo a mis pies	It's a luxury I give my toes
Qué tanto han merecido	that they have richly earned.
Mire, ayer mismo hice un pedido	Look, only yesterday I sent word
De unos zapatos a Ponce	to Ponce for another pair
Ahora, mi número es once,	Size eleven is what I wear
Los callos se me han caído.	Now the hard skin has gone.

By now, José's bar was full. I looked around and it seemed to me that, among the people dancing and drinking, there were many who might have lived through a similar displacement from country to city. After all, Colombia had been transformed in little more than a generation from an undocumented or poorly documented country – Lucho's identity card gave the wrong place of birth; Marlen's had the wrong birth date – to a nation of written records, where families no longer had twenty children or more, but two, or one, or none.

The changes Vivi hadn't been through herself she knew from the collective memory of those around her. Compared with Vivi and her family and the dancers around us in José

Carmona's bar, I sometimes felt the life available to me was claustrophobically small.

Lucho remembered the rhythm of his grandmother and one of her sisters grinding maize in a wooden mortar, in the village of Arjona, his real birthplace, although the documents said Cartagena. It recalled something Marlen had written to Ana over 40 years before:

> He studies a lot and he's very serious. Just think, we fell in love through nothing but looks and telephone calls, and now we can't pass a day without speaking. At times he makes me angry and I snap at him. Then he makes me laugh because he says, 'Careful, you might hit me.' And a while later he tells me off like a favourite child, 'You're bad-mannered today!' I don't think I've told you he was brought up by his grandmother, and at times he makes gestures like a child, although he's a man. But I know it's unconscious, and all because 'the old girl', as he calls her, loved him.

Around us, people were dancing, but not as they did in Medellín or Cali or New York. A couple at one end of the bar, another on the patio, a third across the room had quietly taken to the floor. I thought of taking photographs but there was nothing to see. It was salsa, degree zero, as private physical sensation and no more. To take a photograph seemed somehow inappropriate: this utterly undemonstrative dancing had no visual element. I was the only one who paid it any heed.

In the interior, this way of dancing is known as *amacizado*, 'pressed together'; in Buenaventura and La Costa, it's known as *serrucho*, meaning a saw, or *cobao*, which derives from the verb *covar*, a mining term meaning to excavate a large hole with a metal-tipped pole in search of gold.

José provided every table with an empty beer crate. At the

end of the evening, his patrons paid for the number of empty bottles in it.

'The salsa crowd doesn't like trouble. They just want to dance.'

José's patrons, almost all of whom lived in Barrio Bruselas, were of every age and colour, from white teenagers with their heads virtually inside the speakers, to dark-skinned men and women in their seventies.

'They invent their own steps on the basis of local Afro-Caribbean dances that came before salsa.'

So it was throughout Colombia. The social mobility that makes for standardisation was probably only a generation away, but for the time being there was a wonderfully local quality to salsa: every town had its own response to the music, based on the Afro-Caribbean folk dances of the surrounding countryside.

I had wanted to see Cartagena through Lucho's eyes. I wasn't sure I had. There had been family disputes over the usual matters, and there were people and old haunts he had no interest in revisiting. In any case, Lucho wasn't adept at displaying his life as content for someone else's existence, like a tourist brochure or a theme bar. I had wanted to see the old house where Vivi had learned to dance at her grandmother Julia's feet. But there wasn't time, or we didn't make any.

Before we set off for the overnight drive back to Medellín, we stopped beneath the walls of the old town at a food stand in the street. Nothing set it apart from any other street vendor. But Vivi insisted, so I ordered a prawn cocktail to eat in the car. The stand had been founded in 1954 by a man known as Sincelejo, and taken over, on Sincelejo's death, by his son.

It reminded me of Mama Isabel's, the *pastelillo* truck Mike Amadeo had shown us in the Bronx. They weren't in the tourist guides. I suspected they weren't even part of oral culture, in that people didn't even talk about them. They were simply there and, if you belonged there, you knew about them. I'd been using my habitual visual way of thinking; it was only the prawn cocktail stand that showed me my problem wasn't seeing Cartagena, and salsa, through Lucho's eyes, but feeling them bodily; using the tongue not to speak but to taste.

And Sincelejo's prawn cocktail tasted very good indeed.

8

THE BRITISH BOTTOM

Si yo llego a saber que Perico era sordo,
Yo paro el tren . . .
If I'd known Perico was deaf, I'd have
stopped the train . . .
'*Quítate del a vía, Perico*', composed and
performed by Ismael Rivera with
Cortijo y su Combo

A woman's breathless voice moans, in English, of a lover from a faraway island. He intrigues her with every move. He leaves her helpless.

'Cross body.'

It's Tower Inferno salsa night at Blackpool's famous Tower Ballroom, and the dance floor is crowded. Demonstrating the moves are Jason and Shemayne Parkinson. Jason started dancing young. By the age of twelve, he was competing in the 'Open to World' Championships at Blackpool and by the age of fourteen he had won the first of five British World Open and British National titles as part of the Preston formation team. He and Shemayne have also competed as a couple with great success.

'Change.'

Jason's instructions echo around the hall.

The singing voice cracks in blissful suffering. She can't keep her cool. She slips as they dip into a state of bliss.

Jason grinds his hips and moves Shemayne's hand crotchwards. He flicks back his head in rapture.

'Oooh!'

A ripple of excitement goes around the dance floor.

Then he comes to with a smile and a glisten in his eye, and introduces a new move. 'Round and back.'

They circle each other.

Shemayne bends her knees and sinks slowly to the floor.

Jason shouts, 'Working girls, come on! Show us what you've got!'

She thrusts an outstretched leg between his. Her head is now at crotch height.

Jason whoops.

The audience loves it. Shemayne rises and shrugs her shoulders.

And that's the sequence. Jason makes the call: 'All change!'

He means us to move on to the next partner but it is railwayman's talk too and not out of place because Blackpool has been synonymous with fun by the sea since the completion of the branch line from Poulton in 1846. Working families have been flooding in from Lancashire's cotton industry, Yorkshire's woollen mills and Staffordshire's pottery towns since the nineteenth century, to see waxworks and Chambers of Horrors and freak shows of headless girls and bearded women and three-legged boys and dog-faced men. And, above all, they came to the great dance halls, the Empress Ballroom in the nearby Winter Gardens, which opened in 1896, and the Tower Ballroom, which opened beneath Blackpool Tower three years later.

For much of the twentieth century, dance, along with pub and cinema-going, was the most popular entertainment in the country, and salsa here has as much to do with the long tradition of northern showmen and showgirls working the crowds beside the Irish Sea as with any flux of ancient cultures in the far-off Caribbean.

The resort came into its own between the wars when entire towns took turns to close down and wave off their workforces on special trains for their Wakes Weeks. They re-created their hometowns in Blackpool, which became Glossop or Stalybridge, or Rochdale or Halifax, on Sea. And all the while it remained obdurately itself, with its Ghost Train and palm readers, and the Fun House where gusts of air lifted the giggling mill girls' skirts and the whole town became a distorting mirror, reflecting the working north back at itself, and giving the holiday-makers the kind of joy there is to be derived from being, just for a moment, a little less acutely ourselves.

At the end of the First World War, there were 1.7 million more women in Britain than men. Advice manuals for the 'extra women', as they were called, advised middle-class girls to go where men were by joining a tennis club, or taking lessons in ballroom-dancing and attending dances, which were thought to be the most likely places for encountering members of the opposite sex.

It worked for the industrial classes. In August 1937 80 largely middle-class observers working for the social research organisation Mass Observation descended on the industrial north to study workers on holiday. Their primary motivation in Blackpool seemed to be a somewhat prurient interest in sex-by-the-sea.

They crouched in bushes, crawled under the pier and pretended to be drunk so they could observe couples in the sand. They recorded only three confirmed incidents of actual copulation. One of these involved a member of their own team who had sex up against a wall with a married woman from Leeds.

Between the wars, British entrepreneurs invested huge

sums in dance halls and luxurious cinemas that reassembled exotic fragments into a make-believe world. They were decked out like Moorish citadels, Chinese pagodas, mermaids' gardens or gothic extravaganzas and named after Granada or Luxor or called Palaces or Pyramids. John Betjeman particularly liked the enormous Palace dance hall in Douglas on the Isle of Man, with its parquet floor covering 16,000 square feet, room enough for 5,000 dancers. 'It is in gay baroque style, cream and pink inside, and from the graceful roof hang Japanese lanterns out of a dangling forest of flags.'

The very architecture began to loosen the dancers' ties to their everyday selves. The dances worked them looser still.

'Soon a thousand couples are moving beautifully, the cotton dresses of the girls like vivid tulips in all this pale cream and pink, the sports coats and dark suits of the men a background to so much airy colour.'

Not everyone was so enthusiastic. In his 'rambling but truthful account of what one man saw and heard and felt and thought during a journey through England during the autumn of the year 1933', the Yorkshire novelist and playwright J. B. Priestley divined three distinct Englands. The first England was the slow, benign life of the countryside, what Priestley called 'Old England, the country of the cathedrals and minsters and manor houses and inns, of Parson and Squire; guide-book and quaint highways and byways England'.

The second England was the harsh, ugly industrial city, which he thought of as 'nineteenth-century England, the industrial England of coal, iron, steel, cotton, wool, railways; of thousands of little houses all alike'.

Into what he called 'the third England', Priestley bundled up the 'giant cinemas and dance-halls and cafés' with the new world of 'arterial and by-pass roads' and 'filling stations and factories that look like exhibition buildings' and 'bungalows with tiny garages, cocktail bars,

Woolworths, motor-coaches, wireless, hiking, factory girls looking like actresses. Greyhound racing and dirt tracks, swimming pools and everything given away for cigarette cards'. He had it in for 'swimming costumes and tennis rackets and dancing shoes', too.

He railed against the new, international architecture of the interwar years, which he saw as a surrender of British character to fads from the United States. Among those fads were the dance crazes of the 1920s and '30s. Londoners were doing the foxtrot before the Great War, and the American troops who arrived in 1917 brought jazz and ragtime music, and all manner of new styles: the Jogtrot, the Shimmy, the Missouri Walk, the Vampire, the Black Bottom and the Charleston.

In Priestley's third England, things were stripped of provenance or belonging. All sense of place was under threat. Distant realities became as recognisable as anything closer to hand. A false sense of familiarity arose with film stars and sportsmen, and, for that matter, politicians and world leaders. The grip of the local was loosened. Lineage and inheritance were weakened.

He saw this as the loss of something quintessential, not to say deferential: 'The young people in this England,' he said, no longer 'live vicariously [or] enjoy life at second hand, by telling one another what a wonderful time the young earl is having, or how beautiful Lady Mary looked in her court dress; they get on with their own lives. If they have heroes and heroines, they choose them themselves from the ranks of film stars and sportsmen and the like.'

The Second World War did nothing to quell the fervour for dance. Within months of the war ending, the dance halls were heaving again. In 1953 the *Economist* magazine put annual admissions at about 200 million, which made dancing the second-largest entertainment industry in the country. And dancing meant pair-dancing.

Even within pair-dancing, the first glamorous association

between violence and music began to be felt. At a dance night at St Mary Cray in April 1954, as tension mounted between rival gangs of teddy boys, the MC told police, 'I took the precaution of having the band play only calming music – no quicksteps.'

When Bill Haley's 'Rock Around the Clock' came out in October 1955, it was down in the Decca catalogue as a foxtrot.

'I suppose it did come from America but I don't think we were all that conscious of it.'

We were staying an hour from Blackpool with a friend who had known the Tower Ballroom in the 1950s. The young Joan Lyons had grown up in Bury, Lancashire, and started dancing as a teenager at the local Palais des Danses.

'It was our only recreation really, you know, the cinema and dancing and playing rounders. There was a group of six of us, all girls, and we used to go out to the Palais on Wednesdays and Saturdays. We used to queue up in the freezing weather for hours and hours to get tickets for Christmas Eve and New Year's Eve at the Palais. And once a month we'd all go to Blackpool on this special train, to dance at the Tower Ballroom or the Winter Gardens.'

Working-class girls like Joan had no formal training. They picked up the steps on the dance floor. Joan was confident in the quickstep, foxtrot, waltz, tango and samba, although she couldn't jive, and the *chachachá* didn't really make much sense to her. 'We didn't have anything as sort of sexy as the salsa.'

All the same, it was one of the rituals of growing up.

For men, the dance halls required a uniform-looking shirt and tie. Young women could express themselves in their clothes, and, as there wasn't much money around, Joan used to make her own dresses. And dancing was also an opportunity to experiment with make-up, which meant defying her father. 'I used to go to the house of a friend who lived with her granny. We used to put our lipstick and powder on there. But one day Jean's granny put brown paper over the mirrors so we had to go into the Ladies' toilets just before you got to the Palais and put our lipstick on. I used to have to wipe it off before I got home, though. Dad used to say, "It's common, putting make up on."'

They were innocent times. The girls could leave their handbags in their places confident that no one would take anything. And during the interval, the dance halls served cups of tea and meat pies. There was no alcohol.

When Joan and her friends grew out of going on holiday with their parents, they had to leave town to find an open dance hall, because during Wakes Week everything was closed. 'You had to go to Rochdale or Haywood and that to do your shopping. We used to go to Blackburn or Burnley to dance, the whole gang of us.

'Or we'd go to Butlin's, or the Isle of Man, the Villa Marina. That's where we used to dance to Joe Loss and Ted Heath. It was all live music. Our kind of music was like Nat King Cole and Frank Sinatra. You used to go up and ask the bandleader, "Would you play this music?" and more often than not they would.'

Joan and many of her friends met their future husbands dancing at Bury's Palais des Danses. 'They had a get-together years ago – we didn't go because I think we lived down south at the time – of all the couples that got married that met at the Palais.'

Her beau was a Scottish footballer named Stewart Imlach. 'He was a good dancer, Stewart was. You know, he used to set off at such a speed. He did everything with gusto.'

For Joan, and for most working-class girls of her generation, marriage marked the end of their social dancing. 'Unless we got invited to a do, and then you just had a dance, but mostly that was it, because we moved about such a lot. We never settled anywhere for a long time. It was a shame really because we loved it but, you know, as far as we were concerned, that was part of our youth. It was a different time.

'There was one lad named Brian Goldstone, and all the girls wanted to dance with him, especially the tango, because he was a great dancer. I wonder what happened to him.'

Priestley, the grumbling Yorkshireman, had few good words for things Lancastrian. He had especially strong views on Blackpool. 'There is no less charmingly situated resort anywhere.' But even he had to admit, 'places like Brighton and Margate and Yarmouth are merely playing at being popular seaside resorts. Blackpool has them all licked.' And for that, he said, 'It is entitled to some respect.'

Like the Wakes Weekers, Vivi and I had come here to dance. Tics and spasms, flashing lights, men in white shoes and jackets: it could have been a quarantine ward. Every skin tone, every generation was there: girls with skinny white legs, elegant Caribbean couples perhaps in their seventies, tables of twenty, family groups, men and women alone, five or six hundred of us, all infected by the lunacy of Tower Inferno night at the Tower Ballroom: colour and movement and rhythms transported from the Spanish-speaking Caribbean to the preferred seaside resort of the British working class.

Jason Parkinson was an accomplished northern showman himself. Still sweating from the stage, he told me, 'Not everyone can work a crowd like this. To hold that many people in the palm of your hand, in the world's most famous dance venue, you need to have it. If you don't, you're soon found out.'

Everyone seemed to be dancing with passion: the nubile, the middle-aged and the retired, black, white, coffee-coloured, a lesbian couple in skin-tight leggings, a guy in a rainbow mohican – what a dancer! – even me. It was twenty-first-century Britain at play. Teenage girls in dresses that were obviously too short. More than one woman who could have been their grandmother had drawn the satin too tightly across her rear.

Or take the man across the floor, dressed like a Cuban dandy, with white brogues, trousers and *boina*, the flat cap that is part of the salsa fan's uniform in the Caribbean. Beneath his jacket he is wearing a silk shirt in bold purple. The hypnotic swing of his buttocks attracts the eye to the faint fleshy hue glowing through the seat of his pants, which have turned semi-transparent in the disco lights. Nakedly aware, as I dance with Vivi, that my own performance may look disturbingly similar, I try to look away but fail, my eye caught by the contortions into which he binds one partner after another with the panache of a children's entertainer bending coloured balloons into stegosauruses and Blackpool Towers. Strait-jacketed in their upper limbs like the residents of an old-time lunatic asylum, they spin to freedom as he releases them.

I wondered if it might be some sort of statement. After all, the British buttock is heavy with history, and has for generations been a national obsession. In the eighteenth century, a bottom of generous proportions was a wholly desirable trait. It was the sign of someone not easily swayed, with a solid grounding in reality, what they used to call 'sound fundamentals'. If you ever needed a lawyer, you found one with what they called 'Bottom'. Then old England's once proud haunches went out of fashion and the pronounced rear became an object of ridicule, every caricaturist's signifier for degeneracy. Lowlife characters were depicted forever letting off through flabby, gaping arses.

Having more or less decided how it felt about its own hind quarters, polite society turned to other people's. In the 1910s and '20s, when the pioneers of the ballroom-dance industry saw their own natural clientele seduced by the rhythms and body movements of jazz and ragtime dancing, they decided something had to be done. Before the white middle and upper classes could be allowed to indulge in dances clearly linked to black society, dance celebrities in the United States like Irene and Vernon Castle (once played in a film by Fred Astaire and Ginger Rogers), and their former student Arthur Murray, re-choreographed Afro-American dance. Movements and postures considered too black were recast, and the origins of their dances were obscured.

There was something systematic about the suppression of the Afro-American bottom and the stigmatising of movements suggesting anything sexual. A vaudeville comedian named Harry Fox slowed down ragtime and smoothed its stride to create Mr Fox's Trot, now known as the foxtrot. The Charleston, said to have originated among the black population of South Carolina and denounced by the *Daily Mail* when it reached Britain as 'reminiscent only of Negro orgies', was straightened and whitened into the 'quicktime foxtrot and Charleston', or quickstep, for short. The Lindy Hop was tamed into Swing dancing with the approval of Arthur Murray, who advised his pupils, 'Dancing with hips way back is out of date.' And tango's rising class status in the 1920s is partly explained by the discreet storing of the sacrum in the line of the head, shoulders, rib cage and feet.

When the Castles bowdlerised the Afro-American turkey trot into the One Step, their manager Elizabeth Marbury praised the new white dance for its elegance and wholesomeness, and for eliminating 'all hoppings, all contortions of the body, all flouncing of the elbows, all twisting of the arms, and, above everything else, all fantastic dips'.

In the 1930s, the British bandleader and dance instructor Victor Silvester wrote, 'the most natural and comfortable is always the most graceful and requires the minimum effort'

– meaning, of course, to his white British clients.

Something similar happened to mambo, rumba and samba, all of them originally practised by the darkest and poorest members of their Caribbean and South American communities. Paris was the gateway through which most of these dances had made it to Europe. They were introduced to the British dancing public by a French instructor named Pierre Zurcher-Margolle, known as Monsieur Pierre, and his dance partner, Doris Lavelle. They visited New York, Cuba and Brazil on research trips and, although they took the trouble to study the dances in their home settings, the translation of their observations into a teaching system made drastic reinterpretation unavoidable.

Zurcher-Margolle described rumba, possibly meaning the fast *guaguancó*, as 'so super-rhythmic that it is quite beyond the reach of any European dancer', and considered his pupils incapable of mastering such deeply foreign movements.

In London in the late 1950s, the somewhat dauntingly named Imperial Society of Teachers of Dancing created a new ballroom category called Latin and American Dancing, soon shortened to 'Latin'. It grouped together American jive, and Spanish *paso doble*, Brazilian samba and, from Cuba, rumba and *chachachá* (inexplicably shortened to 'cha cha'), although the new Latin dances had little in common with their originals.

Samba, for example, resembled modern salsa in that the term encompassed a vast range of dances with many regional and class-based variants. Zurcher-Margolle's hybrid version was largely his own invention.

Ballroom rumba is even more of a mystery. No one is quite sure what relationship it bears to the group of dances that emerged in communities of poor blacks living in the Cuban ports of Havana and Matanzas in the mid-nineteenth century. The rot may have started in Cuba itself, where, between 1860 and 1930, white performers blacked up and performed their own travesty of rumba in a blackface theatre tradition called *teatro vernáculo*. A 1943 manual published by the American Rumba Committee identifies American Rumba as an adaptation, not of rumba at all but of Cuban *son*. The English dancer and author Frank Borrows noticed that Monsieur Pierre's 'Cuban System Rumba', which later became English Style rumba and then International Style rumba, was actually mambo. The ballroom historian Juliet McMains agrees: in the early 1950s International Style rumba and American mambo were the same thing.

When the character of the newly co-opted black and Latin American dances differed too drastically from established ballroom technique, it was ignored. Above all, improvisation, which was the basis of all these dance styles, was proscribed. The bottom was driven out of them, and they were introduced into the marketplace shorn of their Afro-American and Afro-Caribbean origins.

Which is why, half-hypnotised by my fellow dancer's gyrating rear, I thought they might not be the tics of a man crazed by the music and the occasion into misguided acts of exhibitionism but rather the deliberate, well-calibrated gestures of a thinking white male confronted by the enormity of history. Which in turn raised a question: what should I do with mine? Go with Victor Silvester and do whatever required the minimum of effort? Or follow the historical thread far enough back to welcome the long-overdue return of the repressed?

In? Or out?

The thing about posing the question in such bald terms is that the conscious mind is not necessarily the most qualified part of the human psyche to intervene in such matters. Too much self-awareness is more a hindrance than a help when you're trying to dance salsa, as the sudden emergence into consciousness of my rear end suggested. Curious to know what freeing my buttocks from their oppressive whiteness would feel like, I held them for a moment in the outward position, at which point the communication between mind and body began to falter. The lines began to fade, and I faced being cut off from my body and feelings. My feeble salsa began to stutter. Within seconds, my body was mechanical, lifeless, fragmented into an assemblage of parts. I stumbled from the dance floor.

Jason Parkinson launched Tower Inferno as a fundraiser for victims of the 2004 Indian Ocean earthquake and tsunami. 'The Tower said, "Have the ballroom for free and we will support you." They had never seen so many young people dancing.

'I said, "This is salsa; it's what people are doing."

'They said, "Would you be interested in working with us and creating something?"

'That's how I created Tower Inferno. And every time we have six, seven, eight hundred people.

'In London it can get a bit serious,' Jason told me. 'There's some towns where they think, you know, this is how it should be danced . . . But here in the north-west we're all colours and creeds, you know? Everybody comes. They come from all over. They love dancing on the floor, looking up and seeing this immense ballroom that's 120 years old that they've only ever dreamed about dancing in, you know, and it's great.'

It was true. The dancers had flooded in from further down the coast and more outlying areas. From Preston, Formby and Liverpool. From Wales, Scotland, even Priestley's Yorkshire, crossing the border into once hostile territory. From Birmingham and the Isle of Man. From the Home Counties in the south but also Italy, Germany, Poland and the Ukraine. I spoke to or danced with 30 or 40 people, in total, and from all of them something similar emanated: a hard-to-define sensation that, no matter the wind gusting bitter salt-spray in from the Irish Sea, the dance floor hosted a blissful floating in a blood-heat brine of otherness. It was a place, not just of tolerance, but of a longing for and a treasuring of difference. It could hardly be otherwise. If you said today that you wanted to introduce to this most monolingual of islands music with foreign lyrics and rhythms and dance forms involving movements of the most unlikely complexity, you'd probably be sectioned. Salsa was Britain's unlikeliest dance craze.

And, to give the man with the British buttocks and the Cuban trousers his due, there was no agreement even over dress code. There were men in jeans and women in evening gowns, tapping out the rhythms in trainers and high heels. There wasn't an absence of codes but an excess of them: everyone brought their own. There were codes everywhere and for everything jostling and mingling as, bodies interlaced, we each stepped forward into someone else's world, then invited them back into our own, everyone crossing someone else's borders. By the time the evening was done, most of us had been woven together by salsa's ingenious rhythmic contrivances, its joyous knots, its seemingly inexhaustible twists and turns, taking on something of our temporary partners, perhaps emerging at the end of it all no longer quite the same people we were when we went in.

In Blackpool's absolute lack of pretension, we found the same atmosphere of easy intimacy and banter that surrounded salsa in Colombia. It was a means to an end: make sure you're having fun and the salsa will take care of itself.

When we left, the party was still in full swing and everyone seemed to be having a good time. There was little alcohol being consumed and there had been no trouble, even on a crowded dance floor, where spouses and lovers were swapping partners and the potential for treading on other people's toes was sky high.

Jason had enthused about the old-style courtesy of the Tower Inferno dance floor at the start of the evening. 'Most people here will dance with 20 people tonight. Everyone will say "Thank you" and leave you alone.'

The evening had proved him right.

We left the dance hall at midnight and stepped back into the drink-sodden, vomit-splattered mess of the traditional British Saturday night.

It had been strange to be in the north-west, which was unknown to me despite the fact that both my parents had been born there, my mother in Southport, from where on a good day you can see Blackpool Tower. And, though my grandparents' siblings in Ormskirk and Liverpool were dead and my mother had long since lost her Lancashire accent, there was a sense of familiarity about the place for me. There were expressions my mother used, an intonation, tiny details of body language that seemed familiar to me.

Soon afterwards, we visited my mother on the Essex coast, where I had grown up. On her shelves I found a book she swore had been there since my childhood: the 1960 revised edition of *The Complete Ballroom Dancer* by Mr Leonard Scrivener. It had belonged to my grandfather and contained 300 pages of tabulated commands which were deafening to read:

'Although the basic balance of the backward walk is the same for the forward walk, the backward walk is principally governed by control of the backward heel.'

Or:

'In Cuba, everybody dances the Ballroom Rumba. This is proof that the Cuban Ballroom Rumba is a practical, natural and enjoyable dance.'

No mention was made of salsa – 1960 was a decade too early – but there was an entry for 'The Cuban Mambo – Cha Cha Cha'. It started:

Gentleman

1. L. forward	Count 2
2. Replace weight on R.	Count 3
3. L. to side – small step – turning slightly to left	Count 4
4. Move R. towards L.	Count 'and'
5. L. to side – very small step	Count 1
6. R. back	Count 2
7. Replace weight forward on L.	Count 3
8. R. to side – small step – turning slightly to left.	Count 4
9. Move L. towards R.	Counts 'and'
10. R. to side – very small step.	Count 1

Repeat above ten steps ad lib.

Even as a purely mechanical guide to limb placement, it was close to useless: so many surface movements taken absolutely literally, their tale told as if it were the only tale to tell. *The Complete Ballroom Dancer* spoke about bodies the way minds without bodies might speak. I imagined the author comparing 'The Family Salsa of Colombia's Caribbean Coast' with 'The Cuban Mambo – Cha Cha Cha' or 'The Basic Steps of the Cuban-system Ballroom Rumba,' and coming up with a list of instructions that would never even had occurred to Vivi and her family.

All the same, my grandfather's book had an introduction by Victor Silvester, the dancer, bandleader and one of the pioneers of ballroom dancing in Britain. My mother told me my grandfather had taken lessons with Silvester. 'He was a wonderful dancer, your grandfather, when he was younger.'

I wasn't sure if I'd forgotten this, or if it was something I'd never known in the first place. But I wondered if the attraction of salsa had something to do with him, the grandfather in whose vicarage I had grown up and who in 1978 had taken a group of pilgrims to retrace the steps of St Paul in Greece, suffered a heart attack there and died. I was 13 and inconsolable. My wanderlust was probably, at root, either an attempt to pursue him, or a shell-shocked fleeing, 20 or 30 years later, from the pain of knowing he was dead. Either way, salsa, which for Vivi was a family tradition, had also taken me back to the continuum of my bloodline too.

9

EXOTIC GOODS

Es un amor que llevo muy dentro.
Y que heredé de mi abuelo.
It's love I carry deep inside,
That I inherited from my grandfather.
     '*Nido de Amor*', composed by Octavio
     Daza, performed by El Gran Combo

Buoyed by the fun we had had in Blackpool, Vivi and I travelled to Manchester hoping for more of the same at the event which had replaced Paul Young's vast salsa congresses.

As event titles go, GBSEx was pretty explicit about what was up for sale. The congress-goers were all wearing what you might call a tag. Judging by the acronym printed in an ornate, tattoo-like script, our crimes were grievous, bodily and sexual. Emma Moore, a director of Salsology, the company which had worked with Paul Young on the SalsaFest, told me that it was entirely innocent – 'just an acronym that happened to fit'.

'We came up with the name "The Great British Salsa Experience" first, but it is a mouthful, and, even in terms of the web, spelling it out to every supplier and person that enquires is a mouthful. So GBSEx was born. But my mum never approved. She still to this day can't say it.'

Emma's mum notwithstanding, the association between salsa and sex was a fairly systematic one. After years spent cleansing exotic dances of any obviously sexual moves, we had found one with barely any suggestive content and sexed it up out of all recognition. A table at the top of the stairs was covered in glossy fliers advertising bawdy seaside trips: seven days of 'Sun, Sand, Sea & Salsa' in Malaga on the 'Costa del Salsa'; '12 Glorious Days of Sea, Sand, Salsa & Kizomba' in Jamaica; a 'Sexy and Sensual Latin Dance Holiday' promising 'Hot and Sexy Fun in the Sun'.

Every detail of GBSEx had been fine-tuned according to the desires of British salsa consumers. 'We did lengthy research at SalsaFest as to why people were buying tickets and the resounding result was people wanted decent workshops. They weren't that bothered about the shows. People come to GBSEx to learn. And that's a British thing. They really care about decent tuition. In any case, having fewer workshops doesn't actually save you any money. When you pay an artist, you generally pay them "2-and-2", two shows and two classes, and they won't knock their fee down if you only want one class.'

So, responding to the demands of the market, during the three nights and two days that GBSEx filled Manchester Town Hall with a hundred artists and sixty-five volunteers, it offered no less than eighty hours of tuition, distributed among six different halls.

'You're not really reinventing the wheel when you run something like this, on the fundamentals.'

So there was a four-hour intensive course for salsa beginners. There were introductory hours or classes for beginners in *bachata*, tango, *chachachá*, *rueda de casino*, rumba (Afro-Cuban movement), Brazilian/carnival samba, reggaeton, and lessons for threesomes and foursomes. These accounted for 25 of the 80 hours.

Emma Moore continued, 'The types of class on offer have changed only slightly over the years. So people are more interested in things like performing and performance skills and ladies' styling than in the traditional partner-work classes.

'We had a number of students who had got so far in their learning On-1, they didn't want to go back to being beginners, effectively, even though it isn't actually that. But now we have had students asking whether there was going to be an introduction to On-1, instead of the usual introduction to On-2.'

Accordingly, there were two classes in leading and following, one in performance and choreography (the only one that addressed the overall structure of the dance) and, surprisingly, only one in music interpretation.

There were 10 hours of ladies' styling workshops, with 120 minutes each dedicated to body movement and arm-work. And there were two hours of styling for men. Micro-crazes were made of toe or finger movements. Every incidental had been broken down, recombined and reheated for salsa's international trade in the bizarre.

That left 39 hours of classes. Two were devoted to Eddie Torres-style shines and the remaining 37 were dedicated to turn patterns and spins. There were workshops in turn patterns with styling, turn patterns with shines, turn patterns for beginners and improvers, for the intermediate and advanced. There were turn patterns On-1 and On-2, Cuban style and Colombian style, meaning from Cali. There were two special turn patterns masterclasses. And a couple of classes in ladies' spinning technique.

In Cartagena I had seen perhaps one or two simple, slow turns to heighten the pleasure of returning to the dancing embrace. In Manchester, the dancers rarely, if ever, came together. It looked like a dance for partners who wanted to spend as little time as possible in each other's company, although I thought it was something else.

Salsa didn't go without saying at GBSEx the way it had in Cartagena. It wasn't a matter of unpretentious fun either, as it had been in Blackpool. The insistence here on technical mastery seemed to be a way of displaying a deep personal commitment to something that was, essentially, a matter of personal enthusiasm. The dozens of workshops represented the replacement of the hereditary principle by technique.

Like Cressida Childs, Emma Moore had a background in exercise culture. She had taught 'aerobics, Pilates; you name it, really', to supplement her income when she was studying performing arts at the London Studio Centre, and the version of salsa she came to combined both interests. 'My sister Kate and I took up salsa and got hooked. It was a nice way to stay fit.'

After dancing professionally, she had moved into the health industry and worked her way up the Esporta group of health clubs until she was a studio manager responsible for about 60 health clubs. Then there was a merger and redundancies, and Emma went back to university and took a postgraduate qualification in marketing.

Emma and Kate started dancing a Cuban style of salsa, On-1. That was the style they began to teach. Then they switched to On-2. 'We wanted to be able to dance with dancers we respected and admired, and in order to be able to dance with them we had to speak their language and their language was On-2, and as a lady we don't get the choice, so you know you really need to be able to dance all styles, because you're being asked by somebody to dance, and, if you're going to dance with that person, you really need to be able to dance their style, simple as that.'

The New York style, I hazarded, also offered a more developed market that the dance teachers could plug into.

'Well,' said Emma, 'that's right.'

There were stands selling salsa clothes, salsa jewellery and a range of holistic therapies that had somehow connected themselves to the dance scene. And there were thousands of fliers advertising outlandish new combinations of old ingredients: Brazilian lambada had been fused with *zouk* from the French-speaking Caribbean to form *lamba-zouk*. *Bachata*, from the Dominican Republic, and Argentinean tango had been blended into *bacha-tango*.

In this latest phase of the centuries-old trade in exotic goods, history seemed to be repeating itself. Once the products concerned were silk, spices, precious stones, fragrances and rare woods. A hundred years ago, tango had crossed from Argentina to Paris and found a place in the French erotic imagination alongside the can-can and the belly dance. Today, they were *soca, zouk, zumba, kizomba*, the '*k*'s and '*z*'s and '*mba*'s replicated into ever longer sequences and ever more genres, mined from the poor world and reworked to fit our rich-world consumer trends.

Emma Moore was after what she called 'a festival feel, happenings throughout the event, like the spinning world record, or impromptu *ruedas*, you know, just to make it a little more fun and unusual, and more of an experience really'.

It looked to me as if Caribbean and African practices were almost being analysed for their active ingredients. These were, in one context, steps, turns, patterns, and, in another, the 'festival feel', the 'experience'. The role of these salsa congresses was to refine and package the results, and sell them on the open market.

We found the corridors periodically full of excited women, glittered, sequinned and tanned. Their performances, before an audience of instructors and students, were the end-product, *or* an end-product, of a considerable financial investment in salsa. They had come, it appeared, to submit themselves to public judgement.

So too had the dancers on the landing above one of the great spiral staircases, with a mosaic floor that depicted those symbols of nineteenth-century Mancunian industry, The Bees. The area had been designated a free-dance or practice space and five couples were practising moves they may, judging by the dense class schedule, have acquired in Tony and Yuko's On-1 Intermediate-to-Advanced Turn Patterns workshop.

It was quite a performance. And it *was* a performance: the dancers were alert to their onlookers' eyes. I looked up from my notes and within ten seconds I had made eye contact with three female dancers in the course of their gyrations. One of them was a girl dancing barefoot and wearing her long black hair down. To the music of the Colombian band Guayacán, she was sending out provocative pelvic ripples.

When she was done, she sat down in the seat next to mine.

I didn't know what language to use.

She told me she spoke Punjabi and German, but not Spanish.

'You don't dance to the lyrics anyway,' she said. 'You dance to the rhythm. One, two, three; five, six, seven. It's the music that makes you move, not the lyrics. One, two, three; five, six, seven. One, two, three; five, six, seven,' she repeated.

Alert to the tone and music of the voice but bereft of any sensitivity to the words, she made me feel rather sad. She could never say, as dancers always have, 'It's our song,' because for her the song was simply an abstraction.

I had taken up residence on the table by the rehearsal space hoping to talk to as many salsa dancers as possible. Vivi had left me to it. She didn't want to hang around the dance floor for fear of being asked to dance, which would have meant either enduring the yanking of limbs and jerking of torso that Brit salsa inflicts on its female participants, or saying no, which would have been just as discomfiting.

I'd drawn up a questionnaire to help me gather data. The

Punjabi girl's dance partner, who had been leading her through an athletic series of turns and spins, and mixing it with plenty of his own, wiped the sweat from his brow and took one of my lists of questions.

The first question asked how people described the salsa they dance. I included Cali style and Cuba style, Los Angeles and New York style, On-1, On-2, *rueda de casino* and cross body. Thinking more laterally, Colombian (which I doubted any Colombian would select), British (which I doubted any Britons would), Puerto Rican, because you never know, and, thinking of Vivi, an invented category: family salsa.

'Yes, yes, yes! That's it!' he said, jabbing the page with his finger, animated, smiling and Venezuelan. He was a university student, not much more than 20, and he had learned at home, dancing with his family members as a very young child.

'It wasn't till I came here that I started taking it seriously. I started dancing again in London where I have Colombian friends. I learned New York style but I mix it up. My dad dances but he never went to classes and, when he sees me dance, he laughs at me. He says I'm very showy! My mum sees me dance and says, "What do you think you're doing?!"'

He was quickly on his feet again, guiding another dance partner through a flamboyant sequence of turns.

I spoke to about 30 GBSEx customers. About a third of them described themselves as non-white and fewer than half came from the United Kingdom. I met Europeans from Belgium, Germany, Poland, Bulgaria, Greece, the Irish Republic and the Ukraine; Caribbeans from Jamaica, Grenada and Barbados; one African, from Ghana, two Indians and one person from each of Iran, Indonesia, Malaysia, and Vietnam. Two were members of salsa's carrier communities: one was from the Dominican Republic and the other was my Venezuelan friend. I wondered where else you would find such a cross-section of the people in Britain today. There were voices abroad declaiming the failure of multi-culturalism but here the new, non-traditional salsa public seemed to find it a pretty good idea.

Vivi had asked me to go to the evening party on my own. I was afraid of being seduced by the sheer Britishness of it all, so I'd insisted that she come with me, and we entered the dance hall together.

In the queue, I said hello to a friendly and immensely tall dancer from Germany and got into a discussion about authenticity. There was a German Christmas market in the square outside Manchester Town Hall. The stands were flat-pack timber huts and the stallholders were wearing folk costumes. It was crammed with shoppers, hurrying past each other in the crowded aisles.

He complained that it was a caricature. Christmas in Germany wasn't anything like this. 'It is actually quite oppressive. You spend the time with family members you don't particularly like and you all pretend to get along. And it is a sober time of the year for us. If you took away the alcohol and the haste and the pushing and shoving, it might look a bit like a German Christmas market.'

When we got inside the dance hall, we found Cuban flags and images of Che Guevara everywhere, although, like Dave Shimeld's old fashion store, it was anything but revolutionary. It was a place of spectacular abundance, like something after Babel. Incompatible dance forms jostled with each other for space on the temporary sprung dance floor.

Although it was a Saturday night, there was no obvious sense of a night off. After a day of workshops in styling and turn patterns and spinning technique, dozens of couples were rehearsing long sequences of intricately wrought moves. The incessant fabrication, formulated by and answerable only to itself, seemed to engender only more and more of its own abundance. Salsa had become a technology with its own inescapable law, embodying studied algorithms in complex entanglements. It had to be dance at its most cerebral.

The sense of sight, the most abstract and easily deceived of the senses, had been elevated to the pre-eminence once occupied by the sense of touch. Carefully twisted together, preoccupied not by each other but by the dance, the paired-off dancers, the heroic masters and possessors of their own fully conscious adventures, displayed each other as entangled subjects and objects. They seemed to dance transfixed by the thought of what a photograph or film of their dance would look like. It was salsa as a charm bracelet jangling with icons, each one of which had cost a small fortune to acquire. A trained eye could have added up the sums invested in each move and given a value to each routine. The proliferation of faddish trinkets and gadgets, traded back and forth as valued collectibles, equipped the dancers with vast repertoires of gestures which were not their own. The more tightly they arranged them into their own dance sequences, the more they were excluded from them.

The overabundance, purposefully multiplied to the limits of the possible, had the effect of making the family salsa of the Spanish-speaking Caribbean appear underdeveloped by comparison. But in Colombia each movement contained within it the universe of everyone's body language, like choice words or metaphors that sound right because the web of language that gives them their sense somehow resonates to them. 'Getting it right' was not a technical matter that could be explained simply in terms of success in a task.

Vivi and I looked on in amazement. None of this seemed to have anything to do with us. I was quite incapable of joining in, so we went back to our hotel early.

The following morning we fell into conversation with a couple whose faces I had seen on a poster. They were living and teaching in Dubai but it turned out they were from Medellín. Colombians always seem to find a family or neighbourhood dimension to things and it took Vivi 30 seconds to learn that Eider Rúa, the director of El Firulete, one of the world's leading salsa companies, had started his career working for my teacher José Fernando González in the school opposite Marlen's flat.

Eider had grown up in Comuna 13 where Vivi's mother used to do social work. It was once the most violent part of Medellín, notorious for gang shootings and violence. His parents had been born in the countryside and came to Medellín as adults. His father, a self-taught guitarist, played traditional peasant music from the Antioquian countryside.

'My parents didn't dance much. My uncles did, but they danced it as they heard it and that was all. I always liked dancing, but normal, natural dance, nothing complicated.'

Aged 12 his father took him out of school and sent him to work. 'I found a job with some people who painted big advertising hoardings. Opposite where I worked, there was a dance school. I saw people dancing through the windows and that was where my interest was born. I told the owner I would paint a board for the school if he would teach me to dance.'

This was in 1990. When he was 13, his father ordered him to give up dancing. Eider decided to leave home. 'My father said if I left home he would drag me back by my hair and lock me in.'

Eider went anyway. He fled to Bogotá and found work as a dance teacher. After two years, missing his family and friends, he returned to Medellín and taught at La Magia de Tus Bailes, the dance academy run by my teacher José Fernando González.

Eider was not yet 17, but he was already dancing competitive tango. 'But I also liked salsa so, when I won a tango competition and they invited me to perform in a show in Cali, I found out who was the best dancer in Cali and asked him for classes.'

The teacher Eider chose was El Mulato, the flamboyant director of the Swing Latino dance troupe. Later, with his partner, Luisa Suaza, Eider went back to Cali and won the Colombian championship, dancing El Mulato's classic Cali-style salsa. Then they went to the International Tango Festival in Argentina and, with their dance troupe, they won the Cóndor de Oro.

In November 1999 Eider and Luisa opened their own dance school in Medellín. In 2005 they were invited to Dubai to perform and teach. They went, saw a land of opportunity and decided to move there. 'We went back to Medellín, planned the journey, then four months later, on 1 May 2006, we arrived to open our dance academy.'

The international trade in dance steps had allowed Eider and Luisa to escape from violence and poverty and build successful careers. There was nothing manufactured in Eider's conversation, no marketing jargon or pretence. He wasn't trying to sell me anything. We agreed to stay in touch and said goodbye. The encounter saved our weekend and gave us something to enthuse about.

Days later, Eider called. I ought to meet him in Zürich, he said, at the biggest salsa congress in Europe. If I wanted to speak to the number-one salsa promoter in the world, Zürich was the place to do it.

I packed my things and headed for Switzerland.

10

Euro-Salsa

Qué te hice yo para que tu me amargues la
vida?
What did I do to make you embitter
my life?
> '*Corazón de acero (Eres criminal)*',
> composed and performed
> by Cuco Valoy

Any weekend of the year there are maybe 20 GBSEx-style
congresses going on around the world. Pick a random date
and you find simultaneous functions in Madrid and Cádiz,
Marseille and Tours, Helsinki and Kiev, the smaller Italian
towns of Syracuse and Bellaria, Mendoza in Argentina,
Jersey City in the United States and Fort-de-France in
Martinique.

Each of them attracts thousands of enthusiasts. Some run
into tens of thousands, and convert entire conference centres
and hotel complexes into salsa factories where the production
lines run 24 hours a day. They set the tone for the dance as
practised outside the traditional salsa communities. And
since Europe and North America have no such thing as
family salsa, the elaborate, cabaret version propagated at
these events largely defines salsa in the rest of the world.

The congresses are connected by transcontinental networks with a global reach. For salsa instructors and performers, breaking into one or other of these circuits means regular work through the year. As well as teaching, they get to sell their DVD courses, publicise their online programmes and enjoy a certain amount of adulation. Each instructor or dance-troupe director negotiates their own fee. The teachers who attract the biggest crowds can command appearance fees of $4,000 for an hour's workshop. At the other end of the scale, I knew of couples from Cali who had somehow found the money to travel to the United States and dance for nothing at the congresses, just to be seen and perhaps get the chance to join the circuit.

The first of the international networks was a World Salsa Tour sponsored by Bacardi from 1999 to 2001. Today, the website of an organisation calling itself the World Salsa Federation lists 31 congresses, most of them in the United States and Canada. But if there could be one spokesman for the new, non-traditional, globalised salsa, it was a Brooklyn-born Puerto Rican called Albert Torres who has organised the Los Angeles congress since 1999 and the Tokyo congress since 2000. His portfolio today includes 39 different salsa congresses all over the world.

Torres had been invited as a guest to the annual three-day Salsafestival Switzerland at the Kongresshaus in Zürich, which organisers called 'one of the biggest and most distinguished events of its kind'. They claimed 8,000–10,000 paying customers. Even subtracting a thousand or so for corporate exaggeration, it was big business.

The trip was costing me more than I could afford. The organisers had waived the €320 fee for the full congress pass but, even so, return flights, three nights in a hotel and meals in one of Europe's most expensive cities soon added up. Salsa here had become a very expensive lifestyle indeed.

It was only after I had arrived in Zürich that I heard the

bad news: something had come up at the last minute and Señor Torres would not be coming. My interview was cancelled.

My first thought was: 'What am I going to tell Vivi?'

With time to kill, I mooched around a bookshop by Lake Zürich, then went up to the American coffee franchise on the first floor, and considered my options.

'Ein *Blueberry Muffin*?'

I wasn't sure.

'Oder ein *Pita Rustica*?'

I didn't know what a *Pita Rustica* was.

'*Fladenbrot*' – flat bread – '*mit* Chicken *und Schnittlauchfrischkäse*' – that needed explaining. It turned out to be cream cheese.

The decision not to translate so characteristic a piece of Americana as the blueberry muffin out of its native language and into German was surprising. I wasn't quite sure why 'cream cheese' could be given a German rendering but not 'chicken'. The presumably Swiss-German-speaking marketing men who had composed the menu for the Zürich branch of this American coffee chain appeared to have found a magical resonance in the English terms that might just have made the dish irresistible to the local clientele, sending Zürich's pastry economy through the roof.

'Sorry!' It was the Swiss-German word for 'Excuse me', pronounced the Italian way, with two rolled 'r's. I had been dithering so a girl had pushed past to order '*Ein* Frappuccino *mit extra Karameltopping*'.

She handed over her money and got the Swiss-German word for thank you. '*Mérci.*'

I didn't know what language was native here. There were cappuccinos and frappuccinos and babychinos, of course, but the credentials of pseudo-Italian I could understand, Italian being a long-established, indeed, a self-elected item in the global repertoire of exotic goods. An entire industry had been built around the conviction that hot milk by any other name wouldn't taste as good.

Wondering what to do next, I left the bookshop and walked. In the street, there were German car advertisements with the local counterpart of '*Vorsprung durch Technik*': a slogan in English that read 'Feel the Difference'.

The area around the Kongresshaus was the most expensive in Zürich, with clusters of five-star hotels and the Bahnhofstraße, the city's most ostentatious shopping street, all looking out towards the lake. I headed in the opposite direction, past the main railway station and towards my hotel, mulling over what I might be able to salvage from the trip.

Two black men were coming the other way along the pavement. They caught my eye. One was in a white *boina*, a flat cap, the uniform of the salsa dancer in the Caribbean. The other wore a rapper's baseball cap. As they drew closer, I heard they were speaking Spanish and thought I recognised the accent.

'Dominican Republic?'

'*Sí, señor.*'

'Is there a community here?'

'A big one, *sí, señor.*'

Their names were Juan Carlos and Daniel and they were construction workers, they said, like most of the Dominican men in Zürich.

'Where can I get a bite to eat?'

'Dominican food?'

'Why not?'

They directed me to a small diner called Bar Olif in Langstraße, deep in Zürich's red-light district. When I got there, a television screen at the back of the room was showing a video of the singer Marc Anthony singing '*Tu amor me hace bien*'. The waitress was singing along with him.

I ordered meat with a rice dish they called *moro de*

güandúles – rice with pigeon peas. The waitress explained that it was a traditional Dominican recipe. I asked her if she was going to the concert that evening, at the salsa festival by the lake, where the Puerto Rican star Víctor Manuelle was performing with his band.

She didn't know anything about it. She asked the other ten or twelve customers in the bar. I couldn't make out whether they didn't know the concert was on, or whether they knew about it but didn't feel it had anything much to do with them. Either way, no one had tickets, which surprised me because, if you like *'Tu amor me hace bien'* by Marc Anthony enough to know all the words, the chances are you also like Víctor Manuelle's *'No hace falta nada'* and *'Tengo ganas de volver a enamorarme'*.

There were a few members of the traditional salsa communities at the concert that evening. A line of five or six dark-skinned women a few rows behind me, twenty or thirty Latin Americans crowded around the stage. There were a few Europeans like me who spoke Spanish and seemed, as I did, to know most of the tunes and enough of the lyrics to mime a few snatches. The atmosphere was slightly sterile, although I enjoyed the performance more than I might have in Colombia, where I suspected the singing of the crowd would have drowned out Víctor Manuelle.

Much of the dance floor paid no particular attention to the band. When the lyrics are incomprehensible to you, I reasoned, the vocalist can hardly be a star. To many of the congress patrons, Víctor Manuelle was no one in particular. The real stars were the dance instructors.

All the same, it was a shame the Dominican waitress from Bar Olif wasn't here, because Víctor Manuelle was magnificent. It was a shame Vivi wasn't here too. She knew the words to all his songs, and to another one that he didn't write but which he sang as a tribute to El Gran Combo:

'Júlia', the song she used to hear in Cartagena when she was just beginning to walk, dancing with her cousins at the feet of her grandmother, Julia Carmona.

*

It was hard to get up the following morning and even harder to brave the cold and the drizzle to get to the conference centre. My reward, when I got there, was an encounter with a genius. I was one of four or five hundred people who had turned up to see his workshop.

Mario Hazarika was one of the most in-demand salsa instructors in the business. If Torres was the spokesman of the new, global salsa, this London-raised South Indian Catholic with a white English grandfather could have been its poster boy.

He wanted to see his students dance and get an idea of the right level to pitch at, so he asked the DJ for what he called 'Song number four' and we all danced. After assessing our ability, he decided to teach us a sequence that included an astonishing number of single and double spins, with hands variously gripped above the head, beside the waist and behind the neck. At one point, he guided his dance partner behind his back and forward until she was looking over his right shoulder. With his upper hand, he released his grip, allowing her hand to fall. He quickly lowered his arm and caught her falling hand at rib height, while, at the same time, elevating her other hand above shoulder height, only to let it go once more and catch it lower down. As he completed this second manoeuvre, he was again raising the first pair of clasped hands and repeated the operation. And so it went on, in a waterwheel-like cascade of movement, raising, releasing and catching, three, four, five times, before turning her again, this way and that, and finally coming to rest.

Mario's frame showed no tightness when he danced. He could repeat the sequence flawlessly from any point to any other, over and over again, with instant recall. It was dazzling. Among the learners on the dance floor beneath him, however, the sheer concentration required to decipher the onslaught of physical data caused rigidified torsos, hunched backs, furrowed brows and every kind of bizarre kinetic tremor. We weren't professional dancers and, judging by the misshapen forms that preceded each new lunge, the intricacy of the moves touched the limit of our collective mental processing power.

After 50 minutes or so, Mario called for 'Song number one'. Without attempting to connect the move to any change in sound texture or other musical cue, the swirling, writhing mass of dancers attempted to repeat the entire sequence. Mario surveyed the floor from the stage, reviewing the sequence's component moves and calling out words of correction. The initiates gazed back, checking the positioning of their own body parts against his. The outward-looking angle of the head and eyes was mimicked by those quickest to pick up the sequence, who then surveyed those around them with a proud detachment from the competence of their own bodies. By the end of the hour-long seminar, most of us could more or less reproduce the schematic arrangements of arms and hands and the order and direction of their spins and turns, and everyone seemed to be happy.

I had never heard of Mario Hazarika until that morning, when a Greek couple I had met at breakfast in my hotel raved about him. 'SuperMario', they said, was the greatest salsa teacher in the world. Not, I had thought, to be missed. Now I was thinking of Sisyphus, condemned for all eternity to push an immense boulder up a hill, only to see it roll back down, and his daughter-in-law Ariadne, who spent her days weaving and her nights unravelling her work. This prodigy of self-perpetuating entanglements could have been their incestuous love-child.

When the workshop was over, I sat down with Mario and he told me his story.

After his first ever salsa lesson in 1998, his teacher had told him, 'Keep coming; there's no need to pay.'

Within a year, he was at a salsa congress in Toronto, Canada, when one of the instructors was taken ill and Mario was asked to cover for him. Ever since then, he has been on the road, travelling and teaching, inside the bubble of the world salsa congresses – one a week all year, more or less, in major cities all over the world – where no language is more than a lingua franca and identities in any case are up for grabs. On the basis of his Brooklyn-like '*fie*, six, seven', I had taken him for a New Yorker.

But, wherever he was from, he was a wondrously gifted engineer of entwined human bodies, with a rare talent for the mental and physical processing of extraordinarily complex salsa moves. I'd read a piece in the *New York Times* about a similar prodigy, Ángel Corella, a Spaniard who had joined the American Ballet Theatre as a teenager. Corella could watch a long, complex dance routine once and then immediately reproduce not only his part but everybody else's too.

'Scientists say motor learning like Mr Corella's can actually be observed in the brain. To know precisely where our bodies are in space at any given moment – an ability called proprioception – our brain receives signals about the length of each muscle and the angle of each joint and "does a kind of mental trigonometry",' said Prof. Patrick Haggard of the Institute of Cognitive Neuroscience, University College, London.

Mental trigonometry just about described Mario's brand of salsa. Lacking Corella-like talents, the sheer complexity of his moves left me baffled. All the same, salsa, SuperMario-style, was not a gateway to the cultures of the Spanish-speaking Caribbean. After more than a decade of teaching and dancing to Spanish-language music, SuperMario, the self-proclaimed 'Million-Move Man', professed to knowing nothing of the language. What he did know was mathematics, which he had studied for four years, and accountancy, which he had studied for three. 'Everything in life has to be in a system for me.'

I stumbled out of Mario's class with my head spinning, and then found a workshop with a very different flavour.

Alberto Valdés, once a soloist with the Ballet Tropicana de Cuba, told us, 'Let's give the parts names so we can remember them. *Enrosca. Salgo. Sombrero. Finta*. And again, *finta*.'

After the class, Alberto told me that in the 1990s he had toured Italy three times with his national troupe, performing in theatres and at the San Remo festival, before he was approached and offered work as a dance instructor. He has been living in Milan since 1996. 'In Italy, I met a lot of people who had been to the Tropicana and wanted me to teach show-style *son*. I refused. I told them I'd teach them what my mother and grandmother danced. I'd teach them the truth. Then, when they wanted to put on a show, they would have all the elements. Without the truth, putting on a show is like building a house with no foundations.'

He gave his class in Spanish, a language as strange to many of the participants as the moves themselves. But to Alberto it was the obvious choice. 'Salsa and *bachata* are sung in Spanish. Why would I teach in anything else?'

When he was at his adopted home in Milan, the similarities between Italian and Spanish no doubt helped. But even this uncompromising Cuban had made adaptations, including some of the same concessions made by the early instructors in London. 'To teach salsa in Europe you have to create a new methodology. You have to isolate each element and give it a name so your regular students know what you're talking about. When you come to a place like this, to be accessible to people who've never studied with you before, you have to create yet another language.'

Everything had to be broken down and repeated over and over again. A double frustration, then, for the non-

Spanish speakers grappling with new moves. And yet the workshops were packed and nobody dropped out. Deferred gratification? Of course. A physical working through to a state of satisfaction? Undoubtedly. But the floating uncertainty, the self-imposed unknowing, was not disagreeable. It was the slow solving of an initially impenetrable problem using physical not mental means, and this re-routing of the analytical mind through the body yielded a strange and satisfying pleasure.

After 45 or 50 minutes of fragmentation and disorientation, the individual components of the move gradually began to lose their distinctness and a smooth current of energy that was as much psychic as it was physical flooded through the class. And when, at last, music was added to the mix, the sensation of flow was palpable. Strangest of all, to me, was the feeling that the sequence had only in part been passed down to us by the teacher. It had also, in a less evident way, been brought out of the dancers, awakened from a dormant state somewhere in our bodily being. Ignited by a spark that might just have been the exhilaration of the moment, it had instantly become expressive of our innermost selves. It had been made *authentic*.

A complex, thrilling alchemy. One worth paying dearly for.

My next workshop was with another Cuban master, Seo Fernández, who had been living in Milan for 17 years, although, he told me, he went back to Cuba every year to stay in touch with what he called 'the source'.

'The way we dance and express ourselves in Cuba is different from what we do in Italy. In Cuba, dancing is part of our character. In Europe, it's business. We've had to invent a lot of figures and refine salsa, but that was good, because in Cuba pair-dancing was dying. We've enriched it. We've been able to meet dancers from other countries and create a fusion.'

Seo moved with incredible control of the torso, shimmying

with stunning rapidity, yet the angle of his porkpie hat never altered. I asked him what you called a hat like that in Cuba.

He replied, 'My hat is my style!'

And I asked him something else. 'When did you dance for the first time in your life?'

He just smiled and shook his head.

In the Kongresshaus, the main hall was beginning to fill up. The evening party would start in an hour or so. Meanwhile, there was a lull. Music was playing. The volume suggested it was intended as a background accompaniment. People were standing around. There were tiny miniskirts, high heels, fishnets, knee-length boots, the occasional tiny ballroom outfit. There were men in white suits and *boinas*.

One or two couples began to rehearse sequences I recognised from the workshops. Quick, snappy triple and quadruple turns, involved knots, pulls on shoulders to deliver the impetus required for the spins. It wasn't dancing; it was practising during the in-between time before a consensus had been reached on where to divide the floor into the best place to stand and talk and the area reserved for dancing.

But these movements transformed the unfocused attention of 'looking' into the focused attention of 'looking at'. The dancers seemed to respond with displays of even greater complexity and commitment. But the music was still only background music and the dancers were still only practising, so, even when the song entered a louder, more intense improvised section, they had no response. If anything, their movements diminished in intensity. They had started at such a pitch there was nowhere to go. Which was when it occurred to me that the cues they were responding to were not musical at all but visual: they were moving according to the gazes of the people around them.

I headed back to Bar Olif to eat. Leaving the conference hall was one of the most educational moments of the congress:

to emerge from the self-absorption, the anticipation, the soon-to-be white-hot cauldron of salsa inside, into a city that regarded salsa, if it regarded it at all, as a foreign, irrelevant affair.

On the way out, I picked up a flier for a Salsa Tanzfestival in Bern where a brilliant Peruvian protégé of Eddie Torres named Adolfo Indacochea was due to perform with his Italian partner Carla Voconi. I noticed the flier misidentified Indacochea as a New Yorker. That is, unless they were talking about his dance style. But, if that was the case, Voconi could hardly be described as Italian: there were many strands and strains of salsa but Italian wasn't one of them. More likely, it was a matter of marketing. New York probably sells better than Peru.

There was a general complacency about provenance, nationality, identity in the salsa world. 'No one knows *anyone* by their real names in this business,' someone had told me, not wishing to be named. It was more than that though.

As an adult, I'd never been much of a cinema-goer, but Vivi loved movies so I began to see all the latest general releases. Looking back, the films I'd seen as a child were full of Hollywood certainties, with everyone comfortable in their roles. They all seemed to be about stability of identity: the good man who remains morally steadfast even when it might be easier to compromise.

When I started going again, they all seemed to be about the opposite. They were tales of people who didn't know who they were; substitution stories which turned on the difference between the protagonist's apparent identity and the truth as it later unfolds. They were about amnesiacs who painfully discover their former identities, humans who turn out to be machines or machines who turn out to be oddly human. Or they were about twins or clones or people whose identities are transferred into someone else's body. To be the protagonist in one of these plots, you couldn't be who you appeared to be. Or, to put it the other way around, to be merely who you appeared to be meant you were no kind of protagonist.

I could identify with an oft-repeated scene in which an envelope appears, full of passports from every imaginable nation. The hero opens it up, expecting to learn at last who he really is. Instead, he finds his own photograph in all of them, beside a different name and nationality each time. It doesn't solve the problem of knowing who he is, although it does allow him, for the rest of the story, to assume a new identity whenever and wherever he wants. It was something like the same fantasy that had taken me to Colombia in the first place.

At times, I caught glimpses of myself dancing and imagined myself part of a bizarre community of men and women whose identities were so composite and unclear that the best policy seemed to be to settle on simplified 'nightlife' versions of ourselves that may or may not contain a hefty make-believe element – a nickname, an accent, a hat – and collectively agree not to enquire any further. As if the salsa dance floor were a playground where we could experiment with our identities. As if identity itself were, at root, a mere matter of choice.

Except that the identities we fixed on weren't creations of our unbridled imaginations but rather transparent parodies of other people. This was probably the only reason I didn't take to the floor in a light suit, a Caribbean *guayabera* shirt and a *boina*, done up to look like Alberto Valdés or Seo Fernández.

When I got to Bar Olif, a family party was going on around a couple of tables. Two couples were dancing, not the *bachata* of the 12.15 p.m. workshop across town (Partnerwork, All Levels), but Dominican family *bachata*, all smiles and chatter, between partners and with the others in the group. Arriving here within minutes of leaving the congress hall left me disorientated, almost unsteady. The

Dominicans, who loved their salsa and danced with a natural quality of basic movement, were just around the corner, offering good, inexpensive food, friendly service and non-stop salsa music. But no one bothered with them. They were, to the congress goers, invisible.

The disconnection between the immigrant world of Zürich's Spanish-speaking Caribbeans and the massive salsa event in town was total. They seemed to belong to two quite separate orders of reality, and the contrast between them forced me to acknowledge suspicions I had wanted to deny because they seemed, well, uncharitable.

But there could be no doubt: there was something deeply dysfunctional about what was going on in the congress hall. Among the Dominicans, music and movement, body language and everyday speech were one. In the congress hall, there were Cubans and Colombians from salsa's carrier communities, who were simply being themselves, and there was almost everyone else.

It seemed strange to me that there could be renowned salsa dancers who understood not a word of Spanish and who exhibited none of the physicality that accompanies it – the shadow moves or micro-expressions that attend every dialect and accent. They didn't even understand that these things were implicit in the music, and in the movements it called into being. Their salsa, I felt, was little more than an aping of someone else's way of life.

And there was something else in the frenzy of technicised movement that was being passed on in the salsa congress, and displayed on the dance floor in the evening parties: a straining at the limits of existence, as if there were a way, by adding another element to the already intricate figures, of squeezing more from each moment of life than each moment of life really had to offer.

The simplicity of family salsa expressed an acceptance of things and their underlying unity. Here, a collective effort was being made to achieve a degree of complexity that would allow us to emerge on the other side of it with two, ten, an infinity of simultaneous existences. But in all the self-involved bustle we ran the risk of mislaying the one life we had.

I went back to the congress hall for the show. For the most part, the acts were polished, highly synchronised performances to mainstream salsa music. Then Alberto Valdés came on with the four other male dancers.

They began with a short incantation in the ritual, Yoruba-inflected language of Afro-Cuban religion, then they took up *clave* rods and conga drums and set up a rhythm, over which a voice suddenly drifted: a recording of Francisco Céspedes, a Mexico-based Cuban, singing '*Oye bien la clave*' ('Listen carefully to the *clave*'), a single Afro-Caribbean voice with a minimal accompaniment – *clave* and string bass on the recording and conga drums being played live on stage by a musician with Alberto's troupe. There was little gloss or refinement in their performance. Their dancing mixed *son* with other forms taken from Afro-Cuban folklore. It seemed to me a militant declaration of rooted, inherited identity. His dance company was called Clave Negra. The name and style staked an aggressive, in the circumstances almost truculent, claim to cultural ownership. It read to me like a choreographed rebuke to the others.

It struck me that it was perfectly normal to feel attracted to exotic perfumes and textures, or to hanker after an Eastern piquancy or a Latin tinge. But it seemed rather odd to want to import, from someone else's world, an entire sub-system like a dance, with its music and its vast array of gestures, every element of which, in its original setting, has a history and a meaning which are hopelessly lost in translation.

It seemed more peculiar still, after co-opting a complex cultural practice from someone else, to want to improve on it, even perfect it, from a narrowly technical point of view. It would be frivolous if you lived on another planet from the people whose practices you were parroting. To do so in full view of immigrant communities to whom salsa belongs, without even acknowledging their presence, seemed crass.

I brought this up with one of the highest-profile instructors in British salsa. He told me, and he asked to remain anonymous, that 'they' resented that 'we' have adopted and developed it into our own form of expression. So far, we saw eye to eye. But the conclusion he drew from all this was diametrically opposed to mine. He blamed the Latin Americans for failing to keep abreast of what was happening in salsa.

'They don't keep up to date,' he said. 'Salsa has become more European than Caribbean, these days.'

But in Zürich the vast majority of us seemed to be white Europeans working ourselves loose from our own identities through a mild form of aphasia, listening to songs in an incomprehensible language, that had been set to music devoid of any clearly defined power of evocation except as a form of non-specific exoticism, immersing ourselves in a body language that was not our own, and no doubt feeling that the state of gentle dissociation these practices made possible represented not a bizarre, even dysfunctional form of self-deception, but the intoxicating discovery of our true selves, freed from the useless inhibitions of an outmoded past.

Here, as in Britain, salsa, which had started off as a reaching towards something foreign and attractive, and a welcoming of its immigrant carriers as exotic others, had once seemed a force for bringing people together. It had morphed into a technique for keeping them apart.

I wanted to ask Alberto what it was like, teaching his culture to white Europeans who were playing with their identities. The following day, I got the chance.

I approached him again as he finished his workshop. We sat at a table at the side of the room and, as the next class began, we started to talk. He was bright and animated, periodically taking my pen and notebook to spell out names and draw maps and diagrams. Although only a few minutes seemed to pass, we talked through my next workshop and the one after that.

'My background is in the folk dances of Cuban's Afro-descendants,' he told me. 'We want to keep our culture and essence alive in the world.' As well as his folk inheritance, Alberto venerated his old teacher, Rogelio Martínez Furé, an investigator into the ancient African survivals in black Cuban music and dance. 'You see our hip movements, a figure of eight, from right to left? That's from the Mandinka people, the descendants of the empire of Mali. In Brazil, the hip movements are quite different' – he demonstrated a rapid trembling of the pelvis – 'because the Brazilian slaves were from a different group.'

He told me about religious ceremonies he had seen in Surinam, where many of the elements were familiar to him from Cuba. They used the same gestures and they chanted the same African words. He told me of his desire to visit Africa and see what his master had seen of African body shapes and dance culture.

Dance, in Alberto's eyes, was a making present of the past, a connecting of the present moment with the continuum of lineage. And, in his performance with Clave Negra, his movements had flowed from gesture to gesture with none of the distinct definition between moves that he had taught in his workshop. There was self-expression in his dancing, but it was of a self rooted in a history which provided him with his identity and made that identity possible.

I was something like the opposite of Alberto, used to a hummingbird-like flitting between other people's cultures, zapping restlessly between cultural channels against a background of total self-possession: I could, I imagined, be anyone I wanted to be, whenever I wanted. But Alberto's dancing seemed to say that the things that define us are not things over which we can exercise our right to choose. We do not opt for the body language that gives us our standing in the world, or the intuitions about dignity and guilt, pride and shame, duty and remorse, that make it possible for us to choose. The fantasy of being entirely self-defining, and choosing my own values and loyalties, would in reality have entailed freeing myself from the very things that constituted my identity. My fantasy of dancing my way into total self-possession, Alberto's performance seemed to say, was actually a fantasy of total loss of self.

*

On the flight home, I plugged my personal stereo into my ears and fell asleep. I woke up listening to El Gran Combo's 2002 album *Arroz con Habichuela* ('Rice and Beans'). It was as good an album as any they had recorded in their 40-year history, and the improvisation by the singer Charlie Aponte at the end of the title track could have been addressed directly at the dance instructors and congresses of recent years.

Sabor, sabor, sabor de la vieja escuela:	The taste of the old school:
Salsa caribeña, rumba, plena.	Caribbean salsa, rumba, plena.
No se aprende en la academia más fina:	It isn't taught in the finest academy:
Calle, calle, calle, calle, rumbón de esquina.	Go outside and look for the dancing on the street corner.

Even so, images of SuperMario's workshop still lingered in my mind. The congress schedule had described his class as London-style salsa, and another as in the Paris style. They sounded self-defeating to me, like the dance equivalent of taking a course in – what? – Mandarin Chinese as spoken by Germans.

Mario himself had been typically self-effacing on the subject of London style. 'It was a joke, originally. All it meant was, we lived in London, that's it. A group of us started dancing at about the same time. We were the London guys. So, London style.'

But back home I began to ask around, and found another figure on the international congress circuit who had a rather different take on the issue. Leon Rose had duelled with Mario on the dance floors of Villa Stefano, Salsa! and La Finca in 1999.

He told me, 'We used to make up our own moves and challenge each other in the clubs. We were creating new moves all the time. That was our thing: to create a new move every day.'

Leon had first seen salsa at DJ Dave Hucker's 'Sunday School' club at Villa Stefano. He learned what he called 'a hybrid of Colombian-Cuban style, not the Cuban style that you see at a high level now', with Elder Sánchez and Nelson Batista.

But by the late 1990s new influences were transforming salsa in the United Kingdom. The first British dancers were already travelling to New York and taking classes with Eddie Torres. New York-style salsa was being taught from 1998 at the Pontin's Salsa Weekenders.

At the same time, a new, physically demanding strain of salsa reached London from Los Angeles, built around a structuring manoeuvre in which the male dancer marked time for a step, turned slightly and led his partner firmly past him until they had exchanged positions. They called this move the 'cross-body lead' and in Los Angeles it was interspersed with balletic lifts and throws. The LA style reached Britain in 1998 in the form of Edith Williams, an early salsa blogger who used the name Edie the Salsa Freak and whose website, salsaweb.com, was packed with information and advice.

Leon Rose combined the cross-body style from Los Angeles – 'nothing too flashy, no lifts or crazy stuff like that' – with the close pair work and fast spins of New York salsa, and Cuban-style moves. He blended them all into his own dance idiom. And, since his grandparents had come to London from Trinidad in the 1950s, bringing with them a few cherished calypso records, Leon had grown up dancing *soca* at family parties. He brought that body language to his salsa, then honed his style under Robert Charlemagne, another dancer with family origins in the English-speaking Caribbean. Charlemagne's grandparents were from Saint Lucia and he too had grown up dancing *soca*, calypso and *zouk*. But Charlemagne, who had family in New York, had visited the clubs there and picked up On-2 turn patterns. He passed his new skills on to Leon Rose and, together, they infused London's composite salsa style with an identifiably Caribbean smoothness and fluidity.

As early as 1949, Mass Observation had reported that among young factory girls in the cavernous dance halls there was 'great competition to dance with the blacks' on account of 'their superb sense of rhythm'. Through dancers like Leon and Robert, the body language of black Britons influenced the way the nation danced salsa.

Leon Rose gave this style a name. 'I started marketing myself as doing the "London style". It was good for the branding because everywhere I went people knew I was from London. Plus my style was a little bit different.'

In 2000, as part of the Bacardi Salsa Congress in London, a national salsa competition was announced. The prize was an expenses-paid trip to Puerto Rico for the 2000 World Salsa Congress. Leon entered with Robert Charlemagne's dance partner Susana Montero, and won.

'We decided to put a group together called Ahora Sí! and we went over there to perform. Then it started going kind of crazy for me.'

Like Mario Hazarika, Leon Rose had been drawn into the dizzying schedules of the congress circuit.

Congressional Inquiry

Quién ha visto a un pajarito
Tirándole al cazador.
Who ever saw a little bird
Shoot at its hunter?
'El Pajaro y El Cazador', composed by
Félix Chappotín, performed by
Roberto Roena y su Apollo Sound

I emailed Albert Torres and tried Facebook but got no reply. I was shy of calling his mobile phone, not knowing where he might be, but in the end I texted him and he replied immediately. We talked until his battery ran out.

A raconteur who packs his conversation with well-rehearsed one-liners ('I was in denial of it – D.E.N.I.A.L. as in "Don't even notice I'm lying!"'), he has repeated his story so many times it has acquired a structure and clarity that lives less frequently told rarely achieve. He is also disarmingly open about the turning points in his life which weave sometimes strategic connections.

During the heyday of mambo in the mid-'50s, his Puerto Rican mother danced at New York's Palladium, where Albert claims he was conceived, although he never met his real father. As a Nuyorican child, he initially resisted his mother's attempts to show him how to dance and rejected the Puerto Rican part of his identity. 'I thought, "I'm American, I don't want to be Puerto Rican, I don't want to dance this, I'm gonna hide in my room and listen to Michael Jackson and James Brown and Motown."'

When he was 13 and his mother took him back to Puerto Rico to live in Vega Baja on the north coast, he didn't want to be there. For the first year or two he didn't want to speak the language. He finally decided to embrace his mother's culture when he heard the music coming out of the Fania label and learned the lyrics of Cheo Feliciano's 'El Ratón' by heart.

But with salsa came alcohol and substance abuse, and Torres soon went off the rails. He started taking drugs when he was twelve and began to skip school and hitchhike to San Juan, where he would stay for three or four days, doing whatever he had to do to make twenty or thirty bucks, selling dope and sleeping on the beach. As he grew older, he began to go to the nightclubs where he would dance the Latin hustle for prizes: a bottle of champagne, a trip to Saint Thomas. 'I can't dance the hustle for shit today!'

Aged 17, Torres moved back to the United States, not to New York but to San Francisco. He lived there for a couple of years before deciding it was warmer in LA, where he could sell bigger quantities of 'stuff'. He has been there ever since, except that he stopped dealing and cleaned himself up. He gives the date of his conversion with confessional zeal. 'I've been sober since 14 December 1985 – 25 years, from the age of 29 to now – and I'm going to be 55 next birthday.'

Torres went back to dancing, clean this time, and was part of the movement that forged the Los Angeles cross-body style. In 1990 he was spotted by choreographers with movie-industry connections and given the part of one of the principal dancers in the film *The Mambo Kings*. The song 'Beautiful Maria of My Soul' was nominated for an Oscar in 1993 and Torres danced at the Academy Awards ceremony. There were other film appearances, but in 1991 he began a parallel career promoting salsa clubs in Los Angeles.

At first, he says, no one wanted to know about salsa. But he persisted, and soon he was running successful club nights and gained a reputation for attending to the finest details.

He heard about the first Puerto Rican salsa congress in 1997 when participants from Los Angeles, who had used the event to spread the cross-body and acrobatics-led style, returned home with news of an event that they considered a resounding success, although financially it had flopped. 'They were excited about it, so in 1998 I went along. The stage was a little scary to dance on. I told the organiser, Eli Irizarri, "You can't dance on it, your heels will go right through it."'

The stage was rebuilt and, when the local compère let him down, Irizarri asked the silver-tongued Torres to MC for the evening. He ended up doing the whole weekend. 'And then we talked about coming back to Puerto Rico in '99 and starting the first Los Angeles congress.'

Irizarri had secured sponsorship from Bacardi, and the congress started with a surprise that helped launch the expansion of the whole movement. When Albert Torres walked on stage to open the event, Tito Puente jumped out from behind a curtain. 'I'd seen him the night before at a book signing and invited him over. He said he didn't think he could make it, then he showed up to surprise me. Joaquín Bacardí, who was sponsoring the event at the time, was like, "Wait a minute, I think we got something here. I mean, Tito Puente's here!"'

In 1999 the rum manufacturer extended its sponsorship to a world salsa tour that took Eli Irizarri's Congreso Mundial de la Salsa around the world. Between 1999 and

2001 it visited four US cities, eight in the Caribbean, and Central and South America, eleven cities in Europe – including the London congress where Leon Rose and Susana Montero won the dance competition – as well as Tokyo, Osaka, Bombay, Calcutta and Sydney.

The tour was punctuated by a falling-out between Torres and Irizarri in 2000. Torres kept his Los Angeles congress and the Tokyo event he had organised in 2000 with a local partner, and began to roll out the blueprint along the West Coast. He opened in San Francisco in 2001, Las Vegas in 2004 and San Diego in 2007.

He also began to forge alliances with event organisers around the world. In 2001 he co-organised or endorsed congresses in Guadalupe, Amsterdam and Cuba to add to his portfolio. By 2007 he was organising or co-producing 32 congresses. The figure grew and grew.

Torres depicts himself as the guarantor of quality in salsa events. 'There are organisers who just think that they can do it on their own, and I wish them the best because everyone should be able to live their dream out, but a lot of times the quality isn't there. If the media come in and see it and think that all congresses are like that, it doesn't give salsa the greatest name. We try to . . . not monopolise but at the same time let those that want to do it on their own maybe give it a certain respect instead of making it some street gig.'

*

Among the Puerto Ricans and North Americans who dictated the canon and its legitimacy in the early congresses and competitions, Cali salsa had no place. Carlos Trujillo, the director of a dance school in Cali called Rucafé, remembers the 2002 World Salsa Congress in Puerto Rico. The participants, he says, were divided into two camps, On-1 and On-2, which they had printed on their T-shirts, baseball caps and sleeves. The classic Cali style was neither.

In 2004, Albert Torres organised a competition in Philadelphia. In the cabaret category, El Mulato of Swing Latino took the title, with another Swing Latino couple third. After that dry run, Torres organised his first world championship. It wasn't the first: a Los Angeles disco called Club Mayan began organising world championships in the 1990s, and in 2000 the International Dance Organization held a world salsa championship, the winners of which, Isaac and Laura Altman, then founded their own World Salsa Federation and organised annual world championships themselves.

But Torres secured international television coverage on ESPN.

His championships had four categories, On-1, On-2, Cabaret and Groups. The winners of the Cabaret section helped put Cali-style salsa on the international map.

At a congress in Miami a few weeks before the competition, Torres was introduced to Ricardo Murillo and Viviana Vargas. 'My partner in Miami said, "This couple is from Cali, Colombia, and they're not charging us anything. They just want to perform because they know you're here."

'When I saw them rehearsing, I said, "They're incredible." I had them close the show and they earned a standing ovation. I asked them to come back the next day. I didn't know they didn't even have a place to stay; they were staying on someone's couch.'

Torres invited them to congresses in San Francisco and New York, and then to the world championships in Las Vegas. 'I called them from the airport when I was leaving, and that was when the guy got honest with me: "We'd love to go, but we can't afford the ticket."

'I said, "You know what? I'm going to buy you guys air tickets and let's see what happens from there."'

They travelled across America together, and at Las Vegas Murillo and Vargas became Cali's first world champions dancing the city's classic style. Torres was struck by their humility. 'Even when they won, they were crying and saying, you know, "We want people to look at our country as a place of dance, not of crime," and I said, "You know what? I want to go and visit Colombia."'

But Torres had an all-too-common idea of Colombia as a sort of Wild West. He was, he told me, 'scared shitless, to tell you the truth'.

'I flew out to surprise Ricardo on his birthday. Viviana had it all planned. Soon I met all these dancers and in the process I saw El Mulato.'

Torres had first met the director of Swing Latino at the 1998 Puerto Rico congress and at many subsequent events, including the Philadelphia competition. But Torres's prejudices about Colombia and Colombians got in the way. 'Mulato's a great director and I have a lot of respect for him, but there was always a wall up there. I always felt something funny was going on, like maybe he's coming to the States to bring someone shit. I just didn't know. I didn't want to judge him. But I have to go with my gut feeling, so I always had a wall up.'

El Mulato invited Torres to the national salsa competition at the 2005 Cali Sugarcane Fair. 'There was about 20,000 people and they were totally nuts because they knew me from ESPN.'

They met again in Las Vegas for the 2006 world salsa championships. Swing Latino won first place in Groups and second in couples in the Cabaret category. In 2007 they repeated their success.

Torres attempted to involve himself in Cali's salsa scene. He claims to have been in talks with the government, the City and El Mulato about bringing one of his congresses to the city. He says he brought dancers in from abroad at no charge. Perhaps unaware of the pride Cali takes in its dance culture, his praise assumed a paternalistic edge. Cali, he said, was 'a jewel that just needs to be dusted off'.

'It just needs to be cleaned up because they are doing

things that are incredible. It's something that needs to be acknowledged, even though it may not be the style that I love and prefer or that's the original.'

By standing in judgement over Cali salsa and introducing the profit motive to a city where salsa has always belonged to the poorest communities, he risked trespassing on hallowed ground.

'For me, the more those kids in the *barrios* in Colombia, or in Cali, dance, the more they have something that gives them the hope of maybe one day getting out of that *barrio*. That was my goal going there, and it still is. I've been on the other side so any way that I can keep them off the streets.'

But, to pioneer this vision, he had arrived in Cali 50 years too late.

Whatever happened during the trip – and the talks clearly ended badly – Torres returned to the United States and reconsidered Swing Latino's successes in his championships. 'We realised that the first two years we were all into the "Ahh!" factor. Like, any time they danced, we were just, "Ahh!" Just, "They win. Forget it. Don't even look at the rules."

'The reality was, we weren't being fair to the others because, whether you dance On-1 or On-2 or Cali style, you still need to break on a certain beat. They weren't prepared to do it. It was their way or no way.

'So we started bumping heads over the marking, and I said, "40 per cent is timing, but, instead of making 40 per cent timing, which kind of works against you, what I'll do is make it 20 per cent timing and 20 per cent musicality, which you guys are fantastic with, the way that you interpret the music. So it won't be 40 per cent against you."'

El Mulato tells a different story. He claims that the dominance of troupes from Cali, especially Swing Latino, meant that groups from elsewhere in the world were losing interest in the Cabaret category. 'It isn't my fault that people don't have the resources to put on an attractive show like we do. So he began to look for a way to find an error in the Cali style.'

This, despite the fact that, according to El Mulato, none of the judges at the competition was even qualified to judge Cali style. 'They don't know how we count. Cali style has all the elements that the other categories have. It's just that the judges haven't learned it.'

Even so, at the 2009 world salsa championships at Fort Lauderdale, Florida, El Mulato went along with Swing Latino. The Cabaret division for pairs was won by Jonathan Landa and Jenny Rodríguez, both Swing Latino dancers. Their closest competitors were Eider Rúa and Luisa Suaza, from Medellín, also dancing in the classic Cali style.

But the Group competition was won by a Mexican troupe, and Swing Latino finished no better than third.

Albert Torres told me, 'They didn't like that. They didn't like that at all.'

He was right: they didn't, but this was only in part because they felt that the judges had been turned against them. It was also because Torres still owed them prize money for the 2007 Group and Cabaret categories, which Swing Latino had dominated.

Torres had financial problems. Disneyland had hosted his 2007 championships, and Torres was depending on their sponsorship to pay prize money from the previous year. But in 2008, as the credit crunch bit, Disney pulled out.

'We got scared and cancelled, which was not a great move because a lot of people lost faith in the event. Looking back, we should have held it anyway, because so many people had already bought their airline tickets. Instead, we stuck our tail between our legs.'

Torres broke with his partners and organised a small event he called the World Latin Dance Competition in San

Diego. 'Everybody got paid, everything was cool. ESPN checked it out, and this year what I've done is, I've signed for the next two years at the Tropicana Hotel, Las Vegas. It's from the 14th to the 17th, and ESPN have signed on, ESPN International and ESPN Deportes, and ESPN 3 is about to sign on, which would then be live, they'll be following me around on the Saturday night from six to nine o'clock Eastern time. That's where we're at with that. I'm the sole owner of the World Latin Dance Competition. Now if they want to be angry, they can all be angry at me.'

Alongside his own events, Torres brought his foreign partners an economy of scale. 'I tell the dancers, "I can give you six gigs, so instead of charging me €2,000 I want you to charge me €1,500." If you made the call, they wouldn't go lower than €2,000 or €2,500 because you only have one gig. I just offered one guy eight gigs in the next six months. They'll do it for €1,200 or €1,000.'

For driving down the dancers' fees, he charged the organisers a commission. It was a successful formula. Torres travels 48 weeks of the year. 'I fly into Los Angeles on Monday evenings, spend my Tuesdays in meetings with my employees while my clothes are washed and dry-cleaned, repack and fly out again on Wednesdays. I usually arrive on Thursdays, depending on the destination, spend Thursday to Sunday at the congress, and fly home again on Monday morning.'

Like Albert Torres, the polished, theatrical, non-traditional salsa of the congresses spends its time in conference centres, hotel chains, airports and the skein of cable and wireless networks that mobilise extra-terrestrial space for the purposes of communications: places where all sense of identity, all connection to family and upbringing, all sense of being absorbed into a greater continuum, have been carefully framed out.

I put this to him, perhaps wording it badly, because he took it as a question about knowledge.

'In all the congresses I go to, I give a seminar about music from Ignacio Piñeiro, via Machito and Tito Puente, to Fania. I always do it at 12 o'clock when there's no other workshop happening, and we still only get maybe 20 or 30 people. It used to piss me off because they're not, unfortunately . . .' His answer tailed off.

He started again. 'I ask the question, "How many of you know who Tito Puente is?" Usually 10 to 20 per cent raise their hands. I won't even ask how many know Johnny Pacheco because maybe one person will raise their hand. Without these pioneers, we wouldn't have what we have today.'

But that was the answer to another question, and Torres shrugged off any scepticism about the congress culture he has done so much to promote. 'I've been told that I've created a monster. "Look what you've done!" Yeah, I've been told that a few times.'

But monsters have a vital, spiritual resonance. They connect us to a primitive energy. The explicit form of salsa taught in the congresses had no such resonance for me. It was something in which I could muster no interest. However technically accomplished, its literalism seemed deadeningly light in subjective complexity and bereft of enriching metaphor and ambiguity.

*

I wasn't the only one dismayed at the turn salsa had taken. I canvassed some of the more influential figures in the British scene, and found a consensus.

Elder Sánchez, one of London's earliest teachers, complained, 'People don't know if they want to be social dancers or performers.'

Lubín Reyes, who opened the first dance venues for working-class Colombians in London, went further. 'I see Brits dancing salsa and I think, "This isn't salsa."'

It wasn't just Colombians who thought this. Jason

Parkinson, the creator of the Tower Inferno salsa night in Blackpool, agreed that salsa dancing here risked becoming a joyless technique. 'Salsa's very easy. We make it hard. People try and do too much with it.'

And Leon Rose had scathing words on the subject: 'English people are not natural dancers. The thing about salsa is that you don't even have to have good, natural rhythm but, if you understand the timing and you know how to lead, you're going to look impressive. I remember a guy who couldn't dance at all but he was able to manipulate women into all sorts of crazy moves. He looked very impressive on the dance floor and women were lining up to dance with him.'

Rose even accepted partial responsibility for the situation: 'When me and Mario [Hazarika, a.k.a. SuperMario] started teaching, we were giving the people what they wanted, which was moves. We would teach new moves in every class. That's London: everyone just wants new moves. They don't want to work on anything specific. They want new moves all the time. That is why social dancing is the way that it is.'

Rose was now living in Paris, which, he said, was quite different. 'When I moved there, I had to change my style completely. I have a technique class where people just learn the basic moves, and that's very popular, and then, where I teach regularly, I teach the same routine over a period of two weeks to make sure it sticks.'

The first, more complex spins had begun to enter London salsa in the early 1990s. Xihomara Granados attributed them to Salsa Fusion, a weekly class and Latin night run by one of her former students, an English dancer named Stephanie Lipton and her partner, a Caleño named Julio Martín.

'My salsa was very Colombian with much more dancing together and a very few simple spins. Nothing like what you see now. Some of my students went to Salsa Fusion;

others began to visit Eddie Torres in New York. People really took a fancy to it and things started to kind of melt down.'

But even Eddie Torres was admitting that things had gone too far. I found an interview in the *New York Times* in which the man who had done so much to make salsa a dance for specialists now admitted, 'You see people spinning like tops and flying in the air and gyrating, and doing this amazing movement and you want to run for your life. It's gotten so sophisticated. Before, we'd give the girls a little turn here, a little turn there. Now we start her off with 14 spins in the first bar.'

The music too seemed to be going through a similar transition towards a kind of deadening technicism. The Afro-Cuban traditions had always had an improvised feel, and in the 1960s and '70s New York salsa adopted a song structure that came from Cuban *son montuno*. The first part of the composition had a song form with verses and some sort of chorus or refrain. The second part consisted of a series of vocal and instrumental sections, each of which had its own character. The mambo was a written section, often involving harmonised rhythmic figures played by all the horns. The *moña* was a jazzy section during which one or more instrumentalists soloed while the horns played short vamps. But the main improvised section was the *montuno* in which the band played a rhythmic figure, the backing vocalists sang a short, prearranged line and the lead singer responded with an improvised burst of witty words to spontaneously invented melodies. The older bands were full of improvisers who could respond in music to the atmosphere. If the dance floor was full, they could extend the song by inserting an extra *moña*, vocal and instrumental, to lengthen the song for the dancers.

In the mouth of a master improviser like Héctor Lavoe, the *montuno* could provoke hysterical laughter or even melancholy. Perhaps the greatest exponent of the *montuno* today is the Venezuelan composer and bandleader Óscar D'León, a magical performer who plays the string bass while dancing and performing vocal improvisations of stunning verbal and melodic creativity. Vivi and I saw him once in Cali's Jorge Isaacs Theatre. Vivi had stitches in her abdomen after an operation but the rhythm left her with no choice but to dance, despite the pain.

There seemed to be no topic D'León couldn't turn instantly into music, in a Nat King Cole-like voice that was all swing, style and humour. He serenaded women and complimented their hair and legs. He dished out hairdressing advice for men – shave your head, go bald like me, and you won't show the years! He complained that his agent, Oswaldo, wouldn't let him out at night in Cali. He urged us to our feet and then asked a young woman who was still sitting what was wrong, then realised she was pregnant and apologised and congratulated her, all in improvised verses set to improvised melodies.

He eulogised a local craftsman who had constructed three basses for him. He talked – sang – movingly about the death of his father. At one point, there was a pop and his microphone went silent. He picked up a replacement, complained about the sound quality and brought the sound engineer on to the stage to sort it out – all in improvised song.

But Óscar D'León was an old-style performer. In the 1980s, when salsa faced its first commercial lull, record companies responded by looking for young, white or light-skinned male vocalists, who were easier to market. Bands became increasingly singer-led, lyrics became romantic, the gangster imagery of the album covers was replaced by sexy poster photography. This new generation of lead vocalists had never learned to improvise and, since, in the song structure, instrumental sections are topped and tailed by *montunos*, they had no way of expanding them and building on them when they played live.

The *moñas* were changing too. Originally they were made up of improvised riffs played by the horns over the harmonic progression of the *montuno*. But arrangers began to write every note and continued the trend away from improvisation.

At the same time, a gulf grew between performing styles and recording styles. Studio techniques and standards developed in the pop-music industry were adopted and tracks began to be recorded independently, not just one instrument at a time but one phrase, sometimes even one note at a time. The trombonist Chris Washburne describes a recording session for the New York-based producer and arranger Ricky González. It took twenty-three hours over three days to record two trombone parts. 'Each phrase was played several times and then polished so that the attack, sustain and release of every note was executed to perfection.'

Technological solutions were preferred to the natural micro-dynamics of genuine musical interaction. Producers began to correct pitch and timing electronically. There was no longer any room for the indefinable complexity of spontaneous musical interaction. By retreating into the safety of technical criteria and standardisation, salsa music and dance both seemed to be losing contact with the ancient sources of intuition that had once inspired them.

The same commercial considerations created other pressures. Artists who put English lyrics to salsa rhythms, like Paul Simon with his 1980 release 'Late in the Evening', had been greeted by outrage, but at the end of the 1980s a controversy blew up that put two of salsa's own stars, the Nuyorican Willie Colón and the Harvard-educated Rubén Blades from Panamá, in opposing camps. In 1978, Colón and Blades had worked together on *Siembra*, the biggest-selling salsa album of all time, packed from start to finish with classics. By the mid-1980s, Blades was building a career for himself in Hollywood as an actor and looking for crossover appeal by recording albums with the likes of Linda Ronstadt and Joe Jackson. Then in 1988 he released a solo album of his own called *Nothing but the Truth*, which included nothing but English-language salsa songs. A year later, another of America's highest-profile musicians, the Talking Heads star David Byrne, included his own composition 'The Rose Tattoo', a salsa song with English verses and a Spanish chorus, on the album *Rei Momo*.

Willie Colón vented his feelings in the pages of *Billboard* magazine: 'What will we do when Anglo-Salsa becomes bigger than the music we have lived and liked for so long? When Latin America swings to Ronstadt and [Paul] Simon in English, and the Salsa Festival at Madison Square Gardens is headlined by [David] Byrne? When America says: "Salsa? Oh, you mean like Paul Simon?" How will it affect the salsa genre when all its biggest stars are white and singing in English? Another way of not being able to love ourselves for what we are.'

According to Frances Aparicio, a Puerto Rican academic, at a Latin music festival held in Chicago in 1989, 'Blades apologised to the mostly working-class Latina/o audience for supposedly abandoning *el pueblo* . . .'

It was the nothingness of salsa that interested me, the redundancy of all accessories or equipment apart from the body. Along the path it seemed to offer towards a form of un-intellectualised embodiment, there was almost nothing there to make money out of. Unfortunately, the profits it has managed to generate have been almost systematically channelled away from the musicians.

And the economics of salsa were in a state of collapse. Roberto Pla had told me, 'New York in the 1970s wasn't like New York today.'

Ángel Fernández, a musician and arranger who played with Ray Barretto, Celia Cruz and Marc Anthony, elaborated: 'In the mid-'70s, a band could play every night of the week.

There were many bands here, with many different styles: *son, charanga,* big band, *conjunto, merengue,* etc. Today's salsa scene in New York is almost non-existent. Now, a band may play once a month and there are really maybe only three bands in New York.'

Jerry Rivas had told me the same story for Puerto Rico, and Seo Fernández had told me that pair-dancing was dying out in Cuba.

The only major market for the music was Colombia. Richie Ray and Bobby Cruz were now recording in Cali and during the annual festival bands flew in from around the world to perform several times a day all through the week. The practice did not always guarantee high quality. Vivi and I went to see Gilberto Santa Rosa there, only to find that the concert started late but ended on time because Santa Rosa had another performance that evening. For our £35, we had an hour and a half and no encore.

But even Cali couldn't supply the solution salsa needed. In the Music Park, I bought T-shirts that reproduced album covers, as well as pirated CDs and DVDs that had been reproduced in industrial quantities. On stage, bands were covering songs by Grupo Niche and Guayacán. I had no idea whether any intellectual property rights were being paid on any of this, but I had my doubts. There should have been a police raid. We should all have been under arrest. The press covering the event said nothing. No one was pointing out the blindingly obvious. It was as if the city's confidence was so fragile that any criticism, however self-evident, would bring it to its knees. Cali, it seemed to me, was as much of a problem to salsa as it was the solution.

Even the international dance events were beginning to lose popularity. I had been told to expect 8,500 people at Zürich. I doubted there were half that many at the Víctor Manuelle concert. And, in Britain, GBSEx could no longer command the attendances of the earlier congresses. Emma Moore admitted that barely a thousand paying customers had turned up in 2010, fewer than half the number claimed by the BritFests and scarcely a quarter the number attracted by the congresses. 'But they were unusual dates in the calendar and they attracted very, very big numbers. At that time, the salsa scene was really thriving.'

The British salsa market had been contracting since about 2005, and the calendar was saturated. 'GBSEx wasn't a success financially. The market is flooded with wannabe promoters running weekenders, and every time I see another one, I just think, we'll probably only lose ten people, but they all add up. The problem is, a lot of amateur promoters feel it's something that's going to earn them a lot of money, which is a big mistake.'

She had decided not to organise a Great British Salsa Experience in 2011.

The big dance events, of course, were latecomers, even in the globalising phase of salsa history. First had come the music. Then came the mass dispersion of Colombians, starting in the 1960s, accelerated by economic recession in the '80s, and the spread of guerrilla and paramilitary violence in the '90s. By the time of the 2005 census, there were 3.3 million Colombian citizens living abroad. Include those who had given up their citizenship, and their children, and the total diaspora was much bigger. They had taken their family salsa around the world with them.

Cubans had followed in smaller numbers, although much more visibly, some of them highly trained dancers like Alberto Valdés or Seo Fernández. Only then did the congresses arrive, capitalising on the salsa scenes created by the Latin American migrant communities. Britain received salsa as a gift borne by its early Colombian community. The same had happened elsewhere: at a club called La Isla in Stockholm, I had met the Colombian family who had introduced salsa to Sweden. In Beijing, I had met a Bogotano, Lucho Roa, who had done the same there. In every area, the migrants adapted themselves and their dances in response to local pressures and perceptions.

Then the big promoters moved in, splitting the dance off from its broader cultural surround and transforming it into something more easily marketable. What had started out among the British as a wonderful fascination with the music and movements of the immigrant Colombian community soon lost that potential for respectful contact and withdrew into a highly technical, culturally vacuous and rather expensive pursuit. There are no blue plaques at 21 Gledhow Gardens, or on the building in Denmark Place where all those people died in 1980. London's Colombian community may be 150,000 strong now. But that great pool of salsa passion was no longer available to the salsa promoters, now the market was contracting. Like the Zürich festival, which had forged no connections with the Dominican community to which salsa was native, British salsa had cut itself off from its roots.

LOST LANGUAGES

Ay mamá, Tiburón!
Mummy, there's a shark!
'*Tiburón*', composed and performed
by Israel Cachao López

Alberto Valdés had made a great impression on me, and I tried to find out more about the habits of movement inherited from ancient Africa. But little seemed to have been written about that great flow of rhythm and body wisdom that had originated in West Africa and had, over the centuries of mass human trafficking, spread across the Atlantic to the Americas. Even so, snatches of it had been half-translated into Afro-American strains of music and dance or repackaged into forms that had spread to Europe and around the world.

I did, however, discover an art historian at Yale, Robert Farris Thompson, who had begun the necessary research. On a visit to Congo-Brazzaville in 1987, he saw a dance marking the passage of young girls into marriageable women:

> The grand initiator breaks ranks. . . . Her shoulders tremble. To the initiated, this communicates that she herself is not dancing. She is being danced (*kinuswa*) by unseen high forces. . . . Acolytes in the circle begin to

vibrate their shoulders, their breasts, and the *kitanda*,
the cloth that covers their breasts. They too are being
'danced.' Their shoulders roll in response to the spirit.

In the Ki-Kongo language spoken in the tropical forests of
Angola and the Democratic Republic of the Congo – the
language of many of the Africans who were kidnapped,
transported to the Americas and sold as slaves – this ecstatic
trembling of the shoulders had a name: *mayembo*, meaning
'possession by the spirit'.

Africa bequeathed *mayembo* to the rumba of black Cuba,
which passed it down to mambo and on to salsa in the 1960s
and '70s. Alberto Valdés knew *mayembo* and had
demonstrated it to me: an up-and-down shudder of the
upper chest, like a vertical shimmy.

Farris Thompson found other survivals. Afro-Cubans
perform on the balls of their feet, as the Kongos did. This
may be a hangover from the earlier stage of the slave trade,
between 1580 and 1640, when exchange centred mostly on
Africans kidnapped from the basin of the Congo: Tekés,
Manicongos and Ngola.

The shuffling step of the Colombian *cumbia* may betray
the influence of Yoruba or Fon styles, brought over from
Africa after 1640, when the slave trade shifted its focus to
the Gulfs of Benin and Biafra, bringing Fon and Yoruba
slaves to Colombia, as well as members of the Ashanti,
Mina, Arará, Xwlá and Ibo peoples.

A rubbing together of the genitals known as 'winding' in
the Bahamas, *gouyade* in Haiti and, tellingly, the Kongo in
Trinidad has a precursor in a traditional Ki-Kongo figure
called *tienga*, which mimes the pelvic movements in sexual
action and is said to gather the heat and the circular motion
of the sun into the hips.

Many musical instruments are seen as living male or
female entities by the communities in which they play an
important ritual role. This is the case with the two *clave*

rods, for instance, and the two bongo drums. There is even brain scan data suggesting that the brains of accomplished musicians come to regard their instruments with the attention we reserve for living organisms. By separating the living into independent individuals (right hemisphere) or objects of use, prey, 'things', and so on (left hemisphere), and sorting musical instruments into the first group, our brains, it seems, may use more mystical ways of thinking than our conscious, rational, secular modes of thought are prepared to admit.

If our spinning and circling motions bind us into the greater totality of the universe, and our instruments blur the distinction between the living and the dead, salsa may embody a way of thinking that is far more complex than mere intellect or language, weaving together the animate and the inanimate and securing the well-being of body, community and cosmos. But our ideas of what reason must mean have become so simplistic that we think such things in contradiction with our rational ways of being. For all our sophistication, we lag hopelessly behind primitive thought in all its astonishing complexity.

*

During the Anglo-Ashanti wars in the nineteenth century, in the Akan interior of what is now Ghana, Ashanti warriors besieging a British fort broke into the cellars. With British soldiers trapped upstairs, the Ashanti pulled in their drums and danced to rhythms that pronounced the phrase '*Obueroni bewu abansoro*': 'The white man will die upstairs.'

The West African talking drums are among humanity's more remarkable inventions. During the 1970s an American percussionist named John Miller Chernoff spent several years in Ghana studying with a master-drummer named Gideon. Early in his training, Chernoff was reproducing a basic rhythm under his master's guidance when Gideon suddenly beat out a series of complicated rhythms. Several minutes later, a man who had passed them at that moment returned with two bottles of beer. The drums actually *speak* the language of the tribe.

This is not to say that drumming always reflects current vernaculars. Religious language everywhere tends to use antiquated forms and the drums sometimes speak in dialects that are slipping out of memory. The religious songs of the Ga people of south-eastern Ghana are in the forgotten Obutu dialect, and some of the most important music of the Dagomba people in northern Ghana is in a language the drummers no longer understand.

Some years after his training had begun, when Chernoff had acquired a degree of mastery, he visited Haiti and met drummers there. He demonstrated several Yeve Cult rhythms. The Haitians said they knew the rhythms well. They even had local names: a beat known in Ghana as *Edahu* was *Yanvlou* in Haiti. Another called *Sohu* in Ghana was *Banda* in Haiti. It is clear that African drumming and dancing survived the middle passage. In 1760 a Danish slave-ship captain noted in his memoir, 'Drums . . . are brought along from the Coast and the slaves are allowed to dance at a certain time on deck, one group after another.'

From the point of view of their kidnappers, the slaves were 'danced' on deck, still in their shackles, to keep them in acceptable physical shape so that they would command good prices at auction in the New World. From the point of view of the slaves, of course, the dance had other meanings.

Chernoff emphasises that dance is implicit in the drum beat. 'When you ask an African friend whether or not he "understands" a certain type of music, he will say yes if he knows the dance that goes with it.'

With the rhythms and ancient drum languages and fading meanings that survived the voyage from West Africa to the New World came repertoires of gesture and movement entirely unnoticed by the non-Africans who then received them.

The languages of the old rhythms have been forgotten. It is hard to know the workings of creative misremembering, but might not the congas and bongos, like their older cousins the talking drums, be uttering fragmented syllables of lost dialects? When I danced with Vivi, then, was it not at root a conversation, however uncomprehending, with those ancient African voices? I began to think of salsa as a way of establishing communication between the centuries by diving to the most primitive and obscure levels and returning enriched to the surface. In salsa, we listen to Africa's languages and dance in Africa's footsteps. We hear their whisper, we mimic their movements. We cannot know what they mean.

The one dimension of the technical salsa I had seen at the congresses that seemed to have no known African antecedents were the intricate hand movements. Nor did the hands perform any similar operations in the traditional salsa of its carrier communities, whose movements are centred on the body's vertical axis and the trunk.

The importance of the hands to hold and steer our partner only comes to the fore in the salsa of the congresses and formal dance classes, transmitted from teacher to pupil in explicit instructions. The relation between articulacy and manual dexterity may not be casual. In babies and young children, pointing and babbling occur together. Children point at the things they name and only name things when they point. Even in adults, speech loses fluency and nuance when hand movements are restricted. The suggestion is that referential language is closely related to hand movements, and specifically to motions that have to do with grasping. Both facilities are believed to be controlled by the motor speech area on the surface of the brain's left frontal lobe.

If speech is the vehicle of a disengaged awareness of our surroundings, lifting us out of our situation, the psychiatrist

Iain McGilchrist believes that grasping, which similarly entails wresting an object away from its context and holding it fast so that we can focus on it, deploys some of the specialities of the left hemisphere in the brain, the hemisphere that enables us to isolate and manipulate elements of the world around us.

McGilchrist holds that in a well-balanced mind thoughts have their origins in the right hemisphere, which is alert and responsive to the wider world, and are passed to the technically gifted but blinkered left hemisphere to be unpacked and enshrined in words, before being handed back to the right to be integrated into our understanding and experience.

However, in our technology-fixated culture, we are heavily skewed towards the strategies of the left hemisphere, which in some cases refuses to return its formulations to the right hemisphere to be reconnected to reality. As a result, we see the world in fragmentary, technical terms, not using holistic, empathic ways of thought.

McGilchrist believes language started out as something akin to the singing voice mothers use to speak to infants, and at some point in evolution metamorphosed into a more referential, verbal medium, migrating away from the right-hemisphere centres where music is processed and settling in the left-hemisphere areas where hand and finger movements are controlled. It is tempting to see salsa making the same journey, because the transition seems to describe the two ways of dancing salsa perfectly.

At a family party when a father and his daughter dance their simple steps in attentive engagement with each other, sharing feelings, showing interest in each other through the disposition of the eyes, body and attention, both hemispheres seem to be working in harmony.

Salsa tends towards abstraction only when it is sequestered by the left hemisphere, which experiences the space around us not through the body, first-hand, as an individual's bridge to the world, but as something that requires measuring and categorising according to abstract criteria. It treats our bodies as pieces of equipment which it uses to carry out essentially mechanical tasks. So, when the Euro-American individualist, for whom salsa is fundamentally a technical matter, pays more attention to the moves than to his partner, he is dancing left-hemisphere salsa. His clarity of movement, his distinctness of step, are left-hemisphere traits.

For one group, it is a technique with no past worth worrying about. For the other, it is one of the imagination's vital supply lines to the store of ancient intuitions and wisdom. McGilchrist could be talking about family salsa when he writes,

> The movement of the right hemisphere is not the unidirectional, instrumental gesture of grasp, but the musical, whole-bodied, socially generative, movement of dance, which is never in a straight line towards something, but always ultimately returns to its origins.

For non-traditional, technical dancers, the onus of generating meaning falls not on the community but on the individual. Perhaps this is why we have to spend so much, acquire so many moves, try so desperately hard.

John Miller Chernoff's Ghanaian drum teacher instructed him not to be ostentatious and virtuosic. True style, he said, consisted in the subtle perfection of strictly respected form. The same went for dancing.

> A dancer should not try to do too much or he will lose clarity or become pretentious. A dancer's subtle refinement and good taste will enliven the music by enriching the occasion, pulling the whole scene into movements rather than attempting to project the strength of one performer. Good dancers get into the

grooves provided by the rhythms and add their bodies to the elaboration of rhythmic sophistication and power.

Unfortunately, as Chernoff writes,

> . . . we will have to wait a long time before all the data is in and we can demonstrate how free Africans who became slaves in Brazil, Haiti and Cuba managed to continue beating the same rhythms for four centuries; how the patrilineal, Muslim Dagomabas and the matrilineal, pagan Ashanti established such a deep history of mutual musical influence; how the daughters of Ga fishermen and Krobo farmers dance to the same Otofu drumming; how freedom-loving Ghanaians can listen to recordings of South Africa's Dark City Sisters; how Cuban Rumba beats did not change after the revolutions; and so on. The point . . . is that we can discuss these matters to an extent, but only to an extent.

It seemed clear to me, though, that Colombia's most African sense of taste had been handed down to Vivi via the cultures of the Chocó, through her mother, and the Caribbean coast, via her father. And that Marlen's aesthetic, the aesthetic of humble, Colombian family salsa, was also that of an ancient African ideal.

Compared with this overwhelming bodily sensation of being immersed in the flux of time, the sense of history I felt around me in Britain seemed disturbingly weak. Here, the recent past – the '60s, the '70s, the '80s – became 'historical' almost as soon as it had been lived, and current affairs were constantly being described as going down in history, as if history consisted of the last 48 hours of news. In Colombia, remembrance worked very differently.

Cali called itself 'the city of musical memory', and it was

true that Cuban music and dance forms from the 1930s and '40s, like the New York crazes of the '50s and '60s, had never gone out of fashion there, even among the young. In Cartagena, too, the *picós* of the Caribbean coast played African music that had been long forgotten in the mother continent.

A South African DJ named Donald 'Jumbo' Vanrenen told me how he had started supplying them with African music. 'On Facebook, someone had posted some music from a Cartagena *picó* recorded 30 years ago. I recognised it as South African *Shangaan* music by Makhubela. Since then, guys have been sending me tunes to identify. I can't say I have been that successful, but I've been swapping obscure Kenyan records for classic coastal records, swapping old Congolese records for new *champeta* CDs. I love the knowledge and dedication of these guys.'

Soon, technology began to allow DJs to sample old African songs and create new ones, or insert Colombian vocals in place of the original Zulu. All of this existed in the submerged economy, in breach of the copyright laws.

Jumbo had retired from deejaying, but the cultural memory of Colombia's Caribbean coast changed that. 'I have Colombian friends in Cape Town who come round and dance to old Colombian music, and have helped to turn my academic interest into a fun dancing experience and I have reactivated my DJ activities and continue to play old 1980s African, reggae, *zouk*, and Latin music.'

The next time we were in Colombia, we headed for a destination where even Alberto Valdés would have been impressed by the retention of ancient body languages.

13
Mama-U

Agua que va a caer, ay, vení mojáme.
Rainwater coming down, aye, come
    and fall on me.
    '*A Golpe de Folklore*', composed by Jairo
    Varela, performed by El Grupo Niche

Every time we passed through Medellín airport – not the international hub but the one in the city serving national destinations – the Quibdó flight drew my attention. I was thinking of Vivi's mother and her childhood in the capital of the Chocó, Colombia's poorest department.

Marlen had been sent from Palmar, high in the mountains, to study at an exclusive convent school run by the Sisters of the Presentation of Mary. It had a reputation for exclusiveness and it was there that she received her secondary education. The journey to Palmar lasted two days so, at the weekends when the convent school was closed, there was no returning home. As a result, Marlen saw little of her mother during her teenage years. She regretted this all her life.

Instead, she would stay in an adobe house near the town centre with a couple she called Uncle Manuel and Aunt Rufina. Manuel and Rufina had a son, Gonzalo, a light-skinned Chocoano who had joined a religious community called the Missionary Sons of the Immaculate Heart of Mary, or the Claretians, in the 1940s. A brilliant scholar of Hebrew and Greek, he had been dispatched to the Vatican on a career path that might have made him a bishop, then an archbishop in Colombia, and perhaps taken him back to Rome as a cardinal. But Gonzalo had rejected the road chosen by his superiors and returned to the Chocó where he disappeared into the forest to work among the indigenous people and the descendants of the slaves.

I wanted to meet Gonzalo but I also wanted to visit the source of the Chocó's inexhaustible supply of rhythmic body movement that feeds the rest of Colombia: the *currulao*, the dance that most synthesises the African inheritance from the slaves who settled on the Pacific coast; the *abozao*, with African roots but also influenced by belly dancing; the *bambaleo, bambazú, makerule, urupina* and the five types of *jota*, of which the folk manuals all repeat the same phrase: 'regarding origin, tradition, area of dispersion or current use, no known data'.

They were just the documented forms. No other Colombian region is so rich in African-influenced dance, yet none is less studied. The origins of the slaves transported there are known only vaguely and the history of their gestures, the counterparts of *mayembo* or *tienga* or of the Mandinka-derived swaying of the hips, remains obscure. Only a few scattered priests and brothers from the Claretian Order have taken much of an interest in the people and their remarkable culture.

Our small plane strained to clear the mountains around Medellín, then lost nearly two miles in altitude before it swooped over the rainforest and down into the clearing where Quibdó squatted flat against the fast-flowing Atrato River. The rain held off as we landed but even so the humidity was suffocating.

Mean annual rainfall here is 280 inches and local

schoolchildren are taught that they live in the second rainiest place in the world after Cherrapunji, India. It is a point of local pride, like the Atrato itself, not the longest of rivers but one of the world's great reservoirs of fresh water and biodiversity. On the 416-mile journey from its source in the Andes to the Caribbean coast, an astonishing quantity of water flows into it, forming perilous eddies and whirlpools which are echoed in the many dances of the Chocoanos, who live mostly on its banks.

We were met by Gonzalo's niece, Alicia, and her partner Rafa. They helped us with our bags and we took a taxi from the airport. Our driver made no concessions to other road users. We improvised a path between the potholes. Cars, minibuses and motorbikes came at us from every direction, although each apparently inevitable collision passed without any actual contact. El Jardín, 'The Garden', was one of Quibdó's better areas yet the mud tracks were nearly impassable. The weight of a burly driver and four passengers, on roads constantly eroded by the downpour, held little hope for the car's life expectancy. Its doors had already rusted through. We made it to the house where I took the first of many cold showers.

Vivi had been to Quibdó only once, as a child, but she had family roots there: as well as the place where her mother had spent her youth, Quibdó was her grandmother Colomba's birthplace. So, for Vivi, the sense of homecoming was deep, and it occurred to me that, as well as homes away from home, there are homes away from them and homes away from *them*, and the entity that is our *original* home, whatever that is, place, person or intuition – to a mother, her child; to a child, its mother; to lovers, perhaps, each other – doesn't so much recede as expand with each displacement.

Quibdó was the blackest place I had visited outside Africa: 85 per cent of the population is Afro-descendent, 8 per cent indigenous and 7 per cent mixed race. After the abolition of slavery, British and US companies exploited the gold mines to exhaustion, then sold them as barren cavities back to Colombia. The Chocó had been left to wallow in under-development, while a local white elite and a few outside entrepreneurs used the cheap labour to extract its remaining natural resources. To strangers like me, black Chocoan society was understandably closed, although I met only warmth and openness, perhaps because my guide, Alicia's partner Rafa, occupied a unique position there. Rafa had arrived in Quibdó in 1991 after studying to become a priest with the Claretians, before opting instead to become a lay brother and devote his life to social causes.

The Claretian Order, committed by its constitution to being 'open-minded, receptive and respectful of the religious and cultural customs and values of the people', was the only voluntary organisation of any longevity in the region. Since reaching the department in 1909, they had championed music and dance there. In 1935 a priest and music teacher named Fr Isaac Rodríguez had arrived from Spain. He organised a male choir, and in 1948 established a parish music school that was unique in the region. Marlen received the Eucharist from Fr Isaac, who was one of the chaplains of her school, although she didn't sing in the choir or study music with him. If she had, she might have met Jairo Varela and Alexis Lozano, the future founders of Grupo Niche and Guayacán, whom Fr Isaac was teaching in those same years.

In 1998, following in Fr Isaac's footsteps, Rafa, along with Alicia's uncle, Gonzalo, created a cultural centre called Mama-U to recover, preserve and disseminate the cultures of the Chocó. Rafa also became involved in the human rights movement. In the mid-1990s a territorial war had broken out between the guerrillas and the paramilitaries, who started a river blockade that deprived isolated communities of a vital resource. The fish caught during the *subienda*, when they swam upriver to mate, were either sold fresh or dried and salted. Without salt, which they could only buy in Quibdó, the Chocó's poor had no food security.

Rafa used the degree of impunity his religious vocation gave him, more a flimsy veil than a bulletproof vest, to defend Chocoan communities from the men of violence. He started travelling with poor families on their river journeys in defiance of the blockade. The paramilitary leader, Carlos Castaño, threatened him repeatedly. One evening in 1999 Castaño's thugs, in a high-tech speed boat, caught Rafa's motor launch in their spotlights and rammed it. A priest on board was killed instantly. A young mother and her three children were thrown into the river. Seriously injured, Rafa managed to empty the fuel tanks into the water and sling them over to the children to keep them afloat. They clung to the tanks and survived. A Spanish aid worker was less fortunate. He too had been badly hurt by the impact, which had flung him into the Atrato. He called and called for help but the night was too black and the current too strong, and Rafa could only listen until the cries stopped.

After the attack, it was no longer safe for Rafa to negotiate with the paras so he devoted his energies to running Mama-U and organising a local arts festival for Quibdó's musicians and dancers.

The day after we arrived, he took me to a bar in central Quibdó called Café y Borojó, managed and run by a women's group, where a group of social workers enthused to me about the variation of Chocoan dance genres. Rafa introduced me to Emilia Caicedo, a huge woman who directed a dance group called Grupo Papitú. She took my hand to greet me and, as if it explained everything, told me, 'Dance is our inheritance of African happiness. Africa is our mother.'

Grupo Papitú was rehearsing that afternoon, and Emilia invited me along.

In Central Quibdó, salsa seemed to come from every doorway. The town itself was drab and the cathedral was a dark, military khaki. It was hard to believe. I kept drifting back to it, imagining the rain would wash the colour off, but it didn't. How can you paint when it rarely stops falling?

The headquarters of the Claretian Order occupied the site of the house that had provided Marlen with a refuge from the suffocating regime of the nuns. She and her friends had had to earn the right to monthly visits from their parents by winning points for punctuality, neatness, housekeeping and personal discipline, which basically meant silence. Marlen missed out several times when the nuns found letters sent to her by a suitor.

On national holidays, the girls of the Presentation school marched behind the band of the corresponding school for boys, organised by Fr Isaac. Despite the heat and humidity, it gave them contact with the boys, and with music. Only on the rarest occasion were the girls allowed to dance, and even then, only *porro* and *cumbia* were allowed. The rest of the time, they spent studying. Marlen's parents had decided she should learn secretarial skills but she was drawn to social work and teaching, perhaps influenced by the poverty around her or by Gonzalo, who, at last, I was about to meet.

Slight in stature but full of energy, even in his mid-seventies, he was cogent and direct, scholarly but accessible, and above all a man of action. Driven by a passion for social justice, he had devoted his life to causes such as literacy, food security and, above all, the need for organisations that could represent poor Chocoanos before the government. He travelled all over the region and got to know everyone, storing their names and faces in a prodigious memory that was complemented by a quiet knack for melding people of radically different temperaments and outlooks into tight alliances, which Gonzalo then nurtured into the Chocó's first social institutions.

When, in the early 1980s, logging companies who had

already torn down the forests further south, moved into the central part of the Chocó, it was Gonzalo who orchestrated the resistance, although, when he speaks of it, he simply says, 'People began to move themselves, people began to get organised.'

After fifteen years of struggle, one of the movements he had launched forced the government to recognise the rights of poor communities to the land they and their forefathers had occupied since 1851, when slavery was abolished. Gonzalo's latest project was the Claretian University Foundation, a college for the poor that he was building brick by brick. For this, and much else, he was revered in Quibdó, although he insisted only on his insignificance.

Rafa took me to the local school where Emilia Caicedo and her Grupo Papitú were rehearsing. They danced stock Afro-Cuban routines like the elegant *danzón*, the first genuinely Cuban creation and the principal musical genre there from the 1870s until quite recently. It looked like a slow, repetitive Cuban salsa. They danced narrative forms too, like the *batia*, which describes panning for gold, and the *palenque*, which tells of a group of slaves who have fled captivity.

Their repertoire also covered European dances and musical genres introduced by Spanish slave-owners: quadrilles, minuets and waltzes that were old-fashioned even in the nineteenth century. These had evolved into forms peculiar to the region. With a theatrical array of claps, flailing hands and fixed smiles that mocked the expressions and body language of the slave-owners, they danced a *mazurka*. Then the men took straw hats which they doffed with deep bows, before partners who fluttered fans, and they danced a polka. It was uncanny: Polish dances that had reached polite society in Western Europe in the early nineteenth century, preserved halfway around the world in the Colombian tropics.

The dancers then travelled back to the seventeenth

century for a flirtatious *contradanza*, border-crossing into body shapes born from the eavesdropping slaves' familiarity with their masters' way of life. All the genres that, centuries later, would entwine and dissolve in the salsa embrace had been retained in the eternal present of the Chocó.

A century and a half seemed no time at all here. It was as if slavery had been abolished yesterday. Perhaps, to the descendants of men and women who had arrived here naked and in chains, with nothing of the past but their bodies, no memory could matter more than body-memory.

Nonetheless, preposterous in its biodiversity, fantastically wealthy in its resources of fresh water, the department is Colombia's poorest, and only 10 per cent of Quibdó's homes are served by the water main, when it works. The latest corruption scandal had broken days before our visit: food aid dispatched from Bogotá to the regional authorities for free distribution to the poor had been found on sale in street markets. This, at a time when a number of children had been taken to hospital in Quibdó and diagnosed with severe malnutrition. Several had died. The mayor and treasurer of Quibdó had been arrested on charges of embezzlement and the government had assumed direct administration.

That night, the capricious Atrato was so swollen that it broke its banks, sending floodwater into the timber homesteads of the poor. The following morning, much of the town was inundated, but Rafa wanted to take me to Mama-U, where more of Quibdó's remarkable dancers rehearsed, so we hailed a motorbike taxi each and crossed town between rainstorms, weaving between the lower-lying streets to avoid the flooding.

At Mama-U, I met Milciades Rentería, a dance teacher and theatre director with a degree in applied anthropology. As one of the community leaders at the vanguard of the project, he was creating programmes of ethno-education to safeguard traditional skills and knowledge and told me that in Quibdó, as in Cali, dance was a way of giving the young a passion or vocation that would save them from lives of violence. At a time when the paramilitary organisations were uprooting rural communities, dance was also a way of preserving a way of life so that what was being destroyed might one day be revived. The members of his dance group, Mi Sangre Candente ('My Red-hot Blood'), took their place on the floor as Milciades brought out a large drum. To its rhythm alone they danced a *palenque* full of extraordinary body movements. Their torsos seemed to have articulations that mine lacked and, with incredible fluidity and speed, they performed gestures requiring a degree of co-ordination I found almost unthinkable.

There is an episode in the *palenque* when, with a frantic quivering of the limbs and torso, the dancers shake themselves free from some sort of constriction – a rope, perhaps, or a chain. Arms and legs on opposite sides are thrown upwards and backwards, exploring the spaces of their new freedom. A joyful charge of energy passes through them. Then, there is a change of tempo and heavy rods appear, brandished with hostile intent. The dancing speaks of the escape from slavery by groups who then defended their freedom, and often died doing so.

They rehearsed the sequence through, then Milciades gestured to Rafa, and Rafa asked me if I would like to join the dancers.

I knew that if I danced, I'd sweat, and if I started sweating, I wouldn't stop until nightfall, and it was still morning. But the dancers refused to take no for an answer, and two of the girls, laughing, pulled me into the rehearsal space. They started moving slowly. I copied them, and then our actions became faster and faster, and soon we were dancing. I had a mental picture of myself as one of those nineteenth-century ethnographers who adopted native dress and customs and passed themselves off as Orientals or Amerindians. I wasn't even the coffee colour of 'white'

Colombians. I was the marble white of people who never seek the sun because their skin doesn't tan, the ideal hue of the colonial elites who prided themselves on the purity of their blood.

As far back as my father had been able to trace us, we'd been a family of refugees fleeing the Irish famines, becoming sailors, saddlers or blacksmiths who moved to where the jobs were. We had only ended up in Liverpool in the 1840s, 30 years after the last official slave ship had sailed, and as far as I knew no one in the family tree had been directly involved in the slave trade. The data didn't go back far enough to be certain, though, and there were certainly cotton brokers on both sides of the family later on. One of them, my mother's mother's father, Charlie Palmer, had shuttled back and forth between Liverpool and Rio.

Little was clear except that the dancers and I came from different sides of one of humanity's essential divisions. But when we danced none of that mattered. For the moments I spent with those magical dancers and Milciades on the drum, I too shared in their inheritance of African joy.

I danced and sweated and, although I went back to the house and showered in cold water and changed my clothes, I went on sweating all day. That night Rafa and I left Vivi talking with Alicia, and went to a private party in poor Quibdó. The music was provided by two boys with a drum and a trombone, and I danced again, only salsa this time, and the remarkable thing was that in Quibdó it seemed to be entirely free of any fixed canon of steps. There seemed to be no moves that weren't improvised, not even a basic step. I began to understand that salsa acted as a sort of universal adaptor for almost all the dances I had seen, and the hundreds of folk dances dispersed throughout the Chocó as well, all of which had local variations. Movements from almost any of these forms could be combined in salsa's all-purpose rhythms, which made every salsa a form of time travel along a sequence of quotations from other dances, all belonging to other ages, that anyone with the necessary knowledge would be able to decipher.

It was Easter Day and we went to the Claretian centre for mass. This consisted of a conversation around a table led by Fr Gonzalo. He talked about the gospel, which he read in Greek, and sermonised on the distinction between personal love, *philos*, and love of a cause, *agape*.

As a young man in Rome, Fr Gonzalo had found in the sacred texts not naked statements of belief but a mass of contradictions that opened spaces for spiritual free will and freedom itself. For him, the Bible contained a theology of liberation for his fellow Chocoanos. He transformed his funeral masses into intense questionings of social conditions. He wrote songs, some of which had been recorded, and composed an Afro-Colombian mass full of music and dance. Gonzalo never rejected the institutional Church, but my feeling was that each had taken its distance from the other and the hierarchy had marginalised him to the Chocó, which was where he wanted to be anyway.

The scales were rather different, but Gonzalo faced much the same problem I did: the encounter of two cultures, resulting in the reinterpretation of each by the other, without being unfaithful to either. The churchmen called it 'inculturation': the presentation and re-expression of the Gospel in the language and forms of an alien culture.

It was clear that the people of the Chocó went to mass in great numbers, but Gonzalo said they had their own spiritual practices, unrelated to the teachings of the priests and mostly hidden from view. 'For centuries they have had their own funeral rites, their own novenas, their *alabao* [a spiritual plainsong], their own saints. They come to church but their beliefs are not the orthodox ones. They have their own trustees, singers and prayer leaders.'

But it was a fine line to tread to feel empathy for other people's way of life while maintaining your own. At

Gonzalo's Bible Centre in Quibdó, a mural used the spiritual language of the Chocó as the medium for a new telling of the ancient stories. I wasn't sure that Gonzalo's version of Catholicism and the accommodations that had been made there would have received unqualified approval from the Vatican. But Fr Gonzalo was not among the undoubting. From my standpoint, he seemed to have passed through faith to the other side.

Chocó death rites were central to the cultures of the Chocó. Not all of them had official sanction. When children aged seven or younger die there, they become angels and go straight to heaven. An extraordinary ceremony called *Chigualo* marks their passing. The night before the burial, the dead child is dressed in light clothes and placed before a table decorated with candles and flowers. The women of the community form a semi-circle around the shrine and they sing and dance, accompanied by the *bombo* and *cununo* drums, the *guasá* – a long, thin maraca – and the *marimba*. While they sing, the child's godmother takes up the child's body and invites the women to dance with the lifeless child. The ritual continues all night. The following day, the child is processed to the cemetery, as the women celebrate a new member of the choir of angels.

Brought up in a vicarage, I had since adolescence turned my back on religion. I had certainly danced an atheistic form of salsa, dissociated from all other-worldly evocation. Here, I wondered what requests and divinations in the Chocó's secret spirit-world I might inadvertently have initiated when I had thought I was only dancing.

In the Chocó, dance was woven into every other aspect of life, at the heart of which were the basic components of the human condition: life, death and love. By comparison, the placeless technicism of the congresses assumed its place at salsa's remotest margins. Here, among such people as Rafa and Gonzalo, in the Chocó's eternal present, the barren, inconsolable aloneness proposed by the atheism I subscribed to seemed not so much a self-evident truth as an unattainable ideal. The nothingness it invites us home to seems ill-considered: here, beyond every elsewhere, lies another elsewhere, more distant, more alien. And then another, and another, until they too echo off towards infinity.

14

QUIBDÓ FUNERAL

Mi mamá me ha dicho . . .
My mother told me . . .
> Traditional song from the Chocó,
> arranged by Jairo Varela and
> performed by Grupo Niche

Marlen always spoke nostalgically of Quibdó. She imagined herself returning there and spending her final years as a social worker beside Gonzalo.

In 2005 she came to visit us in England with Ana. We showed them the sights here, then flew to Italy for a week. Marlen loved Rome, although we walked and walked until she had to sit down. When she couldn't get comfortable in the car, we thought she was just tired.

For her sixtieth birthday the following year, we bought her a voucher for eight dance classes with José Fernando. She could never use it. She noted in her diary:

> 1 a.m. I can't sleep because of the excessive pain in the hip and top of my right leg, which I can only move with difficulty when I change position in the bed or stand up. Not so much when I'm walking. These two days have been hard, but active. Yesterday was particularly special: after a long wait . . . they received my papers for oncology.

But she shielded her daughter from the truth and, when Vivi phoned home to wish her many happy returns, she ended the call sobbing silently.

All she could say to me was: 'It's too soon.'

Marlen wrote in her diary: 'My guest doesn't impede my movement, it doesn't create any inconvenience like some that reside in the uterus, pancreas, liver, stomach, throat, brain, bones, lungs. It's in an annex, not a central room.'

Then the cancer metastasised to her liver.

She needed urgent medical attention. Chemotherapy was promised repeatedly, then inexplicably cancelled. Vivi travelled to Colombia and sued the institute for social security and the hospital that should have been treating her. Five months after the diagnosis, the courts ordered both parties to arrange for chemotherapy to begin within forty-eight hours and Vivi flew back to England.

The day before chemotherapy was due to begin, the appointment was cancelled. This happened twice. Each time, the court reissued its order but it made no difference.

To protect Vivi, Marlen played down the severity of her illness. Some weeks later, Vivi prepared to fly back to Medellín, imagining that she would spend the coming weeks nursing her mother through chemotherapy and allowing her older brother Nestor some respite.

During a telephone call, her father decided to come clean with her. There had been a party next door, Nestor had gone to ask them to keep the noise down and, while he was gone, Marlen had fallen. She was no longer eating. Death could come any time. Vivi bought the first available ticket but there were 48 hours to wait.

Vivi broke down only once: 'Why won't time pass?'

We were probably on our way to the airport when the doctor gave her a painkilling injection. The following day, my mobile phone shook:

SALSA FOR PEOPLE WHO PROBABLY SHOULDN'T

From: Vivi
Received: SAT 05:32

Murio antes d yo llegar   She died before I arrived.

An hour, perhaps two, before Marlen died, I ran my hand over my neck for no apparent reason, and found, below and to the right of my Adam's apple, a swelling. Vivi, who had flown to Colombia to be with her mother but had ended up settling her estate and caring for her brothers, flew back to be with me. There was an operation to remove the tumour and, when I was well enough, we flew back to scatter Marlen's ashes.

While we were in Medellín, there was a succession of small earthquakes. Kiwi was sensitive to the premonitory signs and warned us with quiet yelps. For a moment, our nineteenth-storey flat drifted through space. Days later we woke during a long rumble that brought down 20 houses elsewhere in the city. The earth danced beneath our feet.

Marlen's children decided her ashes should go back to Quibdó. Fr Gonzalo conducted the ceremony. Three black dancers dressed in white danced with the casket. They handed out yellow and purple flowers.

An *alabao* was sung which described Marlen as *hija de raíces negras*, 'the daughter of black roots'.

> *Marlen, tu del Chocó te tuviste que ausentar,*
> *Pero siempre tu quisiste de nuevo aquí regresar.*
> *Hoy regresas en cenizas y de manos de tus hijos.*
> Marlen, you had to leave the Chocó,
> although you always wanted to come back.
> Today you have returned as ashes in the hands of
>   your children.

Gonzalo proclaimed her an ancestor and protector, and we cast the flowers and Marlen's remains into the fast-moving Atrato. The sky was the colour of embers still too hot to touch.

15

YENGA YE KUMBA

Start with a phrase: a word, a name, a sentence,
  Yenga ye kumba
and repeat it,
  yenga ye kumba,
  yenga ye kumba,
  yenga ye kumba,
like a mantra or an incantation learned by heart and
repeated until the phrase becomes a rhythm and the rhythm
determines bearing, breathing, heartbeat, the hypnotised
silence of the mind. Then set it to the lilting of Afro-Cuban
rhythms and let it lurch forward and threaten to catch up
on itself before it pulls up short and, finally, meets itself on
the way back, weaving a linked dance, *yenga ye kumba,*
through the ear.

The focus changes with each repetition, from the struggle
to understand to the altered consciousness of surrender,
and the slow dawning that, with each iteration, *yenga ye
kumba,* the universe has continued its expansion, the earth
has turned another notch and we are all further from where
we started out and closer to our ends; in sum, that there is
no repetition and in the strict sense never can be.

So it may be with this shuffle, this periodic movement we

call dance. Even without our intermittent turns, each step to and fro calls into being another with its own place in the order of things, the daily play of question and answer, theme and variation, of 'call and response' – or as Ki-Kongo has it *'yenga ye kumba'* – the formal structure thought to have been handed down to salsa from Central African song.

Call and response run through the structural conventions of the salsa song. This interplay between soloist and chorus makes salsa a game of individual assertion within, even against, the group: in each solo flight, the vocalist challenges the ensemble, defining his various identities as an individual, a member of the collective and as a link in the chain of tradition. As the soloist's improvisation first merges with the background motif then becomes a distinct voice, the boundary lines between the individual and the group are, by turns, reduced and then emphasised.

Yenga ye kumba applies as much to motion as to music, since the song calls the dance into existence. You feel your way together into the music. There is a restructuring of consciousness. Time narrows to the present moment. Psychic energy runs smoothly. We could speak of intensified emotion or cognitive fluidity, of multi-sensory flow, but there are no words here, only the circumvention of, the release from, familiar habits of thought. The self pales until there is only the dance.

Psychotherapists speak of 'somatic intelligence', a skill or body wisdom that makes of the body a bridge between our conscious and unconscious lives. They use eye contact, touch and movement to help the victims of torture reinhabit their bodies. These experimental treatments are only pale versions, perhaps, of the ancient rhythmic rituals that allowed the slaves to survive.

The forms that flow together in salsa share with all pair-dances other features that are full of therapeutic potential: upright posture, an upbeat gait and rhythms that allow the hemispheres of the brain to be re-synchronised. All over Colombia and the Spanish-speaking Caribbean, dance supplies a precious form of social capital, as the psychologists would say. Perhaps it even helped Colombia re-emerge from the shocking violence of the 1980s and '90s. But, in the Chocó, Cali and elsewhere, it offered something more.

Among people historically denied freedom, education and political representation, music and dance had become means of recording and narrating their stories, and representing themselves to others. These were ends served elsewhere by writing and articulate language, which raises the question: if music and dance had also made it possible to survive history, does writing perform that task, too? Does it spring, like dance, from the need to mourn the dead and shake off past traumas, in order to be able to move freely and flourish in the present?

It may have been precisely this lack of somatic intelligence that Xihomara Granados noticed in her students back in the 1980s. It seemed to me that modern Britain had much to learn from Colombia. But if the British had been drawn to salsa by an instinctive desire to recover a forgotten body wisdom, I worried that its life-transforming charge may have been diminished when, instead of stepping into salsa's world, we brought salsa into ours.

In January 2011 I went with Vivi and her family to a club called Tíbiri-Tábara in Medellín's Avenida 70. We arrived early and watched the place fill up. The music was excellent and we all danced. Lucho worked his minimalist magic with his partner and his daughter, and even Nestor took to the floor. But, as the night went on, I noticed that, in the 15 years since I had started visiting Colombia, salsa there had changed. The first signs of a distance from the music had appeared in the younger dancers. There was extravagant spinning, overwrought movement, a hint of an appeal for an audience – the feeling, too, that the world was watching.

Local styles were being affected by international

standards, and couples here were beginning to incorporate other people's criteria into the intimacy they shared between themselves. It was, I supposed, inevitable. The relationship between the West and its exotic Others is an unequal one. Salsa had been exported into foreign contexts where, isolated from its carrier communities, it had developed into something barely recognisable, that was being imported back and adopted by people who wanted to appear in tune with the international scene.

But as salsa took on the aura of the wider world, it was devouring the local dances that had created it. Colombian folk dancers blame salsa for endangering the traditional dances of the Pacific coast. The success of Cali's dance troupes was making salsa a symbol of Colombia abroad, even as it eroded Colombia's own unique traditions and dance forms. Still, given the reputation enjoyed by Colombia among those who mistake news stories for national realities, it could only be an improvement.

Vivi and I stood up to dance. For all the differences between us, in background and language, family circumstances, temperament and education, age and aspiration, we might have been warriors trading blows. Drums beat and we stood opposite one another, moving in parallel, each stepping clear as the other closed in, the way boxers sound out each other's defences. Except that, when we came together, something happened: an easing of the instinctive borders of intimate body space, the soft erosion of the boundaries between us and we became, no longer adversaries, but the opposite: lovers embracing.

She had brought me this gift, this joyful game of opposites, in wilful disregard of the cultural contradictions and the bruised toes, and, if there's something when we dance that bears a passing resemblance to obsessive madness, it is perhaps because love looks that way too. It is after all enough that the stillness shouldn't be absolute, that there should be motion, however slight, for mechanisms that recognise no division between self and other, neurons that fire whether the movement is ours or someone else's, to begin their silent work of coupling minds and bodies, slowly melding two individuals into one.

As we swayed together, other movements locked into our mirror-play. Perhaps before we ourselves knew what was happening, we moved into that state where feeling comes before thinking, body before mind, synchronisation invades every movement and each knows what the other feels because he or she feels it too.

There are still days when I can't dance at all, and there always will be, when defence mechanisms beyond my control repel the rhythm and the presiding voice over the wayward domain I call myself wonders whether any other person, however different, could be as much of a stranger to me as I am.

But that, too, was part of it: at times we embrace, at times we turn away from each other, *yenga ye kumba*.

The next necessary thing (so at least it seems to me) is neither the construction of a universal, Esperanto-like culture, the culture of airports and motor hotels, nor the invention of some vast technology of human management. It is to enlarge the possibility of intelligible discourse between people quite different from one another in interest, outlook, wealth, and power, and yet contained in a world where, tumbled as they are into endless connection, it is increasingly difficult to get out of each other's way.

Clifford Geertz

Notes on Printed Sources

Chapter 1

p. 10 'an air of confidence': Peter Wade, *Blackness and Race Mixture. The Dynamics and Racial Identity in Colombia*, Johns Hopkins UP, London, 1995, p. 260.

Chapter 2

This Chapter builds on Leoncio Caycedo, 'Londres en Salsa o La Salsa en Londres. Sus Orígenes y Desarrollo', B.A. Spanish Dissertation, University of North London, January 1996.

p. 32 'vestiges of Empire': J. M. Evans, 'Immigration Act 1971', in *The Modern Law Review* 35 (5), 1972, p. 508.

p. 33 'Caterers Association': British Hotelier and Restaurateur, February 1973 pp. 10–11.

p. 39 'South American politics': *The Times*, 18 August 1980, p. 1.

pp. 36–40. 'El Dandy': arson attack based on interviews, plus the following printed sources: the *Sunday Times*, 17 August 1980, pp. 1–2; *The Times*, 18 August, p. 1; 19 August, p. 2; 20 August, p. 3; 22 August, p. 2; 3 September, p. 4; 30 April 1981, p. 4; 1 May 1981, p. 3; 6 May, p. 3; 8 May, p, 3; 18 June, p. 5. *Evening Standard*, 18 August 1981, p. 7; John Withington, *London's Disasters from Boudicca to the Banking Crisis*, The History Press, Brimscombe Port Stroud, 2010, pp. 96–9.

p. 45 'cocaine': *The Federal Reporter*, Decisions of the Federal Courts of Appeals, West Publishing, Eagan, Volume 848, 2nd Edition, May–July, 1988, p. 848 F.2d 1352, 23 June 1988.

CHAPTER 3

p. 54 'the law': Wade, *BRM*, p. 307.

CHAPTER 4

p. 68 'Orestes López': Bentacur Álvarez, *Sin Clave y Bongó No Hay Son*, Editorial Universidad de Antioquia, Medellín, 1999, pp. 111–12.

p. 69 'down the line': Marta Moreno Vega, *When the Spirits Dance Mambo*, Three Rivers Press, New York, 2004. pp. 114–15.

p. 73 'his fuckin' nose': Piri Thomas, *Down These Mean Streets*, Vintage Books, New York, pp. 59–60.

p. 74 'sense of timing': Thomas, p. 105.

p. 76 *'bóveda'*: Moreno Vega, pp. 186ff.

p. 77 'howls, and screams': Christopher Washburne, *Sounding Salsa. Performing Latin Music in New York City*, Temple University Press, p. 119.

p. 77 'passages': Washburne, p. 119.

p. 77 'dark': Washburne, p. 118.

p. 78 'experienced': Washburne, p. 117.

p. 83 'followed the congas': *New York Times*, 29 July 2007, Julie Bloom, 'Salsa Spins Beyond Its Roots'.

p. 89 'black bile': Charles Taylor, *A Secular Society*, The Belknap Press, London, 2007, p. 37.

CHAPTER 5

p. 101 'Watusi': Lise Waxer, ed., *Situating Salsa. Global Markets and Local Meaning in Latin Popular Music*, Routledge, London, pp. 254ff; Umberto Valverde, *Quítate de la Vía Perico*, Espasa Narrativa, Bogotá, 2001, p. 62.

p. 101 'style was created': Alejandro Ulloa, *La salsa en Culi*, Collección Crónica y Periodismo, Ediciones Universidad del Valle, 1992, passim.

p. 107 *'cruzada'*: Washburne, pp. 179–183; Lise Waxer, *The City of Musical Memory. Salsa, Record Grooves, and Popular Culture in Cali, Colombia*, Wesleyan UP, 2002, pp. 172–3.

p. 108 'refuse to dance': Washburne, p. 182.

NOTES ON PRINTED SOURCES

p. 109 *'Pachito Eché'*: Peter Wade, *Music, Nation and Race. Música Tropical in Colombia*, Chicago UP, 2000, p. 119.

p. 109 'rectified versions': Waxer, *CMM*, pp. 173–4.

p. 110 *'El Escondite'*: Valverde, pp. 137–8.

p. 110 *'Pasito Cañandonga'*: Valverde, p. 138; Alejandro Ulloa, *El Baile. Un lenguaje del cuerpo*, Collección de Autores Vallecaucanos, Cali, 2005. p. 66.

p. 114 'catchment area': Trudy Harpham, Emma Grant, Carols Rodríguez, Mental health and social capital in Cali Colombia, *Social Science & Medicine* 58 (2004) 2267–77.

p. 120 'Fania's main objective': Washburne, pp. 17–23.

p. 121 'RMM records': Washburne, pp. 27–31.

p. 123 'Kafka': Franz Kafka, 'The Great Wall of China,' in *The Complete Short Stories*, Vintage Classics, 2005, pp. 235–49: quotation, p. 245.

CHAPTER 6

This Chapter draws on Caicedo and on Patria Román Velázquez, *The Making of Latin London. Salsa Music, Place and Identity*, Ashgate, Aldershot, 1999.

p. 126 'done in America': Adapted from Román Velázquez, pp. 86–7.

p. 130 'explain the steps': Adapted from Román Velázquez, p. 117.

p. 133 'authenticity': Román Velázquez, p. 89.

CHAPTER 8

p. 154 'more women in Britain': Juliet Gardiner, *The Thirties: An Intimate History*, Harper Press, London, 2010, Kindle Edition, Location 11471–74.

p. 154 'married woman from Leeds': Gardiner, Location 12322–23.

p. 155 'Betjeman': David Kynaston, *Family Britain*, Bloomsbury, London, 2009, 1951–57, p. 216.

p. 155 'three distinct Englands': J. B. Priestley, English Journey, Heinemann/Gollancz, 1937, pp. 397ff.

p. 156 'the *Economist*': Kynaston, *FB*, p. 198.

p. 157 'St Mary Cray': Kynaston, *FB*, pp. 379–81.

p. 157 'quicksteps': Kynaston, *FB*, p. 380.

p. 157 'Decca catalogue': Kynaston, *FB*, p. 605.

p. 159 'licked': Priestley, p. 266.

p. 162 Zurcher-Margolle': Juliet McMains, *Glamour Addiction. Inside the American Ballroom Industry*, Wesleyan UP, Middletown, 2006, pp. 114–15, 122–8.

p. 162 'Samba': McMains, p. 125.

p. 166 'Cuban Ballroom Rumba': Leonard Scrivener, ed., *The Complete Ballroom Dancer*, Evans Brothers, London, p. 117.

p. 166 'Cha Cha Cha': ibid., 163.

CHAPTER 10

p. 187 'mental trigonometry': Diane Solway, *Learning To Dance, One Chunk At a Time*, New York Times, 27 May 2007, p. 19.

p. 199 'superb sense of rhythm': David Kynaston, *Austerity Britain. A World to Build*, Bloomsbury, London, 2007, Kindle Edition, Location 6629–30.

CHAPTER 11

p. 211 '14 spins': *New York Times*, 29 July 2007.

p. 214 'Blades apologised': Frances R. Aparicio, *Listening to Salsa. Gender, Latin Popular Music and Puerto Rican Cultures*, Wesleyan UP, 1999, pp. 112 and 116.

CHAPTER 12

p. 218 'grand initiator': Robert Farris Thompson, *Tango. The Art History of Love*, Vintage Books, 2005, pp. 73–4.

p. 219 'Ngola': Jaime Arocha, Muntu, Ananse y la diáspora afrocolombiana, in *Colombia, Migraciones, transnacionalismo y desplazamiento*, ed. Gerardo Arila, Universidad Nacional de Colombia, Bogotá, pp. 397–425; p. 410.

p. 219 'Xwlá and Ibo': Arocha, p. 410.

p. 220 'brains of accomplished': Iain McGilchrist, *The Master and His Emissary*, Yale University Press, 2009, Kindle Edition, Location 1491–2.

p. 220 'die upstairs': John Miller Chernoff, *African Rhythm and African Sensibility. Aesthetics and Social Action in African Musical Idioms*. University of Chicago Press, 1979, p. 77.

p. 221 'bottles of beer': Chernoff, p. 75.

p. 221 'the Ga': Chernoff, p. 211, Note 28.

p. 221 'Dagomba': Chernoff, p. 124.

p. 221 'Haiti': Chernoff, p. 29.

p. 221 'on deck': Ned Sublette, *Cuba and its Music. From the First Drums to the Mambo*, Chicago Review Press, 2004, p. 58.

p. 221 'knows the dance': Chernoff, p. 23.

p. 224 'returns to its origins': McGilchrist, Location 11619–25.

p. 224 'good dancers': Chernoff, pp. 148–9.

p. 225 'to an extent': Chernoff, pp. 195–6.

p. 225 'last 48 hours': Marc Augé, *Non-Places. Introduction to an Anthropology of Supermodernity*, Verso, London, 1995, pp. 26–7 and 104–5.

Chapter 13

p. 229 'Cherrapunji': Wade, *BRM*, p. 95.

p. 231 'the cries stopped': Amnesty International, Colombia: Return to hope – forcibly displaced communities of Urabá and Medio Atrato region, AMR 23/023/2000, 31 May 2000.

Chapter 15

p. 243 'Yenga ye kumba': Farris Thompson, p. 66.

p. 244 'somatic intelligence': Bonnie Meekums, Embodiment in dance movement therapy training and practice, in *Dance Movement Therapy. Theory, Research and Practice*, ed. Helen Payne, Routledge, London, 2008, pp. 167–183; pp. 170–1.

p. 246 'endangering': Alberto Londoño, 'Danzas colombianas', Editorial Universidad de Antioquia, Medellín, 1998, p. 261.

p. 248 Clifford Geertz, *Works and Lives. The Anthropologist as Author*, Polity Press, Cambridge, 1989, p. 147

ACKNOWLEDGEMENTS

While researching and writing this book, I have entered into many memorable partnerships but also stepped on many toes. My interlocutors have on the whole tolerated my invasive and not always graceful incursions with humour and, at times, great generosity.

First and foremost, Leoncio Caycedo, one of the few remaining Colombian promoters in London and the expert on the history of the early Colombian community, provided me with a copy of his undergraduate thesis 'Londres en Salsa o La Salsa en Londres. Sus Orígenes y Desarrollo', B.A. Spanish Dissertation, University of North London, January 1996, and helped me almost daily during the drafting of Chapter 2.

Lubín Reyes and his sons Lubín Jr and Stephen were kind and enthusiastic assistants. Lubín's own story could have been a book in its own right.

DJ Dave Hucker provided me with material for the book, and his own fabulous musical compilations to sustain me as I wrote.

Tomasz Zaleski, a.k.a. Tomek, was both a fascinating and extraordinary interviewee, and is a one-man contact zone where people and cultures meet. Tomek put me in touch with a long list of salsa luminaries in the UK and New York.

Nestor García designed the figures and diagrams showing dance steps and rhythms.

Thanks also to the following:

In Medellín: Marlen Toro RIP, Luis García, Luis Fernando García, José Fernando González, Director of La Magia de Tus Bailes, and his dancers.

In London: Xihomara Granados, Nelson Batista, Elder Sánchez, Mina Elliott, Stephanie Lipton, Romero Zapata, David Shimeld, Chris Greenwood, Jim le Messurier, Roberto Pla, Leon Rose, Robert Charlemagne, Alastair Sadler of The Streetbeat Salsa Co., Chris Marques and Jaclyn Spencer.

In Cali: Mercedes Angarita and Gustavo García; authors Alejandro Ulloa, Pablo Delvalle and Umberto Valverde. Luis Eduardo Hernández, a.k.a. El Mulato, Director of Swing Latino, and his dancers; Luis Cela Caicedo, Director of Nueva Dimensión, and his dancers; Diego Rojas, Director of Pioneros del Ritmo, and his dancers; Carlos Fernando Trujillo, director of Rucafé, and his dancers; Javier Leudo, Director of Súper Ballet de la Salsa, and his dancers. Myriam and William; Rafael Ithier, Jerry Rivas, Papo Rosario and the rest of El Gran Combo de Puerto Rico, with their manager Mario Hernández; Bobby Cruz; Óscar D'León and his manager Oswaldo Ponte.

In Cartagena: Julio Pájaro, José Carmona, Cheo Romero.

In Quibdó: Gonzalo María de la Torre, Rafael Gómez RIP, Alicia Elena de la Torre, Justi Victória Sánchez, Milciades Rentería, Director of Mi Sangre Candente, and his dancers; Emilia Caicedo, Director of Grupo Papitú, and her dancers; Sigifredo Toro; Amalia Lú Posso Figueroa.

In Bogotá: Ana Marín, César Pagano, Rosni and José Portaccio, Raúl Arroyave RIP and Ruby Toro.

In Lancashire: Joan Imlach, Barbara Williams, Jason and Shemayne Parkinson, Rohan Brown.

In Manchester: Emma Moore, Eider Rúa and Luisa Suaza, Directors of El Firulete, and their dancers.

In Zürich: Thomas Stadler, Stefano Amato, Alberto Valdés, Seo Fernández, Tammam Shaibani, a.k.a. Tamambo, Mario Hazarika, a.k.a. SuperMario, Adolfo Indacochea.

In New York: Mike Amadeo, Chris Washburne, Ángel Fernández, Eddie Torres and his wife María.

By email and telephone: Lubomir Jovanovic, a.k.a. DJ Lubi, D.A. 'Jumbo' Vanrenen, Cressida Childs, Imogen Moore, Paul Young, Albert Torres, Edie Williams, a.k.a. Edie the Salsa Freak.

Thanks also to Ned Boulting, Sarah Nurse, Tim Goodden, Paul Roberts, Carolyn Viccari, Brian and James Venner, Steve Docherty and Cristian Chiapponi, for financing this book.

To Mike Watkinson, for being an early reader of parts of the manuscript, and, with Jim Howard and Tim Dean, for sharing those early experiences of Irakere at Ronnie Scott's. To Claire Pooley, Gail Willmott, Alex Di Re, John Gregory, Maurizia Garzia, Cristian Chiapponi, for bopping at the Bass Clef.

To Graham Coster, with whom I discussed this book at an early stage, and who helped me shape the initial book project, and to Francine Brody, the editor of an early draft of this book.

Special thanks to Gary Imlach, who, after being the best man at our wedding, volunteered to be the midwife of this book, and had the remarkable personal skills to be simultaneously a meticulous and exigent editor, and also the closest and most supportive of friends. Working with him was a daily masterclass in authorship. All errors and imbalances, and of course all opinions expressed, are my own.

Most of all, to my wife Vivi, for sharing her life, family, dog and dance with me, I say *!Graci' amo'!*